Bright Colors Falsely Seen

Bright Colors Falsely Seen

Synaesthesia and the Search

for Transcendental Knowledge

Kevin T. Dann

Yale University Press

New Haven & London

The passages from SPEAK, MEMORY by Vladimir Nabokov, Copyright © 1989 by the Estate of Vladimir Nabokov, are reprinted by permission of Vintage Books, a Division of Random House, Inc.

Printed in the United States of America

Library of Congress Cataloging-in-Publication Data

Dann, Kevin T., 1956–
Bright colors falsely seen : Synaesthesia and the search for
transcendental knowledge / Kevin T. Dann.
p.   cm.
Includes bibliographical references and index.
ISBN 0-300-06619-8 (hardcover : alk. paper)
1. Synesthesia.   I. Title.
BF495.D36   1998
152.1—dc21   98-15990
                                                                          CIP

A catalogue record for this book is available from the British Library.

The paper in this book meets the guidelines for permanence and durability of the Committee on Production Guidelines for Book Longevity of the Council on Library Resources.

10   9   8   7   6   5   4   3   2   1

Contents

Preface

The first thing that we ask, when someone *sees* something that the rest of us do not, is whether it is "true." Such subjective visions demand evaluation because they call into question our own perceptions about the nature of reality. If others do not dismiss the visions as mere hallucinations, then these frequently take on a certain numinous quality; they are thought to hold *more* truth than the pedestrian perceptions of nonvisionaries. Nearly every contemporary historian, whether sympathetic to it or not, is familiar with Max Weber's view that Western European history is characterized by *die Entzauberung der Welt,* the "disenchantment of the world." In opposition to the "specialists without spirit, sensualists without heart"—Weber's oft-quoted assessment of modern humanity—the Western Romantic tradition has endeavored to rescue human beings from a deadening objectivism by celebrating the subjective, the invisible, the imaginary (Weber, [1904] 1958, p. 182). As materialism established its final stranglehold on Western civilization, Romantics posited the existence of worlds other than the material one. From the visions of William Blake to Swedenborgian Spiritualism to contemporary parapsychology, many of the attempts to make contact with other worlds have been chronicled by historians. Historical treatments have not necessarily had to come to grips with whether the phenomena in question—whether paranormal psychological effects or visions of gods, angels, demons, and other discarnate beings—have any empirical validity, because their existence as cultural and intellectual artifacts alone gives them sufficient ontological weight for historical inquiry. In the eyes of contemporary historians, angels may not have had much effect on history, but the *belief* in them certainly has, and the same goes for the belief in spirits, elves, fairies, and pixies and the invisible realms in which they dwell. Whether seen as barometers of social change, protests against an increasingly rationalist and materialist worldview, or attempts by traditionally disempowered social groups to gain some measure of influence, those Romantic ideas, along with the individuals and organizations devoted to them, have been thoroughly domesticated by historical scholarship, regardless of whether they have been interpreted by historians as successful or unsuccessful. Witches in seventeenth-century New England villages become ciphers in demographic dilemmas, and the disembodied spirits of nineteenth-century séances are turned into players in the gender wars. For most modern historians the force of the transcendent is mostly political, economic, and social, not spiritual. More than all the Romantic literary explorations of the imagination, the phenomena of Spiritualism introduced the disenchanted to the possibilities of an unseen realm. Westerners, no matter how "disenchanted," have exhibited a perennial curiosity about the invisible world. Latter-day Romantics argue that the positivist worldview is limiting to the human spirit and that human cognition needs to include engagement with nonvisible realms; the manifestations of that invisible world are marshaled in evidence. Synaesthesia—the manifestation of an unseen world examined in this book—is not, like paranormal phenomena, ignored or scoffed at by scientists but is thoroughly documented scientifically. Still, it has generated an enormous amount of what can only be described as religious sentiment. I argue that because Western culture has lacked a suitably inclusive model or description of human consciousness, synaesthesia has repeatedly been mistaken for a unique, desirable "higher" state, enjoyed only by exceptional individuals.

Three years ago, I was in a bookstore in Tempe, Arizona. When I came up to the counter with two books to purchase—Robert Sardello's *Facing the World with Soul* (1991) and Daniel Cottom's *Abyss of Reason* (1991), the sales clerk exclaimed "What a dichotomy!" When I asked him what he meant, he said that soul, which he identified with emotion, and reason are antagonistic, polar opposites. I encouraged him to explain. He said that there was a way to reconcile the division between emotion and reason—"synaesthesia." How did he know this word? I asked. He explained that he was reading a new book on synaesthesia, and that it was one of the books he was featuring in that week's display window on psychology. (The bookstore's entire upper floor was devoted to psychology, New Age, and self-help literature.) I probed a bit more about what "synaesthesia" meant for him and why he had offered this obscure Greek word as a solution to the problem of modernity—call it the mind-body problem, the reason-emotion dichotomy, or the war between the head and the heart. In his response he kept pulling in other scientific terms—"synchronicity," "black holes," "chaos"—and used all metaphorically, extending their original meanings into new territory, just as he had done with the word "synaesthesia." He seemed to be performing some of the same imaginative leaps that had been executed for the past century, as Western science and art repeatedly came face to face with the rare psychological phenomenon known as synaesthesia. Once more I asked myself how so many hopes and desires had been pinned on something so idiosyncratic.

As I left, he told me to look at his handiwork in the display window. There in the center of the window was the book on synaesthesia—Richard Cytowic's *Man Who Tasted Shapes*—surrounded by Terence McKenna's *True Hallucinations,* Stanislav Grof's *Beyond the Brain,* Howard Gardner's *Creating Minds,* and a host of other titles—*Gateway to Inner Space: The Self-Aware Universe,* a book about Milton Erickson's hypnosis techniques, another on neurolinguistic programming in psychotherapy, and many others. Though all were ostensibly about the mind, it struck me that the themes uniting the books were the celebration of unseen worlds, the capacity of some people to see extraordinary visions that not all of us can see, and the suggestion that the ability to perceive unseen worlds might represent the "next step" in human consciousness. Out of the many ideas contained in these books, the bookstore clerk had chosen synaesthesia as the path to liberation from the prisonhouse of the senses and their tyrannical overseer, reason. This liberation has been the continual theme in the Romantic fascination with synaesthesia. Synaesthesia has always been a magnet for Romantic ideas, because it seems to validate the belief in the primacy of imagination in human cognition, as well as to ratify the original wholeness, continuity, and interfusion of immediate experience before its division into atomistic sensations. Most of those who have seized on synaesthesia for support have also maintained that the ultimate function of literature and the arts is to manifest this fusion of the senses. Believing in a primal unity of the senses, Romantics have naturally been fascinated by individuals who seem to be living examples of that unity—synaesthetes. Synaesthetes' senses lack the boundaries that for the rest of us segregate seeing from hearing or smelling or tasting or feeling at any given moment. Synaesthesia has been and continues to exercise a powerful attraction for those who want to "reenchant" the world. To the Romantic nonsynaesthete, synaesthetes seem to have escaped the full conse-quences of the fall into rational consciousness suffered by the rest of us.

My own view is that this is a mistaken notion, that most of those who have championed synaesthesia have not understood what it really is, and that the continued appeal of synaesthesia and other apparently anomalous states of consciousness results from Romanticism's never having "come of age." The two-centuries-old Romantic call for new ways of seeing, and with them, new ways of being, has stagnated, often owing to insufficient understanding of how consciousness has evolved. In particular, liberatory Romanticism has routinely ascribed to synaesthetic percepts an absolute, transcendental value, as if these bizarre sensations contained esoteric truths that we needed only to learn how to decipher. Because of its persistence as a Romantic ideal over the last century, synaesthesia—a rare psychological anomaly and the arcane, apparently trivial fancy of a small group of artists and intellectuals—has become a lens through which it is possible to see the limits of modern and postmodern attempts to escape the fetters of the Enlightenment. Synaesthesia invites historical reflec-tion unencumbered by deadening positivism and rationalism, but also by liberatory excess. While debunking a century of extravagant claims about synaesthesia and eideticism as transcendental knowledge, I welcome the possi-bility that these phenomena do point to a new development in human con-sciousness.

It is difficult to set this study within the context of academic cultural history as it is currently practiced. The topics of synaesthesia and eideticism have no historiography. Even as an entry point for a critical study of modern Romantic ideas about the evolution of human consciousness, synaesthesia may seem an arcane choice. It is admittedly abstruse, but as demonstrated by the bookstore clerk's enthusiastic borrowing of synaesthesia as an explanatory principle and tool for cultural critique, synaesthesia is also a modern apparition with a certain irresistible quality that invites speculative thought. Through imaginative spec-ulation, it seems possible to begin to see the unseen, any era's most fundamental Romantic desire.

AKNOWLEDGMENTS

I wish to acknowledge the generous assistance of the following individuals, who answered questions, made suggestions, or offered research support during the research and writing of this book: Betsy Behnke, Chantal Cannon, Richard Cytowic, Sean Day, Bulat Galeyev, Yosi Glicksohn, Bob Gussner, Andreas Heertsch, Harry Hunt, D. Barton Johnson, Jan Klimkowski, Gary Lachman, Jackson Lears, Dean Leary, Christophe-Andreas Lindenberg, Florin Lowndes, Matt Matsuda, Philip Nikolayev, Fred Paddock, Philip Pauly, Peter Rennick, Valdemar Setzer, Carol Steen, Charles Tart, Ed Tenner, and Olivia Walling. Special thanks are due my wife, Joyce, who patiently listened to the ideas and arguments as they developed and who made helpful editorial remarks on an early draft. Susan Abel of Yale University Press skillfully guided the final shaping of the book.

This book is dedicated to my daughter, Jordan.

Introduction

In 1922, Edgar Curtis, the three-and-a-half-year-old son of Professor O. F. Curtis of Cornell University, heard the report of guns from a nearby rifle range and asked his mother, "What is that big black noise?" A few days later, as he was being put to bed on the sleeping porch, Edgar heard a high, shrill chirp and asked, "What is that little white noise?" When his mother told him it was a cricket, he protested, while imitating a typical cricket call: "Not the brown one, but the little white noise," and then imitated this shriller, higher, unfamiliar insect sound. Listening to the resonating buzz of a more distant cricket, Edgar pronounced it to be red. For Edgar, the whirring of electric fans was orange, the humming of vacuum cleaners black, the rhythm of a moving streetcar yellow. Alone in a room with a piano, he tentatively touched the keys, crying out with delight the different colors they produced—middle C red, bass notes black, high notes white. One day, upon seeing a rainbow, Edgar exclaimed, "A song! A song!" (Whitchurch, 1922, pp. 302–303).

"M," the seven-and-a-half-year-old daughter of a Dartmouth professor in the 1930s, also saw colors whenever she heard music. Asked by psychologists to match the colors she saw to a chart of a hundred different hues, she would usually say that the color was not on the chart and would point to two or three hues and suggest that the color she saw was a mixture of them. The blotches of color she saw sometimes seemed to be within her forehead (high tones), sometimes near her ears (low tones). The colors varied in size with the pitch of the tones: middle-range tones were between one and three inches in diameter, the high tone of a whistle "as small as a pea" (Riggs and Karwoski, 1934, p. 31). People were also different colors to her: "K. is grey, sort of silverish. A square would be greyish white or silverish; a circle would be gold. Sometimes shapes of objects give colours but mostly living people. K. is silverish, because his head is sort of square. E. is purplish blue, dark orchid, her head is sort of plump and bobbed haired. My mother is medium purple—sort of plump, her hair goes behind and makes her look that colour to me. S. is white, whitish brown, due to the shape of his face. P. is orange, due to the sharpness of his nose" (p. 31). Asked what color black people were, the girl answered: "I haven't known them well enough to know what colors they are" (p. 31). An audience was "very bright orange with a black outline. All strangers look like that. As I know them better they get mild blue or pinkish orchid" (p. 31). Asked what color Dartmouth students were, she said that they were mild orange, without the black outline, since they knew her better than professors, who were bright orange and outlined. People in motion pictures "move[d] so fast" that she could not make out any colors (p. 31).

In the 1960s, the psychologist A. R. Luria described the case of a certain "S" (for the man's surname—Shereshevsky) who saw voices in different colors. According to Solomon Shereshevsky:

> There are people who seem to have many voices, whose voices seem to be an entire composition, a bouquet. The late S. M. Eisenstein had just such a voice: listening to him, it was as though a flame with fibers protruding from it was advancing right toward me. I got so interested in his voice, I couldn't follow what he was saying. . . . To this day I can't escape from seeing colors when I hear sounds. What first strikes me is the color of someone's voice. Then it fades off . . . for it does interfere. If, say, a person says something, I see the word; but should another person's voice break in, blurs appear. These creep into the syllables of the words and I can't make out what is being said. [Shereshevsky, quoted in Luria, 1976, pp. 24–25]

Shereshevsky had a similarly idiosyncratic response to letters. Here is how he described some of the letters of the Cyrillic alphabet:

> A is something white and long; и moves off somewhere ahead so that you just can't sketch it, whereas й is pointed in form. Ю is also pointed and sharper than е whereas

я is big, so big that you can actually roll right over it. O is a sound that comes from your chest. . . . It's broad, though the sound itself tends to fall. Эй moves off somewhere to the side. I also experience a sense of taste from each sound. And when I see lines, some configuration that has been drawn, these produce sounds. Take the figure ∠＿＿. This is somewhere in between e, ю and й; ᴡᴡᴡ is a vowel sound, but it also resembles the sound *r*—not a pure *r* though. . . . But one thing still isn't clear to me: if the line goes up, I experience a sound, but if it moves in the reverse direction, it no longer comes through as a sound but as some sort of wooden hook for a yoke. The configuration ∪ appears to be something dark, but if it had been drawn slower, it would have seemed different. Had you, say, drawn it like this ∪′, then it would have been the sound e.

Shereshevsky had a strange relationship with numbers as well:

For me, 2, 4, 6, 5 are not just numbers. They have forms. 1 is a pointed number— which has nothing to do with the way it's written. It's because it's somehow firm and complete. 2 is flatter, rectangular, whitish in color, sometimes almost a gray. 3 is a pointed segment which rotates. 4 is also square and dull; it looks like 2 but has more substance to it, it's thicker. 5 is absolutely complete and takes the form of a cone or a tower—something substantial. 6, the first number after 5, has a whitish hue; 8 somehow has a naïve quality, it's milky blue like lime . . . [S. V. Shereshevsky, quoted in Luria, 1976, p. 26]

Carol Steen, an artist, describes the colors she sees when receiving acupuncture treatments:

The first color I might see would be orange and then . . . I might see a purple or a magenta or a red or green. . . . Most often, by the end of the treatment, when the acupuncturist took the needles out, the colors would come full force and they would just be utterly, completely brilliant. Moving colors, swirling around, one chasing the other and pushing the blackness all the way to the edge and sometimes just exploding out of there completely. . . . When she has the needles all in place, often, as I am just lying there quietly, all of a sudden, it's like watching watercolors just moving across a black screen. The black dissolves the white, but the colors are far more brilliant, far more wonderful, these inside colors, than anything that I am able to do with paint. [conversation with Carol Steen, October 27, 1994]

One might add to these statements the testimony of a person for whom a tin whistle gave the impression of "a clear, sweet flavor like Christmas candy or sugar and water. The higher the note, the less pronounced the sweet," or another for whom the lowest tones of the piano sounded "like toast soaked in hot water; the middle regions sweet, like licorice, banana; the high tones thin, insipid" (Cutsforth, 1925, p. 534). None of these people were speaking metaphorically; the colored piano notes, the sweet whistle tones, the explosions of color created by an acupuncturist's needles, were all actual images, as real as any other images formed in their minds. The voices of the children Edgar Curtis and "M" are completely candid, guilelessly reporting what lay before their eyes; it would have been a complete surprise to them that others did not perceive the world in the same manner that they did. The adult voices of Shereshevsky and Carol Steen are equally ingenuous, and if asked when they started to have these strange sensations, they and others like them would invariably answer that the phenomenon began as far back as they could remember, back to Edgar or M's age. But they might also have told another story, one of how private this world came to be. Thomas D. Cutsforth described the case of a "Miss E.," who until she worked in Cutsforth's lab as a senior in college, had always thought of herself as abnormal. She told Cutsforth, himself synaesthetic, of how her efforts to avoid her own synaesthetic mental processes had only hindered her thinking (p. 528). Carol Steen remembers how, beginning in the second grade, when she spoke of colored letters or numbers, her classmates would tell her she was "weird." From then on, she kept her "colors" hidden, speaking of them to no one. Home on a semester break during her junior year of college, while having dinner with her family, she remembers turning to her father and declaring "The number five is yellow." "No, it's yellow-ochre," he replied. While her mother and brother looked at each other, stupefied, Carol told her father that she was having trouble determining whether the number two was blue or green. "It's green," he assured her. But, according to Carol, after that conversation, her father "froze," never saying another word about it, and to this day he denies that the conversation ever took place (though Carol's mother and brother testify otherwise). It was almost thirty years before Carol met another person who saw colors in response to sounds, and when she did, she broke down in tears (conversation with Carol Steen, October 27, 1994). Shereshevsky *never* met another person like himself, though he met with a sympathetic listener in Luria.

In recent years, a neurologist studying this condition has received many letters like the following one from people who have read newspaper articles or heard radio reports about his research:

> I read the article . . . concerning your work. . . . It's an affirmation that I am not nuts and whatever my other problems may have been, being crazy was not one of them. . . .
>
> You have no idea . . . how exciting it is to read someone else's description . . . of an experience that I have never been quite sure wasn't the result of my imagination or

being insane. I have never met anyone else who saw sound. When enough people tell you that you are imagining things it's easy to doubt yourself. I've never been quite sure that I'm not crazy.

I love my colors, can't imagine being without them. One of the things I love about my husband are the colors of his voice and his laugh. It's a wonderful golden brown, with a flavor of crisp, buttery toast. . . .

Would it be possible to meet others? As I said, I have never met anyone else who does these things, and would very much like to, as much for reassurance as for anything else. [Cytowic, 1989, p. 27]

COLORED SOUNDS AND POINTED NUMBERS:
THE PHENOMENOLOGY OF SYNAESTHESIA

All of these voices describe the same phenomenon, synaesthesia, understood by contemporary scientists as "an *involuntary* joining in which the real information of one sense is accompanied by a perception in another sense."[1] As puzzling to the behavioral scientists who have studied this curious linkage of the senses as it is to the people who experience it, synaesthesia has been known to science for more than a century and a half and was for a decade or two at the turn of the century one of the most intensively investigated psychological anomalies. Some of the most prominent psychologists in Europe and North America have done research on synaesthesia—Charles Féré and Alfred Binet (France); Théodore Flournoy (Switzerland); G. T. Fechner, Wilhelm Wundt, Moritz Benedikt, Eugen Bleuler, E. R. Jaensch, and Heinz Werner (Germany); Francis Galton, Charles S. Myers, and MacDonald Critchley (England); Mary Calkins, R. H. Wheeler, A. H. Pierce, Herbert Sidney Langfeld, Theodore Karwoski, and A. R. Luria (United States). After more than a century of theorizing, there are still no widely accepted explanations of either the cause or the mechanism of synaesthesia, but the extensive descriptive literature does suggest a set of diagnostic criteria:

1. Synaesthesia is involuntary and insuppressible, but it cannot be evoked at will. For synaesthetes, the colors, tastes, and other sensations they describe are always present but may not always be clearly discernible. In the words of Carol Steen:

Synaesthesia doesn't come to you full-blown, but develops over time in the same way that you could look at clouds and not truly see them until someone explained their basic taxonomy to you. When I started getting really aware of synaesthesia, I was struck by the sense that the first colors that I saw for numbers and letters were the brightest ones—the reds, orange, and yellows. Green and blue came later, and there was confusion about it. I remember thinking to myself, if some of these letters and numbers have colors, then they *all* ought to have color. Then I started to look, and the blacks came and the whites came, and then finally, the very last colors that I saw were the ones that could be considered low-value or subtle colors, dove-gray, for example, like the letter, *d* or the color of beer for the letter *z*. I have to admit that I don't see purple, and I am being confused a little by the letter *q*. [Conversation with Carol Steen, October 27, 1994]

In Carol's case, fifty years of complete isolation left her somewhat inattentive to her own synaesthetic percepts; once she became aware that others shared her form of perception, talked to researchers who understood it, and even discussed her synaesthesia with other synaesthetes, it became more elaborate, that is, she noticed entire ranges of perception that, though there all along, had been "invisible" to her. As she became more acutely cognizant of the hues of her "photisms" (the term given to the patches of color that seem to swirl about in the synaesthete's visual field), she also detected geometric shapes, and she began to see color in response to music, something she had never done before. Calm, relaxed mental states make synaesthesia more vivid. When distracted or keenly focused on a particular problem, synaesthetes may be totally unaware of their synaesthetic percepts.

2. Synaesthetic images are perceived by the synaesthete as projected externally. In visual forms the synaesthetic percept is felt to be close to the face, while in kinaesthetic forms it is felt to occupy the space immediately surrounding the body.

3. Synaesthetic percepts are stable over the individual's lifetime, and they are both discrete (a photism is not just a "bright" color, but a particular hue), and generic (the percepts are unelaborated—that is, visual photisms are geometric shapes rather than images of actual objects, and gustatory percepts are salty or sweet rather than suggesting specific flavors). These percepts are invariably described by synaesthetes as having begun in early childhood, and they endure over their entire lifetime. Researchers studying synaesthesia have confirmed what synaesthetes themselves attest. In a recent study, when given a list of 130 words, phrases, and letters and asked to describe the color of the associated sensation, only 37 percent of nonsynaesthetes' responses were identical to their original description a week before, while 92 percent of synaesthetes' responses were identical after a full year (Baron-Cohen, Goldstein, and Wyke, 1993, p. 419). Other studies conducted over ten, twenty, or more years yield the same results.

There is some evidence that synaesthetic percepts may decline later in life. Recently, when the *New York Times* ran an article on absolute pitch perception, two readers who had absolute pitch wrote in to speak of their loss of the capacity as they aged. Amazingly, both individuals also mentioned that they experienced visual-auditory synaesthesiae in response to music. Peter C. Lynn spoke of becoming conscious of both his absolute pitch perception and synaesthesia at age six, capacities which were a vital part of his mental and emotional life until his early sixties, when they began to decline. At age seventy-one, he said, he had lost them altogether: "This process, apparently due to aging, is an incredibly painful sensory deprivation. The music I now hear does not match the one engraved in my retentive memory. What I hear no longer corresponds to what the ear 'knows.' . . . Absolute pitch may not matter to those who never had it or are comfortable with relative pitch, but to me it is like the loss of a vital organ, a kind of phantom brain that you reach for but can no longer find." Lynn's diminished synaesthesia may have been a result of diminished hearing acuity, however.[2]

4. Synaesthesia is memorable, such that the synaesthetic percepts are often more easily and vividly remembered than the original stimulus. Synaesthetes with color hearing for numbers frequently memorize the color sequences rather than the digits themselves for telephone numbers, addresses and other numerical information. A number of synaesthetes who are also "lightning calculators" perform mathematical operations by mentally manipulating the colors, not the numbers. Synaesthetic singers and musicians who are also endowed with perfect pitch use their colored photisms to "tune," matching the color produced by a sung or sounded note to the remembered one. When a synaesthete forgets something, it is the color (or other associated synaesthetic percept) which is the last thing to fade from the mind. Although the faculty is a great aid to memory, most synaesthetes occasionally experience episodes in which the vividness and memorability of synaesthesia interferes with the process of logical thought.

5. Synaesthesia is emotional, almost always being associated with a narrowly circumscribed set of strong emotions, particularly certain forms of pleasure or displeasure. Though few if any students of synaesthesia have pointed it out, it seems significant that the two realms of mental images that are most often linked for synaesthetes—color and linguistic symbols—are the realms that have enchanted human beings perhaps for a longer time and more deeply than any others. During the stage of mental development when synaesthetic perception is most prevalent among the population as a whole (before age seven), nearly all objects of thought have an explicit affective dimension, but colors,

letters, numbers, and words are particularly salient emotionally. Children savor letters and numbers, playing with them as if they were the most esteemed objects in all creation.

6. Synaesthesia is nonlinguistic, that is, it is exceedingly difficult to describe in words. This difficulty tends to give synaesthesia a quality of ineffability, both for the synaesthetes themselves and for nonsynaesthetic observers.

7. Synaesthesia occurs in people with normal, noninjured, nondiseased brains. Because of its rarity (recent estimates range from one per twenty-five thousand to one per million adults), synaesthesia has frequently been considered either to be pathological (dysfunctional), or conversely, to be indicative of exceptional mental ability. Synaesthetes are usually of average or above-average intelligence and quite often are highly creative. Synaesthesia seems to be much more common among women than men.[3]

FALSE STARTS: SUPPOSED ORIGINS
OF THE INTEREST IN SYNAESTHESIA

Many of the sources reviewing the history of interest in synaesthesia fix the origin of this interest in the seventeenth or eighteenth century, because they interpret certain philosophical speculations about human sensation and the possible analogies between sound and color as discussions of synaesthesia. Paradoxically, the two individuals most frequently cited in these reviews as "studying" synaesthesia—Isaac Newton and John Locke—are the very thinkers who initiated the philosophical crisis to which Symbolism, with its interest in synaesthesia, was a calculated response. When William Blake, in *Jerusalem* ([1820] 1969, p. 636), surveyed the materialism spreading from England over all of Europe, he saw "the Loom of Locke, whose Woof rages dire, / Wash'd by the Water-wheels of Newton. Black the cloth / In heavy wreaths folds over every Nation." Newtonian physics rationalized the cosmos by reducing its properties to laws of motion and the structure of the atom. Those arenas of human experience which remained unquantifiable were dismissed as illusion, and Locke's philosophy helped to expunge human cognition from coparticipation with the cosmos and paved the way for nineteenth century positivism.

In his *Essay Concerning Human Understanding,* John Locke had discussed "a studious blind man" who declared that the color scarlet was like the sound of a trumpet. Although Locke's comments are frequently cited as an early example of scientific interest in synaesthesia, the passage in question is really Locke's reformulation of the seventeenth-century philosophical conundrum known as the "Molyneux problem": If a man born blind were to gain his sight in later life, would he be able to identify the objects around him by sight alone? Locke, whose philosophy was formulated as an alternative to the "innate ideas" posited by authoritarian and antiexperimental scholastic philosophy, answered Molyneux with an emphatic No. Locke interpreted the example of the blind man as proof that without the requisite sensing ability, it is impossible to understand a particular sensory experience—a supposition that was consistent with his view that there were no innate ideas and that all knowledge derived from (sensory) experience of the external world. By advancing empiricism over idealism, Locke emphasized the importance of sensation, but his answer to the Molyneux problem also served to assign the senses discrete channels, each alien from the others. More important, Locke's empiricism devalued any perceptions that did not issue from the "primary" and "secondary" qualities of material objects. Part of the late nineteenth-century fascination with synaesthesia had to do with its apparent ability to overthrow Locke's separation of the senses both from one another and from creative interaction with the external world. Synaesthesia connected what had been split asunder; scientific study of individual synaesthetes yielded positive proof that the two highest senses—hearing and vision—could at least in some individuals be intertwined, and the artistic exploitation of this possibility suggested that perhaps the unity of the senses could be extended to all people.[4]

Isaac Newton's (1718) thought that the spaces occupied by the seven colors of the spectrum were analogous to the relative intervals between notes in the octave is frequently cited as an example of early research into synaesthesia, as is Father Louis Bertrand Castel's (1740) attempt to apply Newton's observations by experimenting with an instrument that was designed to produce colored light to accompany musical notes, a technology that Erasmus Darwin tried to revive at century's end. None of these speculations were concerned with synaesthesia; they only began to be interpreted as such in the last decade of the nineteenth century, after it became widely known that many synaesthetes saw colored photisms in response to music as well as to language. Newton's color spectrum—musical scale analogy was actually a classic expression of his mechanistic approach to the universe, the exact contrary of Romantic and Symbolist conceptions. Johann Wolfgang von Goethe is also routinely cited as having studied synaesthesia; advocates of such a view cite Goethe's discussion of the relation between sound and color in *Zur Farbenlehre*. Goethe denied the sort of relation that would later be looked for by those interested in synaesthesia, declaring that sound and color are "general, elementary effects acting according to the general laws of separation and tendency to union . . . yet acting thus in wholly different provinces, in different modes, on different elementary mediums, for different senses." Though Goethe did cite a pamphlet by J. L. Hoffman that compared the setting of the colors of the artist's palette to the tuning of the individual instruments in an orchestra (yellow suggested the clarinets, bright red the trumpets, ultramarine the violas, and so on), he was fully aware that Hoffman's example was a simple analogy, not a description of an actual perception. Believing that the eye owed its existence to light and that "a dormant light resides in the eye," Goethe cited as proof the "brightest images" of the imagination, the appearance of objects in dreams as if in daylight, and the so-called pathological colors, a wide range of subjectively produced visual sensations, from "Acyanoblephsia" (the inability to perceive blue hues) to shock- or fever-induced phosphenes, the mental menagerie seen by hypochondriacs, and afterimages of the sun and other objects. The entire purpose of Goethe's theory of color was to bridge the chasm between Newton's emphasis on "objective," physical color and the obvious participation of the individual subject in the experience of color. If Goethe had been familiar with the phenomenon of synaesthesia, he certainly would have mentioned it in *Zur Farbenlehre*. Chromaesthesia, with its spectacular colored visions, would have seemed to furnish additional evidence of the "light-making" ability of the eye.[5]

One final common error made by those attempting to construct a history of investigation for synaesthesia is to equate speculation about sound symbolism—the use of speech to symbolize other sensory domains—with synaesthesia. Among chromaesthetes, the stimulus that most commonly produces a sensation of color in the visual field is the human voice, particularly its sounding of vowels. Among non-synaesthetic individuals, however, vowels are almost universally sensed along a bright-dark continuum (the "front" vowels— *i, e*—seen as relatively bright, the "back" vowels—*o, u*—as dark), and in the nineteenth century the two very distinct phenomena began to be confused. In historical reviews of the subject, investigators cited such sources as an 1821 article in the *Literary Gazette* referring to an author who used Virgil to show the colors and instrumental sounds of the vowels; M. Brés's 1822 *Lettres sur l'harmonie du langage,* which included one letter devoted to the sound symbolism of vowels; E. Castiliano's 1850 treatise on vowel sound symbolism; and Georg Brandes's 1854 poem "The Color of the Vowels." None of these works described true vocalic chromaesthesia rather, they dealt with the feeling-tones associated with the most expressive of human sounds. The works do foreshadow the search for a universal language that later helped generate so much interest in synaesthesia. Though none of these questions—the analogy between sound and color, the independence or interdependence of the senses, the ability of vocalic sounds to represent nonacoustic dimensions of sense experience—involves synaesthesia, all share with synaesthesia the sense of being "about" a set of transcendental properties of human sensory capacity.

The entry for "synaesthesia" in the *Oxford English Dictionary* reflects the word's semantic migration from its home in psychology through several other disciplines. In 1901 "synaesthesia" began to be used in literary scholarship to refer to cross-sensory metaphors, and by the 1940s linguistics had extended its meaning to the relationship between speech sounds and the sensory experiences they are meant to represent. Though some of those semantic extensions are irrelevant to the themes of this book, others reveal the persistent Romantic interpretation of synaesthesia as a coveted visionary faculty. Psychologists frequently distinguish authentic cases of synaesthesia (as identified on the basis of the criteria listed earlier) from the many other uses of the word, by calling it "idiopathic synaesthesia," a term I shall also use.[6]

SYNAESTHESIA AND THE SEARCH FOR UNITY
AND A UNIVERSAL LANGUAGE

If one accepts the division of the senses into five modes, twenty possible combinations may result from pairing them. Theoretically, a tactile stimulus could evoke a color, a sound, a smell, or a taste; a visual stimulus might evoke a sound, smell, taste, or touch sensation; an odor, taste, or sound could similarly create sensations in the other modes. Yet most of these combinations never occur; other than visual synaesthesiae, only tactile-visual (sight-induced sensations of touch), tactile-auditory (sound-induced sensations of touch), and kinaesthetic-olfactory (smell-induced bodily sensations) have been recorded as occurring naturally, and only three others (tactile-olfactory, thermal-visual, and algesic-auditory) have been produced experimentally. By far the most common sense in which synaesthetes experience a "secondary sensation" is vision, all four other senses as well as certain somaesthetic sensations (pain, temperature, and kinaesthesis) having been recorded as producing, either naturally or experimentally, visual synaesthesiae. Since the discovery of synaesthesia in the nineteenth century, scientific interest in intersensory relations has focused on the peculiar phenomenon of *audition coloreé,* or "color[ed] hearing" (*Farbenhören* in German), the rare condition in which certain individuals always see within their visual field distinct, vivid patches of color in conjunction with particular sounds. In these individuals, a variety of auditory stimuli—from vowels or consonants to entire words, musical notes, and other sounds—call forth what seem to nonsynaesthetes fantastic visual displays. A particular voice might be heard as "brownish yellow, the color of a ripe English walnut," another as "yellowish, poorly saturated, like old beeswax"; the sound of an organ might evoke a photism which is "very rich deep black, [of] bluish cast, [with] spots and streaks of brown, with irradiating flames"; the single consonant *b* might produce "a dark, bluish, thick amorphous patch of color, about the size of one's hand." As the most common form of synaesthesia, color hearing is commonly designated by the generic word "synaesthesia."[7]

All these forms of synaesthesia, visual or nonvisual, are mental *images*. As images, they are most closely related to another rare, poorly understood, yet exhaustively studied type of mental imagery—eidetic imagery. The psychological literature has used a variety of characteristics to define the eidetic image, but in most contemporary work the following criteria are accepted as diagnostic: a normal, subjective visual image is experienced with particular vividness; although not dependent on the experience of an actual external object, the eidetic image is "seen" in the mind and is accompanied by bodily engagement with the image (including a sense of its "felt meaning"); the eidetic image is a healthful, not a pathological, manifestation. Like the photisms of color hearing and other synaesthetic percepts, the eidetic image is noteworthy in its vividness and memorability, and in the subjective sense of its being projected. Like synaesthetes, eidetic imagers (*eidetikers,* or eidetics) believe their images to be real, although they share their perception of those images with very few others. A significant number of eidetics (approximately half) are also synaesthetic; proportionately fewer synaesthetes possess eidetic perception. Similarities between eideticism and synaesthesia have been pointed out since Francis Galton's pioneering work on mental imagery *Inquiries into Human Faculty and Its Development* (1883), and in the 1930s, as part of his developmental theory, psychologist Heinz Werner ([1934] 1978) grouped them together as "syncretic" experiences entailing a dedifferentiation (or fusion) of perceptual qualities in subjective experience. Recently (Tellegen and Atkinson, 1974; Rader and Tellegen, 1987), psychologists have considered these two forms of mental imagery in terms of the capacity for "absorption," the ability to engage one's diverse representational resources, including one's imagination and feelings, in perceiving the world. Absorbed states are those which involve a release from the active, volitional, and problem-solving mode of consciousness—the rational, instrumental mind so lamented by the Romantics—for a more passive, less reality-bound, more imaginative mode.[8]

The contemporary scientific definitions of both synaesthesia and eideticism contrast the "actual" or "real" external world with the "subjective" internal world. The apparent release from reality that accompanies synaesthetic and eidetic perception has attracted the attention of a variety of thinkers over the last century, all of whom might be considered "Romantic" in the sense of aspiring to a theory of knowledge that gives primacy to the human imagination. In choosing "Romantic" as a category to help organize the diverse personalities encountered here, I am following the lines of D. G. James's conception of Romanticism: "To possess a mind open to the envisagement of the strange and different, to contemplate unknown modes of being, divine and otherwise, whether God or genii, or demons or angels or a metamorphosed humanity, to refuse to be buckled down to the evidence of the senses, this is essential Romanticism, which is no mere phenomenon that appeared towards the end of the eighteenth century and died out after fifty years" (James, 1963, pp. 168–169).

In some sense, the predominance of so-called synaesthesia in the poetry of many of the core English and German Romantic poets—William Blake, Samuel Taylor Coleridge, William Wordsworth, Percy Bysshe Shelley, Friedrich Schlegel, Ludwig Tieck, Novalis—foreshadows the infatuation of later Romanticism, from French Symbolism to Haight-Ashbury psychedelic culture, with the glorification of sensory experience. In their frequent attempts to express sublime moments of expanded consciousness poetically, these and other Romantics often employed intersensory metaphors. When Coleridge (in "The Eolian Harp") spoke of "A light in sound, a sound-like power in light," or when Shelley used poetic metaphors linking light and music (in "Alastor," "The Revolt of Islam," "To a Skylark," and other poems), they were not, as seven decades of literary criticism has assumed, experiencing synaesthesia but were reaching beyond the bounds of the five senses for language to express the ineffable. All language is ultimately rooted in sensory experience, so after the senses are transcended, there is no language left but that of inventive combination of the senses. If the fundamental impulse of the high Romantic period was one of expanded consciousness, then it is easy to see why so much of its poetic language employed intersensory metaphor. When French Symbolists of the late nineteenth century took their own aim at expanded consciousness, coincident with the scientific discovery of synaesthesia, it was inevitable that they turned to the surprising juxtapositions of the senses experienced by actual synaesthetes for inspiration.[9]

M. H. Abrams (1984, p. 42) has shown how for eighteenth-century English Romantics protesting "single vision and Newton's sleep," the "correspondent breeze" was the perfect metaphor, its invisibility overthrowing the tyranny of the eye and the obsession with material substance, and at the same time providing an image derived from nature, from which post-Cartesian mechanism and dualism had radically severed human consciousness. "Invisibles"— drawn first from the language of Mesmerism, later from physics and other sciences—have continued to be favorite Romantic metaphors, but while these metaphors ebb and flow with scientific knowledge (such invisible entities as cosmic rays, magnetic and morphogenetic fields, the Van Allen radiation belts, and holograms all having had their day), synaesthesia has remained a potent metaphorical vehicle, for in addition to its aura of "invisibility," it adds the important Romantic themes of unity (the uniting of subjectivity and objectivity as well as the uniting of the senses) and liberation (from the physical world). Abrams accurately described Romanticism as the secularization of the Biblical narrative of Eden-Fall-Redemption into innocence-alienation-regeneration; synaesthesia, as a new and expanded form of wholeness, fits neatly into the last term of this triad and so has been seized upon repeatedly by Romantic writers seeking to regenerate what they have seen as the the dying culture of Cartesian dualism. Though I will treat a number of Romantic interpretations of eidetic imagery, eideticism has never generated the exaggerated claims concerning its power that synaesthesia has, a comparison which suggests that even more than the dimension of "seeing the unseen," synaesthesia's seeming affirmation of inherent unity and wholeness is what primarily lends it its attraction for the Romantic sensibility.

Despite overwhelming evidence, available since the initial scientific studies of synaesthesia, that the colors reported for linguistic sounds (and musical tones) were highly idiosyncratic, researchers continue to attempt to prove the existence of certain "absolute" cross-sensory values. The French Symbolists' long argument over the color of the vowels, Wassily Kandinsky's color theory, and the many attempts to create "color music" have all been motivated by a desire to discover a transcendental form of representation, free of the subjective limitations of conventional language. Both art theorists and experimental psychologists had already been searching for universal values for color and line. They saw synaesthetic photisms, because of their apparent objective reality as projected images and their linkage to other sensory attributes, as uniquely and persuasively indicative of some yet-to-be-elaborated transcendental schema. The visually projected nature of eideticism lent it too an elevated status denied typical mental images, as a reality existing "out there"; and because it seemed able to overcome the subjective limits of ordinary memory, it was often interpreted as an absolute form of knowledge. With Vladimir Nabokov, synaesthesia and eideticism combined with an extraordinary literary gift. His work demands that the reader give rather more than the usual credence to the objective reality of imagined worlds; indeed, its effect has often been to move readers to ascribe to Nabokov an ability to actually see the "otherworld," not just to persuasively imagine one. To many observers, synaesthetes and eidetic imagers have been permitted a view of something that seems to hold more truth than their own nonsynaesthetic and noneidetic imagery. For more than a century now, these mysterious faculties have been viewed by many as a "next step" in human cognitive evolution.

The apparent liberatory promise of synaesthesia has been reinforced by the fact that in addition to being the cognitive condition of a few "gifted" individuals, synaesthesia can occasionally be experienced by nonsynaesthetes, during altered states of consciousness. Though the most notorious of these states is the LSD trip, synaesthetic perception commonly accompanies intoxication with other hallucinogens, including mescaline, hashish, and dimethyltryptamine (DMT). In the nineteenth century, when it became widely known that some people saw color in response to sound, those who studied synaesthesia recalled the writings of artists, poets, and other seekers of expanded consciousness that described similar experiences. In 1857, Union College undergraduate FitzHugh Ludlow had published his account of the visions induced by eating cannabis jelly: "Thus the hasheesh-eater knows what it is . . . to *smell* colors, to *see* sounds, and much more frequently, to *see* feelings" (Ludlow, 1857, pp. 149–150). French poet Théophile Gautier had described something similar in 1843: "My hearing was inordinately developed; I heard the sound of colors. Green, red, blue, yellow sounds came to me perfectly distinctly" (quoted in Ludlow, 1857, p. 150). Though much less frequently invoked by those who see it as a state of expanded consciousness, a variety of disparate episodic states of consciousness, including the hypnotic state, schizophrenia, and temporal-lobe epilepsy also occasionally provoke synaesthesia. The emancipation felt by nonsynaesthetes within all these states is essentially freedom from rationality and from a defined sense of self. In most cases, synaesthetes themselves rarely if ever experience such a feeling of ego loss while they are perceiving synaesthetically; yet this distinction is never made by Romantic champions of synaesthetic perception, who have almost invariably assumed that synaesthetes are permanently within the redemption or regeneration mode of Abrams's triad.

Along with those who have been equally enthusiastic about the "expansion" of consciousness through both synaesthesia and hallucinogens, a surprisingly eclectic group of more sober twentieth-century intellectuals—including A. R. Luria, Charles Hartshorne, Maurice Merleau-Ponty, Roman Jakobson, and Sergei Eisenstein—have given synaesthesia a central place in their theoretical approaches. The attractiveness of synaesthesia as an explanatory idea has only increased in recent years. In a 1990 collection of essays attempting to rescue subjective visual phenomena from the realm of the strictly irrational and idio-syncratic, Yale University psychologist Lawrence Marks reiterated his twenty-year-old hypothesis that synaesthesia is the mechanism underlying all meta-phor construction. In 1991, cognitive anthropologist Bradd Shore published a major theoretical article in *Current Anthropology* in which he proposed that all cultural meaning has a "double birth," once through the evolution of spatial and temporal analogies in particular social and historical settings, and once through idiosyncratic schematization in individuals, via the mechanism of synaesthesia. In 1993, New Age publisher J. P. Tarcher published *The Man Who Tasted Shapes,* by neurologist Richard Cytowic, in which synaesthesia functions as a sort of "antidote" to rationality. Despite, or perhaps because of, this continued interdisciplinary interest and its impact on a variety of modern cultural expressions, from the visual arts and literary criticism to contemporary popular occultism, synaesthesia has never been investigated by cultural or intellectual historians other than incidentally, as a part of larger studies. In Stephen Kern's *The Culture of Time and Space, 1880–1918* (1983), synaesthesia is briefly mentioned as a conspicuous ingredient in turn-of-the-century artistic attempts to go beyond existing genre boundaries, but Kern's treatment gives no sense of the philosophical issues brought into focus by both the scientific and the artistic interest in synaesthesia. The nineteenth-century "genealogy" of synaesthesia—from Romanticism to Symbolism to Futurism—set forth by Kern and taken for granted by so many other historians obscures the survival of the faddish fin de siècle atmosphere surrounding synaesthesia in a variety of twentieth-century Romantic projects, continuing up through the most recent incarnation of liberatory Romanticism—cyberculture. As evidenced by the current "cyberpunk" infatuation with synaesthesia, as well as by neurologist Cytowic's use of synaesthesia to announce that we really are primarily emo-tional beings rather than rational machines and Marks's theory of metaphor, the Romantic and Symbolist aspiration to transcend the senses has not dimin-ished in our day.

Chapter 1 From *un Truc* to Occult Truth: The Fascination with Synaesthesia in Fin de Siècle France

For seventy years, after the first full description was published in 1812, synaesthesia was unknown in Europe outside the medical community, where it was considered to be a rare pathology of the visual system. Western culture's wider acquaintance with synaesthesia began in 1883 in a colorful flash of Symbolist light, with Arthur Rimbaud's distillation into sonnet form of French medical literature on subjective visions, and by century's end the visual phantasmagoria of synaesthesia had become something of an intellectual fad. The phenomenon was thus ushered into popular awareness in an atmosphere of magic and mystery. As one bizarre flower in Symbolism's hothouse collection of subjective sensations, ranging from dreams to opium visions, synaesthesia was attractive to those late nineteenth-century artists and intellectuals disaffected with positivism. While some scientists and critics interpreted both actual synaesthetes and their artistic imitators as diseased or degenerate, in the prevailing view of synaesthesia the ability to "see sounds" was esteemed as a special, "higher" form of human vision. The initial association of color hearing with Arthur Rimbaud, the archetypal *voyant* of French Symbolism, and then, through a curious invention of tradition, with Charles Baudelaire, guaranteed that subsequent Romantic thinkers would approach synaesthesia as a privileged form of perception. The metaphysical stance of the Symbolists, summarized in Baudelaire's declaration that "commonsense tells us that the things of the earth exist but very little, and that true reality lies only in dreams" ([1856] 1968, p. 345), predisposed them to favor synaesthesia, which seemed to them to have dreamlike qualities. For the most part, the fin de siècle fascination with syn- aesthesia took little account of phenomenological descriptions by synaesthetes themselves; the Symbolists preferred to *imagine* that a variety of psychological and even religious consequences stemmed from synaesthetic perception. The association of synaesthesia with artistic perception has obscured the origins of scientific and extrascientific knowledge of the phenomenon. These origins suggest that despite the fervent interest in rarefied forms of vision, fin de siècle Europe lacked an adequate schema to interpret synaesthetes and their magical colored apparitions.

THE MEDICAL DISCOVERY AND EARLY
DESCRIPTION OF SYNAESTHESIA

Almost immediately following its discovery and scientific description in the first decades of the nineteenth century, the rare, idiosyncratic, and altogether previously unnoticed psychological phenomenon known as synaesthesia was given a variety of histories by European and American writers, both scientific and nonscientific. Those invented histories, though they convey a limited understanding of the nature of synaesthesia, reveal a great deal about the intellectual, cultural, and spiritual aspirations of the interpreters. Given that writings about synaesthesia have continued to feature such invented histories, it is critical to attempt to understand just where, when, and in what context a systematic study of synaesthesia was originally made, and to trace the early development of scientific thinking on the subject. The first published work dealing with the psychological phenomenon that came to be known as syn- aesthesia was Dr. G. T. L. Sachs's 1812 treatise on his own and his sister's experience of color hearing. Sachs and his sister had highly specific, invariable color sensations associated with vowels, consonants, musical notes, sounds of instruments, numbers, names of cities, days of the week, dates, periods of history, and the stages of human life and saw the colors whenever they heard, saw, or thought of any of these sounds or concepts. Dr. Sachs's phenomenologi- cal description of their chromaesthesia was only a small part of a work whose principal object was to discuss frankly something considerably more monstrous—their albinism. This genetic condition, not the strange colored visions, motivated Sachs's treatise, and it was as an example of one of nature's most dramatic "sports" that it attracted attention. When Sachs's *Historiae naturalis duorum leucaetiopum auctoris ipsius et sororis eius* (Natural history of two albinos, the author and his sister) was translated into German in 1824 by Julius Heinrich Gottlieb Schlegel, it was given the title *Ein Beitrag zur näheren Kenntnis der Albinos*—"A Contribution to Deeper Knowledge of Albinos." Physicians with an interest in the anomalies of vision, however, quickly made note of the treatment of that subject in Sachs's work. Beginning in 1814 with Joseph Capuron and Victor Nysten's *Nouveau dictionnaire de médecine, de chirurgie, de physique, de chimie et d'histoire naturelle,* Sachs's case was routinely cited in medical reference works under one or another entry—such as "Retina," "Hallucinations," "Imagination"—dealing with subjective phenomena of vision. In 1848, in his review of the case of Dr. Sachs, Dr. Edward Cornaz called the abnormal sensation of color *hyperchromatopsie,* a term that was retained in Dr. Louis-Victor Marcé's *Des altérations de la sensibilité* (1860) and in an 1863 publication by Dr. Claude Perroud, which included the first attempt to explain the physiology of color hearing. In 1864, Dr. Ernest Chabalier coined a new term—*pseudochromesthésie*—which suggests how the projected color images of the synaesthete were regarded by the nonsynaesthete, that is, as "false. Chabalier's article described the case of a friend, also a doctor, who had color hearing for vowels, numbers, days of the week, months, and proper names. Chabalier noted that his chromaesthetic friend had had hallucinations and illusions as a child, apparent reinforcement for the view that the photisms of color hearers were a product of an abnormal visual system.[1]

Twenty years later, the terminology regarding synaesthesia was still fluid, an indication of how poorly understood it was, but in any case synaesthesia remained strictly an *optical* problem. In 1882, Dr. Luigi Pedrono in *Les annales d'oculistique* referred to the English expression "colour-hearing," but preferred to coin a new Greek term—*phonopsie* (that is, "sound seeing")—which stressed its visual nature. In all of these works, along with various medical encyclopedias, the colored visions of the synaesthete were considered within the context of other subjective visual sensations—hallucinations, afterimages, and entoptic phenomena. Sachs's synaesthetic visions had come to light just as European thought was becoming more open to the reality of something that the Romantics had been championing for decades—inner vision. Inspired by Goethe's call in *Zur Farbenlehre* for more attention to the productions of the eye, V. J.

Purkinje had, in a series of publications between 1812 and 1829, developed a classification that recognized twenty-eight categories of retinal images. In his *Handbuch der Physiologie des Menschen für Vorlesungen,* Johannes Müller (1838) demonstrated conclusively that a person could produce his own "visual light"; Müller cited as evidence such phenomena as "seeing stars," and drug-induced visions. According to Jonathan Crary (1990), these subjectively produced visual phenomena began to attain the status of optical "truth" by midcentury—and in so doing prepared the way for new conceptions of objectivity and freed sensory perception from the need for an external referent. Still, disagreement continued over just how "true" these inner visions were. Despite the enthusiasm of Romantic writers for what seemed to be increasing accumulation of scientific evidence for the powerful role of the imagination in human cognition, Sachs's and Chabalier's cases, like other cases of rare visual phenomena, were principally discussed by scientists as representing *abnormalities* of the visual system.[2]

Full descriptions of individual cases of color hearing were very slow to appear in the scientific literature. Aside from Sachs's and Chabalier's cases, the medical encyclopedic literature cited only a few rare, anonymous anecdotal observations of cases. The last century of literature on synaesthesia provides ample testimony that early in their lives, unless they have a sibling, parent, or other intimate relation in whom to confide, synaesthetes almost universally hide their condition, having experienced painful ridicule when they spoke of their "visions." For those synaesthetes without such early confidantes, it is not uncommon to go through their entire life without ever meeting another synaesthete. Sachs's almost incidental mention of his and his sister's psychological anomaly became public knowledge because of his commitment to advancing medical knowledge, and for seven decades, practically the only synaesthetes to come forward were, like Sachs, careful scientific observers whose curiosity about their own condition superseded any fear they had of being labeled as delusional or insane. In 1873, the Austrian doctor Jean Nüssbaumer published an essay on his own and his brother's cases of color hearing, making a distinction between "subjective" and "objective" sensations of color induced by sound—"objective" applying to his experience. Nüssbaumer emphasized that although many individuals had a vague sensation of color in response to sound, the true color hearer saw projected in his actual visual field a distinct, specific color, as "real" as any other color perceived. For Nüssbaumer, it was the nonsynaesthete, not the synaesthete, who was "imagining" things. Another Viennese physician, Moritz Benedikt, suggested that the Nüssbaumer brothers' *Farbenempfindungen* was

Bright Colors Falsely Seen

Bright Colors Falsely Seen

Synaesthesia and the Search

for Transcendental Knowledge

Kevin T. Dann

Yale University Press

New Haven & London

that is, those who had never experienced this level of consciousness—sounded like synaesthesia. The occultist Paul Sédir attempted to acquire accurate descriptions of the astral world by hypnotizing a medium, then reciting Hindu mantras and playing notes on the piano for her. In her trance state, she described the mantra (or what to her ears would have been heard as nonsense syllables) "OM! MANI PADME HUM!" as looking like four interlocking pale green circles that gave a cold sensation. A B-minor arpeggio took the form of a green ring, fringed by blue arrowlike shapes. Low C on the piano produced a bright red helmet shape, C♯ a blue rectangle with a green point in the center. Although Sédir took these colored geometric figures to be "inscribed by sounds on the astral canvas," what he was really producing in his hypnotized subject were synaesthetic photisms (Godwin, 1991, pp. 37–38). In *Soul Shapes*, Alice Dew-Smith claimed to "visualize souls," picturing them in four color types: the colors of the "surface" soul were most complex; the "deep" soul evoked a color image that was smaller and dark brown with red patches; the "mixed" soul was an oblong sphere with yellow at the surface; the "blue" soul was the highest and simplest of all. In her preface, Dew-Smith alluded to Francis Galton's work on projected mental imagery and suggested that her "soul seeing" was related to numerical, calendrical, or other mental forms (Dew-Smith, 1890, p. 7).

Just as Symbolists had invented a tradition linking universal correspondences with synaesthesia, "evolutionary occultists" linked synaesthesia with descriptions of the astral world. According to Victor Segalen, "the Initiates attribute to each of their letters a specific color. Colored hearing did not wait for the very famous sonnet 'Vowels' to illustrate the Kabbalah" (Segalen, 1902, p. 145). Segalen cited an article about "sound, light, and color in the astral" in the occultist journal *L'Initiation* as his source for this observation. The journal's full title—*Revue philosophique indépendente des hautes études, hypnotisme, force psychique, théosophie, kabbale gnose, franc-maçonnerie, sciences occultes*—gives some idea of the range of interests of its readers, who were also reading speculative occult syncretism in the *Revue spirite: Journal d'études psychologiques; La curiosité: Journal de l'occultisme scientifique; Revue de l'hypnotisme;* and *Annales des sciences psychiques* (the most widely read French journal of psychic research, which became *Revue métapsychique* in 1919). Jules Millet's 1892 work on audition colorée had noted that of late synaesthesia had been given a "cosmic conception": given that both sound and light were vibrations, and that light (color) was of a higher vibration, perhaps the resonating bodies that produced sound also produced light, which could be seen only by those with more refined nervous systems. In support of this explanation, Millet cited a passage in an

1888 article by occultist Franz Hartmann which read: "If the movement of the ether goes from thousands of vibrations per second to many billions, you will have light instead of sound" (Millet, 1892, p. 65). Millet found this plausible and believed that in the future humans would begin to see the many vibrations of the ether that at the time escaped human perception. Superficially, the descriptions of astral "vibrations" *did* sound like descriptions of synaesthetic photisms, as in this passage from one of Annie Besant's works:

> These vibrations, which shape the matter of the plane into thought-forms, give rise also—from their swiftness and subtlety—to the most exquisite and constantly changing colours, waves of varying shades like the rainbow hues in mother-of-pearl, etherealized and brightened to an indescribable extent, sweeping over and through every form, so that each presents a harmony of rippling, living, luminous, delicate colours, including many not even known to earth. Words can give no idea of the exquisite beauty and radiance shown in combinations of this subtle matter, instinct with life and motion. Every seer who has witnessed it, Hindu, Buddhist, Christian, speaks in rapturous terms of its glorious beauty. [Besant, 1897, p. 146]

KANDINSKY'S INVENTION AS SYNAESTHETE

This new confusion—between synaesthesia and "astral" perception—was perpetuated by Wassily Kandinsky's *Über das Geistige in der Kunst* (Concerning the spiritual in art, [1912] 1947), writings he first assembled in 1908–1909, which served as both a primer on his theories of art and a manifesto for Kandinsky's anticipated "Epoch of the Great Spiritual." Opening with a frontal attack on materialism, Kandinsky lamented that even art had succumbed to the materialism of the age: "During periods when art has no champion, when true spiritual food is wanting, there is retrogression in the spiritual world" (p. 28; Kandinsky, [1912] 1947, is henceforth cited parenthetically in text by page number only). Kandinsky gave an approving nod toward his fellow crusaders for the "nonmaterial"—the Spiritualists Johann Karl Friedrich Zöllner and William Crookes, the psychic investigator Charles Richet, the criminologist Cesare Lombroso, the ectoplasmic wonder Eusapia Palladino, Theosophical Society founder Helena Petrovna Blavatsky, and the Anthroposophical Society founder Rudolf Steiner. Kandinsky imagined Western culture as a "spiritual pyramid" filled with materialist philistines, except at the very apex, where a few nonmaterialist spiritual adepts hovered. Chief among these adepts was Mme. Blavatsky, whose methods were, according to Kandinsky, "in opposition to positivism, derive[d] from an ancient wisdom, which has been formulated with relative precision" (p. 32). Part of Kandinsky's and others' sense of the imminence of the "Great Spiritual" was derived from Theosophical literature, which posited 1899 as the end of the Kali Yuga, the long age in which human beings descended increasingly into matter. After this, according to Blavatsky, humankind was destined to enter an era of increasing spiritualization. Literature, music, and art, declared Kandinsky, would be the domains where this spiritual transformation would first become noticeable. He conceived of all artistic genres as capable of producing transhistorical forms of aesthetic meaning for the "sensitive" soul; the more the work of art transcended a particular set of idiosyncratic cultural meanings, the more resonance it would have for such sensitives, who were expected to become more numerous under the joint tutelage of the Theosophical Society and aesthetic theorists like Kandinsky. Aural sensations, for example, would transcend the limitations of language and become "pure sound . . . [exercising] a direct influence on the soul" (p. 34).

This aesthete's aesthetic, rooted in Symbolist principles of artistic excellence, was particularly conspicuous in Kandinsky's approach to color. The effects of color were hierarchical, depending on the "level of [spiritual] development" of the individual. People at a low stage of development experienced only fleeting "superficial" effects due to color, while those at a higher level experienced "a more profound effect, which occasions a deep emotional response" (p. 44). In such people, color "call[ed] forth a vibration from the soul." As with pure sound, pure color could, in the right people, communicate directly, unmediated by symbolic conventions. Red, for example, "may cause a spiritual vibration like flame, since red is the color of flame" (p. 44). What is most remarkable about this passage is that Kandinsky, who had such an intimate relationship with color, should call a flame "red." Speculating about the effects of color on the other senses, he chose the rather uninspired possibility that bright yellow might produce a "sour effect" by association with lemons. Beyond such fairly obvious associative effects of color, Kandinsky was particularly interested in effects that violated common convention, citing as example a case of the peculiar form of synaesthesia known as "colored gustation." A Dr. Franz Freudenberg had published the case of one of his patients, for whom a certain sauce had a "blue" taste. Freudenberg's article, which also contained a discussion of audition colorée, was not from the by then vast scientific literature on synaesthesia, but from a German occultist journal, *Die übersinnliche Welt: Monatsschrift für okkultische Forschung.* Freudenberg noted that the woman was "spiritually, unusually highly developed," a perception that deeply impressed Kandinsky, who underlined this characterization in his copy of the article.[6]

This single example was evidence enough for Kandinsky, who in his theory of synaesthesia posited that

> in the case of such highly developed people the paths leading to the soul are so direct, and the impressions it receives are so quickly produced, that an effect immediately communicated to the soul via the medium of taste sets up vibrations along the corresponding paths leading away from the soul to the other sensory organs (in this case, the eye). The effect would be a sort of echo or resonance, as in the case of musical instruments, which without themselves being touched, vibrate in sympathy with another instrument being played. Such highly sensitive people are like good, much-played violins, which vibrate in all their parts and fibers at every touch of the bow. [p. 45]

Kandinsky fancied himself one of these fine violins, and he followed with his own cross-sensory sensitivity to the haptic (prickly versus smooth) and thermal (cold versus warm) properties of colors. He also noted the fairly universal tendency to link bright colors with high musical tones and dark colors with low tones and cited Russian occultist Aleksandra Zakharin-Unkovskaia, who had developed a method to teach children how to "hear color" and "see sounds."[7] Though acknowledging that Freudenberg argued against any general laws of color-sound equivalence, Kandinsky cited an article by Leonid Sabaneiev, a devotee of Aleksandr Scriabin, expressing hope that such laws would soon be established. Kandinsky found Scriabin's table of correlations for his work *Prometheus* and Zakharin-Unkovskaia's work at the St. Petersburg Conservatory as promising "empirically a table of equivalent tones in color and music" Whatever might eventually prove to be the correct set of correspondences for the "sensitive" soul, color was a "keyboard," and it was the artist's job to "purposefully set the soul vibrating by means of this or that key." Kandinsky never dealt with the fact that every color hearer had a completely idiosyncratic set of colors; his desire was for a sort of mathematics of color, whereby the spiritually advanced artist like himself could pluck the strings and evoke the appropriate response. The descriptions of astral colors that Kandinsky read in the occult literature held extraordinary promise because they testified to an "absolute" form of representation, free of the possibility of artifice or misrepresentation. The abstract canvases that Kandinsky began to produce almost simultaneously with the publication of *Concerning the Spiritual in Art* were immediately attacked as hermetic depictions that could mean something to Kandinsky and no one else. By appealing to a transcendent color schema, Kandinsky attempted to defuse these criticisms. In an autobiographical note in a 1913 catalog, Kandinsky vigorously refuted what he claimed were the two most common misconceptions about his abstract paintings—that he wanted to "paint music," and that he was merely painting his own inner psychic states. He said that he was instead "mak[ing] the inner element sound forth more strongly by limiting the external" (p. 46). The "innere Notwendigkeit," variously translated as the "inner element" or "inner necessity," was an inalienable "spiritual" truth accessible to artists like Kandinsky, who supposedly brought it forth for all to see in his paintings.

All of Kandinsky's speculations about synaesthesia and nonrepresentational art would probably be long forgotten had Kandinsky not, by the time that *On the Spiritual in Art* was published in 1912, succeeded in producing his first, and arguably *the* first, completely abstract paintings. Anyone who had a passing familiarity with Theosophical or anthroposophical ideas was aware of the "new gnosis" embraced by Kandinsky and other Expressionists, but contemporaries did not necessarily perceive a causal relationship between occult ideas and the art appearing on Expressionist canvases. Art critic and historian Gustav Hartlaub, himself a student of occult thought (though he identified himself as among the "non-Theosophists"), believed that the "curious spiritual upheaval" in Europe could be seen nowhere more clearly than in Expressionist art. He noted the employment of color to achieve gnosis: "Colors . . . are symbols for feelings, sometimes for thoughts too, direct revelations of inner states of being, even if naturally awakened by the seen, felt experience of the sensual world, like sounds in music. Munch was the first one to grasp them in this sense. Today such a grasp is almost common property of a generation of artists . . . Marc, Kandinsky, Kokoschka, Muche, Chagall, Metzinger, or Klee" (Hartlaub, quoted in Long, 1993, p. 92). Though Hartlaub touched on Theosophical ideas and mentioned Rudolf Steiner in particular, he nowhere suggested that the Expressionists had drawn their inspiration from such ideas. Rather, the Expressionists' ideal of a visual art that freed color and line from historical and cultural limitations was seen as an independent validation of occult beliefs: "What is offered to us today in Expressionist art and poetry is what we may recognize as a manifestation analogous to a neo-gnostic orientation. Entirely without direct contact, something is being realized on the aesthetic plane: . . . the gradual growth of a new and expanded consciousness!" (p. 93). Hartlaub pointed to specific themes and patterns in Expressionist painting—auras in Marc and Kokoschka, Klee's astral colors, Marc's cosmic animal world—and wondered whether such depictions did not seem "clairvoyant in the occult sense to the Theosophist." But Hartlaub remained clearly determined to protect these artists from accusations of mere occultism: "The artist remains completely in

the aesthetic realm, if out of purely artistic considerations, without even knowing about the occult, he redirects his attention from the physical object, from
visual content, to 'seeing' itself as an inner act of the soul. It is exactly this,
however, if we may believe the initiates, that always leads to a kind of colorful,
astral clairvoyancy" (p. 94). According to Hartlaub, artists like Kandinsky
reached higher planes of consciousness strictly through the practice of their art,
not through any particular occult methods of altering consciousness. Kandinsky, by dwelling on his self-proclaimed innate sensitivity to color, intended to
advance this same reading.

Criticism of and historical scholarship on Expressionist art in the following
decades occasionally examined the relation between the rise of abstraction and
Theosophical and other occult sources, but they seldom gave a specifically
occult interpretation of synaesthesia. Then in 1966 an article by art historian
Sixten Ringbom appeared in the *Journal of the Warburg and Courtauld Institutes*
that drew particular attention to Kandinsky's views on synaesthesia. Ringbom,
who was himself a student of occultism, focused particularly on the influence
on Kandinsky of Rudolf Steiner and Theosophical writers Helen P. Blavatsky,
Annie Besant, and C. W. Leadbeater. Ringbom was especially interested in
what these writers had to say about "thought-forms," the colored geometric
forms that were visible to true clairvoyants (that is, not the "atavistically"
mediumistic, but "advanced" clairvoyants, who retain full ego consciousness).
According to Theosophical writings, thought-forms were a (supersensorily)
visible representation of the emotional and spiritual condition of the person
who generated them. Ringbom pointed out that Besant and Leadbeater's 1901
book *Thought-Forms* and Leadbeater's 1902 work *Man Visible and Invisible,*
which not only detailed the occult theory of the supersensory world of colors
and forms but included colored plates illustrating them, were available to
Kandinsky in German translation in 1908. Ringbom stressed the importance of
these works to Kandinsky's ideas about the relation between colors and tones,
and thus between painting and music, a focal subject of *On the Spiritual in Art.*
Ringbom's thesis was that Kandinsky was at least partially synaesthetic and had
drawn on *Thought-Forms* for an explanation of synaesthesia that offered an
alternative to positivistic theories. As evidence Ringbom included a lengthy
passage from the closing section of *Thought-Forms* describing "Forms Built by
Music," which included the statement that "when . . . a musical note is
sounded, a flash of colour corresponding to it may be seen by those whose finer
senses are already to some extent developed."[8]

Thought-Forms described and illustrated three examples of musical thought-forms perceived by an astral clairvoyant for Mendelssohn's "Songs Without Words" no. 9, the soldier's chorus from Gounod's "Faust," and the overture to Wagner's *Die Meistersinger*. While the Mendelssohn composition produced a linear form in the three primary colors, and Gounod's chorus a globelike form radiant with the entire spectrum, Wagner produced a "vast bell-shaped erection, fully nine hundred feet in height":

> The resemblance to the successively retreating ramparts of a mountain is almost perfect, and it is heightened by the billowy masses of cloud which roll between the crags and give the effect of perspective . . . the broad result is that each mountain-peak has its own brilliant hue—a splendid splash of vivid colour, glowing with the glory of its own living light, spreading its resplendent radiance over all the country round. Yet in each of these masses of colour other colours are constantly flickering, as they do over the surface of molten metal, so that the coruscations and scintillations of these wondrous astral edifices are far beyond the power of any physical words to describe. [Besant and Leadbeater, [1901] 1961, p. 64]

The attraction of such spectacular color visions, particularly because of Besant and Leadbeater's claim that they were representative of the spiritual values of the different compositions, was no doubt irresistible to Kandinsky, who was searching for his own transcendental language of color. Struck by the superficial similarity between synaesthetic photisms and astral thought-forms, Kandinsky transferred the objective authority attributed to the thought-forms to the swirling colors of the color hearer. Ringbom recapitulated Kandinsky's reasoning—and then added the claim that Kandinsky was himself synaesthetic. Kandinsky and Ringbom both made the same error that had been made by Baudelaire, or at least by Baudelaire's interpreters, mistaking descriptions of the spiritual, *supersensible* world for descriptions of the material, *sensible* world. In their eagerness to discover evidence of a nonvisible spiritual world, both the artist and the art historian invented their own positivist and materialist interpretations of synaesthesia, even though they were advancing them to protest against materialism and positivism.

Ringbom's thesis won wide acceptance among art historians during the 1970s and 1980s. E. H. Gombrich, despite his skepticism about Theosophical descriptions of thought-forms and other clairvoyant phenomena, supported Ringbom's thesis, particularly his highlighting of Kandinsky's interest in synaesthesia.[9] Though less impressed than Ringbom with the impact *Thought-Forms* had had on Kandinsky, Rose-Carol Washton Long mentioned in her *Kandinsky: The Development of an Abstract Style* (1980) the interest in synaesthesia among both Symbolists and Theosophists and chronicled Kandinsky's and others' attempts at a synaesthetic *Gesamtkunstwerk*.[10] Tracing the history of Kandinsky's theories on the synthesis of the arts in *Kandinsky and Schoenberg: Letters, Pictures, Documents* (1984), Jelena Hahl-Koch speaks of Kandinsky's "synesthetic gift" and also identifies Kandinsky as "a true eidetic."[11] Without specifically commenting on the validity of Ringbom's thesis, Bettina Knapp goes much further even than Kandinsky and Ringbom in her interpretation of synaesthesia as a higher form of consciousness:

> Synesthesia may be looked upon as a giant awakening, a psychic happening, and a flaring up of forces within the unconscious. Such a process enables the artist to experience the simultaneity of sense impressions, to see the work of art coming into being, and to come into contact with new languages, forgotten species, and preformal life. So that the synesthetic experience may bear its full fruit, the artist must be willing to undergo a momentary eclipse of his conscious personality and a dissociation of the ego, allowing him to be engulfed by the powers of the collective unconscious. Then the inner eye and ear can feel cadences and aromas, as well as the material fullness and aerated atomizations of sublimated spheres. [Knapp, 1988, pp. 83–84]

Knapp pairs her extravagant view of synaesthesia with Kandinsky's "soul reverberation" theory and then details Kandinsky's "synaesthetic" technique in his collection of prose poems, "Klänge" ("Sounds"), which she sees as "forays into the synesthetic experience [that] capture life in its flux, and action in its counteraction" (Knapp, 1988, p. 84). The imperative to acknowledge a nonvisible realm is so great that these authors find it unnecessary to discriminate between vastly dissimilar ideas and experiences. Since the appearance in the late nineteenth century of the first works explicitly describing supersensible realms, the tendency of people without direct experience of these realms, but looking to validate them, has been to conflate them with other phenomena. Romantic thinkers have been especially attracted to phenomena described by science, perhaps to counteract the common perception of their positivist critics that they are anti-science. Unfortunately, a sort of Law of Minimization of Mystery is at work in twentieth-century Romantic borrowings of scientific ideas about consciousness. The best contemporary example is the use by New Age Romantics of popularized notions about quantum physics: Consciousness is mysterious. Quantum mechanics is mysterious. Therefore, they must be similar. The "holographic paradigm," equating consciousness with a hologram, came about through the same sort of reasoning. Such correlating of mysteries was common at the turn of the century, when speculation about new forms of consciousness was rife. Synaesthesia was a mystery. The astral realm was a mystery. Because both seemed to be "about" colors visible to a select few, they were lumped together.[12]

In the introduction to a recent collection of articles gathered by the Los Angeles County Museum of Art to accompany the exhibit "The Spiritual in Art: Abstract Painting, 1890–1925," volume editor Maurice Tuchman, after a brief review of Western occult thought beginning with Plotinus and ending with Baudelaire, claimed that

> a fascination with synesthesia, the overlap between the senses—'sounds ring musically, colors speak'—absorbed the energies of numerous writers and thinkers throughout the ages. By extension, the energy flow and vibrations pervading the physical world concerned many theorists. Baudelaire, for example, used vibrational imagery as an integral part of his vocabulary and interpreted the world as constantly in motion: 'the more vigilant senses perceive more reverberating sensations' in which 'all sublime thought is accompanied by a nervous shaking.' [Tuchman, 1986, p. 20]

According to Tuchman, as twentieth-century artists, led by Kandinsky and his fellow Expressionists, moved toward abstraction, they never abandoned meaning but rather attempted to reach deeper levels of meaning, those which were hidden or "occult." Tuchman acknowledged the pioneering work of Sixten Ringbom in elucidating these hidden meanings, and the volume included an article by Ringbom, "Transcending the Visible: The Generation of the Abstract Pioneers," which largely recapitulated the ideas presented in his earlier publications on Kandinsky. Again, Ringbom stressed the influence of Rudolf Steiner on Kandinsky, and again he linked synaesthesia with the meditative techniques outlined in Steiner's writings: Kandinsky "believed that one could produce synesthesia by exercise. He thought that by screening off accidental impressions, a procedure that is the classic preliminary to mystical meditation, one could learn to receive higher stimuli. It was in the hope of achieving such higher perception that Kandinsky wrote meticulous notes after he read Steiner's occult texts." Further on in the article, after reviewing Steiner's and Leadbeater's descriptions of the clairvoyant sights of the astral plane, Ringbom states: "For Kandinsky an experience like the sights described by these authors would have made almost any amount of spiritual exercise worthwhile" (quoted in Tuchman, 1986, p. 132).

According to Ringbom, Long, Tuchman, and other scholars, Kandinsky found in Rudolf Steiner's writings support for his belief that synaesthesia permitted sensations from the nonmaterial world to reach the physical world. Ringbom, after quoting Kandinsky's notes on Steiner's instructions for achieving supersensible cognition, asks: "What, apart from synaesthesia, did Kandinsky hope to gain by the exercise of such precepts?" Long points to a passage in Steiner's *Theosophy* (1904) asserting that in the "spirit land," "each color, each perception of light represents a spiritual tone, and every combination of colors corresponds with a harmony, a melody" (Long, 1980, p. 109). Steiner's language here and elsewhere, whenever he spoke of the association of tones and colors, always referred to phenomena of *supersensible* perception, as he was constantly careful to point out: "It must be noted that by seeing a color, spiritual seeing is meant. When the clairvoyant speaks of 'seeing red,' he means: 'I have an experience, in a psycho-spiritual way, which is equivalent to the physical experience when an impression of red is received.' . . . If this point is overlooked, a mere color-vision may easily be mistaken for a genuine clairvoyant experience" (Steiner, [1900] 1947, p. 133). In his book *Theosophy*, the text that Ringbom contends so influenced Kandinsky, Steiner goes to great lengths to caution against the confusion of the material world perceivable by the bodily senses with the spiritual world, which can be experienced only with spiritual, non-bodily faculties. In the section "Thought-Forms and the Human Aura" in *Theosophy*, Steiner states that "misunderstandings can arise in men . . . in regard to the nature of what is here described as the aura. We might imagine that what are here described as colors would stand before the soul just as the physical colors stand before the physical eye. But such a soul color would be nothing but hallucination. With hallucinatory impressions, spiritual science is not in the least concerned" (Steiner, [1900] 1947, p. 203). Such misunderstandings were common enough that Steiner added a lengthy appendix to later editions of *Theosophy* to reinforce the distinction.

For Steiner, there really was a transcendental world of spiritual truth, but it was in no way accessible via the sorts of strictly subjective methods employed by Kandinsky. Steiner's epistemology of "objective idealism" maintained that at a certain level thinking becomes "intellektuelle Anschauung," intellectual, or "sense-free," perception of a realm of concepts that have objective content of their own. More than a theory of knowledge, this epistemology was for Steiner a means of attaining higher cognitive levels. According to Steiner, spiritual science, or anthroposophy, was capable of studying objective but transcendental phenomena by cognitive modes beyond the physical senses. The perennial problem was that Kandinsky and others who were eager to penetrate the material world to reach this "sense-free" realm of objective truth chose inappropriate methods. In his painting Kandinsky erased the object by reducing or eliminating thought and immersing himself in pure feeling, while Steiner called for the infusion of clear thinking *with* feeling, to attain knowledge of the higher worlds. Calling spiritual science both *Wissenschaft* (systematic knowledge, science) and *Erkenntnis* (cognition, perception), Steiner outlined a three-stage system through which anyone attempting to secure valid and comprehensive knowledge of higher worlds would pass. In progressing along this contemplative path, a person was increasingly liberated from the phenomenal world and not only entered supersensible realms but developed the ability to interpret the experience of them correctly. One of the reasons that Steiner's work was of interest to Kandinsky was that Steiner's account of the individual attainment of higher cognition, like Blavatsky and Besant's, was based on the assumption of an evolution in consciousness: humanity was entering the period when it must consciously choose to pursue spiritual development through *intellektuelle Anschauung*. Kandinsky interpreted this thesis as a validation of his own art and art theories, including his conception of synaesthesia as a form of higher cognition.[13]

As the third prominent European artist to be "invented" as a synaesthetc, Kandinsky, along with his admirers, furthered the explicit association of synaesthesia with creative artistic perception and "higher consciousness." Indeed, Kandinsky has replaced Rimbaud as the synaesthete of choice in contemporary discussions of the nature of synaesthesia. In his recent book on synaesthesia, Richard Cytowic offers a sketch of Kandinsky that reinforces the Romantic myth of synaesthetic perception:

> Vasily Kandinsky (1866–1944) was a synesthetic artist who perhaps had the deepest understanding of sensory fusion. . . . Kandinsky was among the first to step off the well-beaten path of representation that Western art had followed for five hundred years, and his model to express his transcendent vision was music. . . . Kandinsky absorbed the teachings of Theosophy and Eastern thought, and the ideas he encountered in both scientific and esoteric writings confirmed a spiritual view of the world. . . . Kandinsky wished to push aside analytic explanations and move himself and his audience closer to the quality of direct experience that synesthesia represented. [Cytowic, 1994, pp. 55–56]

SYNAESTHESIA AND THE ASTRAL WORLD:
THE CONFUSION PERSISTS

Cytowic's serious consideration of Kandinsky's occult interests is an uncommonly open-minded gesture for a contemporary behavioral scientist. Whether a century ago or today, natural science has little interest in the speculative claims of popular occultism other than as a competing worldview that challenges its status as supreme elucidator of all phenomena, normal or paranormal. The "astral" has no place within modern natural scientific explanatory apparatus; among mainstream scientists, the word itself has become a sort of pejorative, a code word signifying flaky pseudoscience. The conflation of synaesthetic photisms with astral visions only helped drive materialist science and its anti-materialist critics further apart and ensured that synaesthesia and other scientific mysteries would continue to provoke Romantic claims about the unseen and our rudimentary ability to see it. At the same time, scientists could deride astral enthusiasts in the effort to arrogate all epistemological authority to science. As a phenomenon at the edge of both scientific and extrascientific explanatory abilities, synaesthesia continues to draw our attention to the incompleteness of our understanding of the interface between ourselves and the wider world.

Chapter 3 The Meaning of Synaesthesia Is Meaning

The artistic interest in idiopathic synaesthesia as a possible model for a transcendental language migrated through the arts at the turn of the century, moving from poetry and theater to painting and then to music. In each of these arts, cross-sensory analogies were assumed to exist between color and musical tone, and through them, artists hoped to express the "inner necessity"—objective spiritual truth—spoken of by Kandinsky. For many of these artists, a satisfying synthesis of colored light and sound, or in some cases, moving color alone, was seen as a substitute for the "higher consciousness" possessed by the actual synaesthete. After 1883 and the post-"Voyelles" fascination with color hearing, all the painters, musicians, and tinkerers who were interested in creating color music acquainted themselves with the scientific literature on synaesthesia, and scientists often took note of color music when they surveyed the subject. In 1889 Louis Favre, who published several articles on chromaesthesia, requested permission to give a performance of color music at the illuminated fountains of the Paris exhibition. Favre was the first of many "color musicians" who, charmed by the idea that a few people saw moving, brightly colored abstract forms as they listened to music, were determined to make the same experience available to everyone. Russian composer Aleksandr Scriabin's *Prometheus,* widely assumed to have been inspired by his own synaesthetic ability, showed that such synthetic performances were in no way transcendental, either in the sense of being universally comprehensible or in the sense of portraying any absolute reality beyond the physical. The true role of synaesthesia in human consciousness remained obscure; synaesthesia remained caught between the Romantic interpretation of it as a higher form of consciousness conveying transcendent meaning, and the positivist denial that such meaning existed.

AN ART OF MOBILE COLOR

Endeavors to bring together sight and sound in works of art long antedated scientific interest in synaesthesia. Chronologies of such attempts usually begin with Père Castel's invention of a *clavecin oculaire* in 1741. Castel received his inspiration for the instrument at least in part from an earlier Jesuit priest-professor, Athanasius Kircher, who had called sound "the ape of light," and in his *Musurgia universalis* (1650) wrote: "If at the time of a fine concert we could see the air stirred by all the vibrations communicated to it by the voices and instruments, we should be surprised to see it filled with the liveliest and most finely blended colors." Castel made the mistake of assuming that Kircher referred to the visible spectrum, whereas Kircher was actually describing the colors produced by sound in the *astral* realm, which were "visible" only to clairvoyants. Discussion and experimentation focused (as it would after the publication of Rimbaud's "Voyelles") on whether absolute correspondences existed between colors and musical notes, and how those correspondences might be best represented by means of a keyboard device that projected colored light. Natural philosophers's interest quickly shifted to the general public, who were taken with the possibilities of color music as a form of entertainment. In the early 1800s, Sir David Brewster experimented with creating a device that might put colors into motion so artfully that they would resemble music. His efforts led him to predict that "combinations of forms and colours may be made to succeed each other in such a manner as to excite sentiments and ideas with such vivacity as those which are excited by musical composition." Brewster came up with such a device in 1818, but before he could patent it, the patent officer showed it to an optician, and within three months over two hundred thousand of the devices—the first kaleidoscopes—had been sold in London and Paris. Italian theater artist Pietro Gonzaga's observation that fireworks predated Castel and others' instruments as the original "music for the eyes" suggests that it is the perennial delight in the visual magic of mobile color in motion that has sustained interest in color music for so long. Color music was a diversion of the same order as such natural displays as rainbows, sunrises and sunsets, or the northern lights, replicated artificially in fireworks, Bengal lights, illuminated vapors, colored steam, 'fairy fountains,' and similar exhibitions in the open air. Color music merely added sound to the visual spectacle. In 1877, P. T. Barnum put one of Bainbridge Bishop's color organs in his museum, and for the next half-century variations on the device were constantly being incorporated into popular theatrical entertainments in Europe and North America.[1]

Though Castel and the many inventors who followed him never claimed that their instruments made the spiritual realm visible, they often spoke as if they had brought the heavens down to earth. Their enthusiasm for color music showed through in their pronouncements about the "new" art they believed they were pioneering. Arthur W. Rimington, who first demonstrated his color organ in London in 1895, saw himself as the inventor of mobile color, which he took to be the vanguard of a revolutionary, wholly abstract art: "We have not yet had pictures in which there is neither form nor subject, but only pure color." He felt that the purpose of the new art, "the extent and grandeur of whose developments it is simply impossible to estimate," was "to ennoble, to refine, to increase the pleasures and interests of life, to educate the special sense or senses to which they minister." Twenty years later M. Luckiesh also expected "that mobile color will become a distinct art. Why not? Color apart from sound— and all by itself—can thrill humanity. Best of all, its appeal is sensual before it is intellectual." Mary Hallock Greenewalt, a concert pianist who became interested in color music about 1906, gave her first color music concert in Philadelphia in 1911, and eventually designed her own devices. She told a convention of the Illuminating Engineers' Society in 1918 that color music was "an art that can play at will on the spinal marrow of the human being, remind him of the Holy Ghost and the utter sheerness of beauty." The effusive mysticism typical of the creators of color music often met with indifference or incredulity from critics and the public. At one of Rimington's performances in the Manchester Free Trade Hall, the show was interrupted when a man stood up and accused Rimington of fraud. Reviews in Manchester called Rimington's invention a "glorified magic lantern," and "an ingenious toy." For over thirty years, an argument over the validity of color music's artistic and technical premises was carried on sporadically in newspapers and magazines; after nearly every concert, readers would write in either to praise the unearthly beauty of the performances or to ridicule the idea of an analogy between sound and color. Throughout these debates, the existence of idiopathic synaesthesia was routinely cited as evidence that such an analogy might be possible, and color music supporters helped to reinforce the image of color hearers as aesthetically gifted, by constantly invoking the names of Baudelaire, Rimbaud, and later Kandinsky.[2]

At the same time as these experiments in color music were being carried out, Expressionist artists extended the initiative into drama. Influenced by the Symbolists and their own interest in synaesthesia, Wassily Kandinsky (with *Der gelbe Klang*, written in 1909) and Arnold Schoenberg (with *Die glückliche Hand*, begun in 1910) attempted artworks that incorporated "synaesthetic" effects. In both these abstract stage compositions, projected colored light was supposed to reinforce the emotional tones of the music and the sparse libretto and stage action. Whether by coincidence or by design, Schoenberg's color-emotion schema matched Kandinsky's as outlined in *On the Spiritual in Art*, thus creating the impression that their choice of colors had some objective authority. But both men had done little to alter traditional color symbolism—brown, green, and violet for passivity; red, orange, and yellow for increasing activity; and vaporous blue for celestial apotheosis. The minimalist plots of both works can be seen as expressing an "evolutionary" movement from dense materiality to increasingly exalted and ethereal spirituality, the movement that Kandinsky and Schoenberg expected to arrive imminently in the world at large.[3]

Historians and critics looking back at these works have invariably linked them to Richard Wagner's hope for a future synthesis of the arts, and some have even assumed that Wagner, because of his interest in the Gesamtkunstwerk, had color hearing! Usually these authors have erroneously cited aesthetic precursors as well; for example, in the chapter "Synesthetic Symbolism" in his survey of twentieth-century music, Glenn Watkins identifies Kandinsky's, Schoenberg's, and a number of other musical works with "the notion of spiritual and material correspondences and intrasensory relationships—ideas directly traceable to Swedenborg's *Arcana coelestia* (1749–1756) and Goethe's *Farbenlehre* (1805–1710)." Rather than see *Der gelbe Klang* and *Die glückliche Hand* as Symbolist endeavors that crudely employed color and music to represent transcendence in artistic language, Watkins and others have granted them a spiritual and intellectual authority to which they have no claim.

After the turn of the century, color music theorists occasionally located both Swedenborg's celestial arcana and the chromatic arcana of synaesthesia in the "fourth dimension." The reasoning was that because in the world of three dimensions these and other phenomena were not visible to everyone, they must take place in a higher, fourth dimension; many considered the "astral" realm of Theosophy to be identical with the fourth dimension. The examination of synaesthesia and synthetic artworks (that is to say, works that attempted to fuse sensory data) gives some notion about the degree to which these two concepts were linked at the time. In James Gibbons Huneker's 1902 story "The Disenchanted Symphony," speculation about the fourth dimension is prefaced with a passage that reveals the status of earlier ideas about synaesthesia:

> He [Pobloff, Huneker's fictional Russian composer] did not credit the theory of the alienists that the confusion of tone and color—*audition colorée*—betrayed the existence of a slight mental lesion; and he laughed consumedly at the notion of confusing musicians with madmen. . . . Why should the highly organized brain of a musician be considered abnormal because it could see tone, hear color, and out of a mixture of sound and silence, fashion images of awe and sweetness for a wondering, unbelieving world? If man is a being afloat in an ocean of vibrations, as Maurice de Fleury wrote, then any or all vibrations are possible. Why not a synthesis? Why not a transposition of the *neurons?* [Huneker, [1902] 1969, p. 329]

Pobloff tries to express audition colorée and a fourth spatial dimension in a symphony he composes entitled *The Abysm,* whose final notes cause the orchestra to disappear into a fourth-dimensional abyss of its own, from which they are called back when Pobloff plays the symphony backwards on the piano. Or so it appears to Pobloff, who has actually fallen off his conductor's riser, been knocked unconscious, and *dreamed* the entire sequence of events.[5]

Huneker's satirization of hyperspace theories and, seemingly, of artistic conceptions of color hearing as a mark of genius rather than madness, may give the impression that he was a diehard positivist skeptical about the existence of any transcendental realm, whether musical or mathematical. Huneker was as much a Romantic as the composer he invented. He had left his native Philadelphia for Paris in the 1890s, where he was infected with the "synthetic" bug. His principal theme in all his critical and fictional writing was the nature of artistic genius. He stayed abreast of the popular occultist ideas of the day and set out to demolish those he found wanting.[6] Despite a certain playful skepticism about the promise of synthetic art and its theoretical underpinnings, Huneker's frequent return to the theme suggests that he never quite abandoned his youthful infatuation with the possibility of such a synthesis. In a 1905 story entitled "The Medium," Mrs. Whistler, a woman with "supernormal" (which she and Huneker distinguish from "supernatural") powers unleashes a fantastic "symphony" of perfumes. Another of Huneker's artistic geniuses declares, "I can produce blazing symphonies. I will prove to you that colour is also music. This sounds as if I were a victim to that lesion of the brain called 'coloured-audition.' Perhaps. Not Helmholtz or Chevreul can tell me anything new in the science of optics. I am possessor of the rainbow secrets" (Huneker, 1905, p. 96).

The American architect Claude Bragdon, perhaps the most vocal advocate of a spatial fourth dimension, was equally passionate about color music. Lamenting the vulgarizations of colored light in the "sky signs" of upper Broadway in New York and on the Chicago lakefront, he argued for "an art of mobile color, not as a moving picture show—a thing of quick-passing concrete images, to shock, startle, or to charm—but as a rich and various language in which light, proverbially the symbol of the spirit, is made to speak, through the senses, some healing message to the soul" (Bragdon, 1926, p. 101). Bragdon, whose desire for a transcendental language found a congenial home in the Theosophical Society as well as in his speculations on the fourth dimension, insisted that this art of mobile color be realized through abstract, four-dimensional geometric forms, "remote . . . from the things of sense, from knowledge and experience" (p. 102). Drawing on François Delsarte's ideas about the relation between color and human physiology (ideas themselves influenced by occult thought), C. W. Leadbeater's descriptions of the colors of the "auric egg" surrounding humans, and Louis Wilson's occult scale correlating colors and musical tones, Bragdon attempted to forge a theory of color music that would be sufficiently immaterial but at the same time accessible to those who could not of their own accord peer into the fourth dimension. Bragdon imagined "an art of mobile color unconditioned by considerations of mechanical difficulty or of expense. . . . Sunsets, solar coronas, star spectra, auroras such as were never seen on sea or land; rainbows, bubbles, rippling water; flaming volcanoes, lava streams of living light—these and a hundred other enthralling and perfectly realizable effects suggest themselves. What Israel of the future will pour on mortals this new 'music of the spheres'?" (p. 112).

In 1919, Bragdon joined with the painter Van Deering Perrine and the Danish folksinger Thomas Wilfred to form the Prometheans, which they envisioned as an international society devoted to creating an art of abstract, mobile color. Working out of a studio built for them by patron Walter Kirkpatrick Brice on his Long Island estate, they attempted to perfect a color music instrument. Wilfred quickly became the most active of the group, and developed a device he called the "Clavilux," for projecting "lumia," kinetic color projections that he believed to be the realization of Bragdon's dream of fourth-dimensional forms.[7] The critic Sheldon Cheney's review of a studio demonstration of the Clavilux suggests that with each new technical development, believers felt a renewed sense of the transcendental promise of color music. In terms familiar to devotees of abstract mysticism, Cheney wrote: "One had that feeling of detachment, of ecstasy, which is a response only to the most solemn religious or aesthetic experience. . . . Perhaps this is the beginning of the greatest, the most spiritual and radiant art of all" (Cheney, 1934, p. 187). Cheney saw Wilfred's lumia as another manifestation of the evolutionary advance he detected in Expressionist abstraction; "in its finite way," according to Cheney, abstraction "echoes . . . one further push of evolutionary achievement, the harmonious order of the infinite" (Cheney, 1934, p. 323). The association of synaesthesia with so many synthetic artistic projects, real or imagined, particularly given their "ecstatic" overtones, has contributed to the Romantic interpretation of synaesthesia as a liberatory form of perception.

SCRIABIN: SYNAESTHESIA OR MEGALOMANIA?

Of all of the synthetic color and music productions that have helped to strengthen the liberatory Romantic view of synaesthesia, Aleksandr Scriabin's composition *Prometheus: The Poem of Fire* has had the greatest impact. When Scriabin wrote *Prometheus* in 1910, he included a "light-line" (*Tastiera per luce*) in the score, which was intended to indicate changes in projected colored light to accompany the music's tonal dynamics. According to nearly every writer on both synaesthesia and Scriabin, Scriabin was a chromaesthete, and the color arrangement for *Prometheus* followed his individual schema of color-sound equivalences. Though Richard Cytowic in his recent book on synaesthesia carefully distinguishes the many cross-sensory artistic experiments from idiopathic or "involuntary" synaesthesia, he states that "Scriabin specifically sought to express his own synesthesiae in his 1922 [sic] symphony *Prometheus, The Poem of Fire* (Cytowic, 1993, pp. 54–55). There is actually no evidence that Scriabin was a a synaesthete, and considerable evidence to the contrary. Scriabin's equivalences of color and tones rather too neatly follow a circle of fifths, that is, his "colors" proceed in intervals of a fifth (rather than stepwise diatonically) up the scale as they increase in wavelength. Thus, red = C, orange = G, yellow = D, green = A, blue = E, indigo = B, and violet = F$^\sharp$. No true chromaesthete has such a systematic arrangement of color-tone equivalences. When asked to describe their photisms verbally or to match them to color charts, chromaesthetes never choose the seven conventional color terms of the

Newtonian rainbow; they invariably include black or white in their photism descriptions, along with dozens of highly idiosyncratic color terms—"beeswax yellow," "mouse color," "mixture of yellow and grey, like new rope." Typically their tone-photisms include some mixture of hues and they qualify each with adjectives indicating the degree of saturation of the colors—"light," "dark," "pale." Chromaesthetes also usually describe their photisms in geometric terms—"sparks," "spots," "lines," "streaks," "zigzags." (For example, Michael J. Zigler [1930] reported on two female undergraduates at Wellesley College who saw three-dimensional geometric forms when they heard musical instruments played. As in all other cases of synaesthesia, the forms were always the same for any particular instrument, although sometimes they were in color and sometimes not. Hearing the sound of a flute, one subject saw a photism resembling a thimble or an acorn cup, the other a hollow tube; a bugle produced a morning glory and a sphere with an opening on its upper side; piano produced quadrangular blocks or spheres. Forms for other instruments included a mass which burst into jagged splinters, lumpy dough, ribbons, streamers, and daggers.) Frequently the colors carry affective or emotional significance; colors are "happy," "sad," "energetic," "angry." Finally, synaesthetic photisms obey dynamic laws that Scriabin would certainly have noticed and exploited if he had been a true chromaesthete: high tones produce small, faint-hued photisms, while low tones give large, dark photisms, with intermediate tones falling somewhere between; the size and brightness of the photisms for tones vary with the intensity of the sound; combinations of tones result in a superposition of colors and sometimes in a mixture. None of these characteristics were ever noted by Scriabin, nor were they provided for in his *luce* instructions for *Prometheus*. Also, whereas the photisms of true chromaesthetes are invariable over time, Scriabin altered his arrangement to fit his artistic needs, at least for *Prometheus*. That Scriabin did not possess absolute pitch also argues against his being a synaesthete. The literature on synaesthesia is filled with descriptions of "tonal" chromaesthetes who use their photisms to correct their pitch. Singers are alerted to deviations in vocal pitch because they "see" that their photism is of the wrong hue; when they modulate their voice to the right pitch, the color is corrected. Instrumentalists who are chromaesthetic report that they automatically use the same technique. While not all tonal chromaesthetes have this ability, it seems that those with any aptitude for or training in music come to rely on their photisms for guidance in pitch.[8]

The assumption that Scriabin was a synaesthete may have begun with an article written in 1914 by British psychologist Charles S. Myers. Myers, who was especially interested in synaesthetes' perception of music, interviewed Scriabin in 1914 when he was in London for performances of *Prometheus* and his *Poème de l'Extase*. Myers reported that Scriabin had no other forms—such as lexical or vocalic—of color hearing and that his musical chromaesthesia was for tonalities, not individual notes. A reading of Myers' description, however, shows that what Scriabin described were mere affective-symbolic associations, not the automatic and unvarying chromatisms of color hearing. Myers' "Two Cases of Synaesthesia" (1914) published in the *British Journal of Psychology*, actually described only one case of synaesthesia, and it was *not* Scriabin. Adding to the confusion were Scriabin's occult interests and their influence on *Prometheus.* Introduced to Theosophical literature in Paris in 1906, Scriabin became a devotee of Blavatsky, and, to a lesser degree, Annie Besant and C. W. Leadbeater. Although he completely changed many Theosophical tenets to suit his personal philosophy, he adopted wholesale the table of color-note correspondences from Blavatsky's *Secret Doctrine:* "C—Red . . . corresponding to Power; D—Orange . . . Energy; E—Yellow . . . Intellect; F—Green . . . Sympathy; G—Blue . . . Devotion; A—Indigo . . . Selfless Love; B—Violet . . . Psychism." Reading Blavatsky's accompanying assertion that "the best psychics . . . can perceive colours produced by the vibrations of musical instruments, every note suggesting a different colour" (Blavatsky, 1888, vol. 3, p. 145), Scriabin assumed these colors as his own, employing the colors for keys, not individual notes. Listeners to and critics of Scriabin who placed any stock in Theosophical beliefs assumed that Scriabin's colors were the "correct" ones because they believed that he had privileged access to the higher realms. As with Baudelaire, Rimbaud, and Kandinsky, the perception of synaesthesia as a faculty of the aesthetically gifted or the spiritually advanced helped to invent Scriabin as a synaesthete.[9]

The assumption that color hearing was a mark of spiritual prowess even led one of Scriabin's biographers to claim that he had had his own experience of "sporadic synaesthesia." Echoing Kandinsky's description of his *Lohengrin* vision, Faubion Bowers told of how

> on two occasions I have seen radiant flashes of blinding colours and lights during performances of Scriabin's music. I was neither prepared for them, nor was I able to repeat them at any other time. They happened; I saw light unexpectedly and for no explicable or useful purpose. The experiences lasted for not more than a few seconds and were gone. They were quite different from a thrill of sensation, tears of pleasure, or usual emotions associated with beautiful music. I was more surprised than pleased. They have not recurred. But I have not forgotten them.[10]

Kandinsky had the same reaction to his spontaneous color vision while listening to Wagner, interpreting it as both synaesthetic and sublime. The mixture of the mistaken attribution of synaesthesia to Scriabin, his interest in occult literature, and the still-thriving occult interpretation of synaesthesia have combined to make Scriabin every contemporary occultist's favorite "synaesthete." Wilson Lyle, a music critic with a penchant for the occult, typifies this view. In an article surveying color music attempts, he makes the materialist error of placing "psychic sight" (presumably the ability to see astral colors) on the electromagnetic spectrum: "The scale of aural sound roughly spans from 32 vibrations per second to somewhere around 16,000, the vibrations on either side not being receivable *via* the ear. As a comparison, developed psychic sight has a range of vision far wider than that of, say, photographic film and extends to approximately twice the scale of average vision through the naked eye." Then he confuses synaesthesia with "psychic sight": "One friend of mine perceives a certain psychic colour in response to a particular musical pitch and from that will say what the note or key he is hearing represents. When a piano is out of tune or a gramophone record pressing is off-pitch, he proceeds to emit a series of lowing sounds or different vibrations until, somehow, he discovers by means of psychic sense or colour what the correct key should be. And he can work within finer limits than semitones." Finally, going on to describe Scriabin's *Prometheus,* Lyle attributes this "psychic sense" of color to Scriabin and says that all of the controversy about the color-sound arrangement for *Prometheus* misses the fact that Scriabin was elaborating "psychic impressions": "Skryabin cannot therefore properly be judged alongside other [color music] composers by musicians, critics, and laymen, however talented, *unless they too have explored the mystical way*" (Lyle, 1982, p. 263).

Occultist and composer Cyril Scott saw the synaesthete as "one who has awakened the latent faculties of the pineal gland and pituitary body" such that he could "see auras above the orchestra pit" (Scott quoted in Birren, 1941, p. 290). Both as a Theosophist and as a musician, Scott strove to communicate with the spiritual world, and he assumed that the synaesthete's color visions represented music as it would be perceived on the astral plane, where the spiritual, rather than strictly sensual, values of music were apparent. He also believed that Scriabin's color effects for *Prometheus* were intended to express these astral colors: "It was because Scriabin was inspired so forcibly to express the Deva-evolution that he felt the necessity for employing the 'keyboard of light' in conjunction with the orchestra; his intense predilection for trills arose from the same cause. Those endowed with a sufficiently high type of clairvoyance to see the Devas on the more rarefied planes tell us that they scintillate with the most superb colours" (Scott, [1930] 1950, p. 134). Scott distinguished "trained clairvoyants'" scale-colors from the colors of those who had "an elementary form of clairvoyance much tainted by imagination" (1917, pp. 114–115). By this he meant synaesthetes, and he cited examples from Galton's *Inquiries into Human Faculty* that did not jibe with the scales of true clairvoyants, who he maintained were "unanimous" in their tone-color (and tone-vowel) associations. Scott compared synaesthesia with astral clairvoyance specifically to denigrate the perceptual abilities of idiopathic synaesthetes.[11]

Though Scriabin was obviously not a synaesthete and *Prometheus* has as little to do with synaesthetic perception as Rimbaud's "Voyelles" or Kandinsky's paintings, they are worth a closer examination because of their prominent place in the mythical lineage of synaesthesia as a higher form of consciousness. *Prometheus* was not actually performed with the light effects until March 1915, in New York, where the Russian Symphony Orchestra was conducted by Modest Altschuler. A reviewer of the performance was singularly unimpressed with the intended "synaesthetic" effect: "During the performance the lights in the auditorium were extinguished, and a white sheet at the back of the platform and above the heads of the players was illuminated by streaks and spots of light of various colors which had no possible connection with the music, but which served to divert the senses of the audience from a too concentrated attention on the music." The reviewer for the *Nation* had a similar reaction:[12]

> Although he endeavored to show that certain colors, singly or in contrast, will produce similar effects on the senses and emotions as certain musical tones or chords, [Scriabin] has failed to make such connection clear to the spectator and hearer. His musical score, moreover, represents the very extreme of ultra-modern cacophony, all harmonic euphony being avoided with a zeal worthy of a better cause. . . . It is not likely that Scriabin's experiment will be repeated by other composers; moving-picture shows offer much better opportunities.

The complaint about the incomprehensibility of the tone-color associations was an echo of the complaints leveled against "synaesthesia" in Symbolist poetry and drama; they were essentially self-contained, just as any particular synaesthete's were for any other people. Two of the very first authors on chromaesthesia—Sachs in 1812 and Nüssbaumer in 1873—had noted how they had argued with their synaesthetic siblings over the details of their photisms, and the prodigious literature on synaesthesia, though it may by 1910 have had little to say about the cause of the curious perceptual style, could at least state definitively that there was no consensus among synaesthetes when it came to the correspondence between their colors and musical tones, words, vowels, or any other stimulus. And yet Scriabin and the other creators of color music were intent on projecting particular color-tone configurations that would be meaningful to the nonsynaesthetic audience, not to mention the occasional synaesthete who sat there enjoying his or her own colors.

The tendency to hermeticism that was evident in *Prometheus* paled in comparison to the grander work that Scriabin had been planning since 1902, and this work shows the true nature of Scriabin's desire for a synthetic work of art. This never completed chef d'oeuvre was to be called *Mysterium,* and although as with any mystery its exact details were largely undisclosed, it was fundamentally a dream of the unification of all of humanity in a single moment of ecstatic revelation. The work was intended by Scriabin to engage, along with vision and hearing, all the "inferior" senses—touch, taste, and smell. Even more dramatically than the association of color and music in *Prometheus,* Scriabin's multisensory extravaganza was doomed to fail artistically, since the specific properties of those other senses cannot be universally systematized, any more than can the association of tones and colors. Scriabin's planned *Mysterium* was the endpoint of the literal reading of the Baudelairean dictum that "sounds, colors, scents correspond." The other barrier to the universal mystical catharsis Scriabin planned was language; for all nations to participate, he needed a truly international language. Because Sanskrit was believed to be the primordial Aryan language, he purchased a Sanskrit grammar and began to study it, but he soon realized it would take too much time for him to learn and gave it up. He then had the idea of giving special courses to organize the mass of participants to learn a synthetic Ur-language of his own devising. All of these impossible aesthetic goals sprang from Scriabin's fundamental belief that a realm of Platonic absolutes was accessible to him, and through his artistic act, to all others.

Scriabin, both in his most orgiastic erotic moments (such as the *Poème orgiaque*—"Poem of Ecstasy" [1906]) and in his most orgiastic "religious" moments, reached for synaesthetic expression to heighten the ecstatic feeling of oneness he so craved, just as the Romantic lyricists had done more than a century before. The two moments were never far apart; in his diary Scriabin remarked that just as "man during the moment of ecstasy in the sexual act loses *consciousness and his whole organism* experiences bliss at all points, so too God-man, experiencing ecstasy, fills the universe with bliss and kindles the flame. Man-God is the bearer of universal consciousness" (quoted in Matlaw, 1979, p. 14; emphasis in the original). According to Boris de Schloezer, Scriabin "intended to achieve human and cosmic oneness; his ideology was essentially a theory of oneness and the means by which it could be achieved" (de Schloezer, 1987, p. 63). Though none of the other yearners after a "synaesthetic" Gesamtkunstwerk were prey to Scriabin's apocalyptic excess, they did sometimes display a certain eschatological excitement. They were like Scriabin in their use of light to achieve their symbolic purposes. There is no more dramatic mode of expressing the poles of unity and fragmentation; light can be split into multiple colors and then reunited in the totality of whiteness. The common thread running through all the supposedly "synaesthetic" compositions, from the most mundane color music productions to the esoterically inspired work of Scriabin, Kandinsky, Wilfred, and others, was a movement upward, outward, and toward unity, most often represented by a final merger in white light.

THE UNITY OF THE SENSES

At the time of the experiments by Scriabin, Wilfred, and others in representing a transcendental world by fusing sight and sound, the scientific study of synaesthesia had progressed very little, although new cases continued to be documented and occasional feeble explanations proposed. In 1914, the same year in which Charles Myers described Scriabin as a synaesthete, I. H. Coriat (1913, 1914) published reports of two new cases, one of color hearing and another of "colored pain," while H. S. Langfeld, who contributed summaries of research on synaesthesia to each issue of the *Psychological Bulletin,* published his own description of a chromaesthetic woman musician (1914). Langfeld's study, which retested the subject's color-tone associations after an interval of seven years, indicates that the consistency in synaesthetes' cross-sensory associations over time was still a subject of considerable interest to psychologists. Both Coriat and Langfeld, along with most other contemporary researchers, subscribed to a physiological explanation of the mechanism of synaesthesia; variously called by its proponents the irradiation, neural, or sensory-reflex theory, this explanation held that connections existed between specific sensory fibers of distinct but adjoining cortical areas in the brain. Eugen Bleuler, who with his chromaesthetic student Karl Lehmann had written one of the earliest scientific descriptions of synaesthesia more than thirty years previously, published a long theoretical discussion of synaesthesia arguing in favor of some sort of neural crossover (Bleuler, 1913).

Many psychologists, however, interpreted synaesthesia not as an anomaly of the nervous system but rather as an indication of some fundamental interrelation of the sensory modes. Aside from its idiosyncratic appeal, the phenomenon of synaesthesia had originally drawn much of its interest from the possibility it seemed to offer for explaining the relation of human linguistic symbolization to the phenomenal world. Whether expressed in jewel-like Symbolist sonnets or psychological studies of people with color hearing, synaesthesia clearly offered no set of absolute correspondences between sound, particularly human speech, and various aesthetic dimensions; yet the expectation persisted that general laws describing the relation between sound and sense could be established. Long after the burst of descriptive literature between 1880 and 1920, reports continued to appear occasionally maintaining that reliable correlations existed between sound and at least one important aesthetic quality—color. As mentioned earlier, many of these reports noted the correspondence between auditory pitch and visual brightness: the higher the pitch of a sound, the brighter the color associated with it. A third of the thirty-four studies between 1920 and 1975 listed in Lawrence Marks's review of visual-auditory synaesthesia confirmed this correlation (1975, pp. 306–307). Marks's paper did not distinguish on this point between the reports of synaesthetes and the studies of nonsynaesthetes that also demonstrated this relation between high-pitched sounds and bright hues; perhaps for this reason, he failed to recognize that a large number of the so-called color hearers who were the subjects of the early studies were describing not actual synaesthetic impressions but merely mental associations between sounds and colors.

This conflation of descriptions of the mental processes of synaesthetes with those of nonsynaesthetes was especially marked in the work of C. E. Osgood (1953, 1960), who attempted to measure on a scale not only the brightness, but the relative heaviness, goodness, strength, energy, and other seemingly "cross-sensory" attributes of given words. Although these scientific studies were not infused with the religious longing so evident in the nonscientific descriptions of synaesthesia, their authors also reached for the transcendental in their tacit belief that some absolute table of equivalencies could be established for the different senses.

Many students of synaesthesia believed that German psychologist Erich von Hornbostel provided experimental corroboration of the unity of the senses by means of a series of experiments he conducted in 1925. Subjects first matched differently hued (from black to white) papers to the equivalently "bright" odor of different concentrations of a benzol solution. Then they attempted to match these odors with a graded series of audible tones for brightness. Finally, the variegated papers were matched to tones. Hornbostel was astounded to find an almost identical match between the three sensory dimensions. Brightness, it seemed, was a universal sensory attribute. When Hornbostel first reported his discovery, he did so in true Romantic fashion. His article began with a disavowal of the assertion that for the deaf there is no music; Hornbostel (1927, p. 83), who did "not pretend to have seen tones or heard colors," described the visual music produced by the movements of a veiled dancer. The "primitive" nature of the unity of the senses was alluded to throughout: Hornbostel told of an African tribe who had but a single word to describe the four "lesser" senses— hearing, taste, smell, and touch; the archaic unity of the senses was preserved in the French verb *sentir*, which carried simultaneously the meanings "to smell," "to touch," and "to feel"; the word "bright" had been a strictly adjective for an aural sensation until the period of Middle High German, when it became a visual descriptor as well. Feeling was the original sense, which science had only recently split into five discrete senses. Hornbostel pointed out that "an octave chord feels consonant on the skin in contrast to a seventh" (p. 84); this he attributed to a vestige of hearing latent in the sense of touch. Although he did not explicitly assert that his experiment explained the cross-sensory associations of synaesthesia, Hornbostel did allude to the specific case of a mother and daughter, both synaesthetes, who differed in their color-vowel associations; Hornbostel dismissed the discrepancy by saying that both agreed that a particular vowel was "bright, clear, and sharp" (p. 85).

Hornbostel saw primitive thought as full of natural, rather than contrived, synaesthetic expression. A primitive person, Hornbostel said, "does not put soul into things, because soul has not yet been taken out of them." The unmediated iconicity of words in primal tongues was still audible in the phonemes of modern languages, where sound symbolism was obvious in the "dull, dark, . . . blunt, heavy, dense, thick . . . full, round, swelling" sounds of words with *m* or *mb* in them, or the opposite impressions communicated by the words "bright, sharp, light, blank" (Hornbostel, 1927, p. 87).

Even before Hornbostel posited in 1925 that brightness was a universal dimension of all sensory experience, several psychologists who were not specifically studying synaesthesia had proposed that precise analogies could be drawn between vision and hearing. In 1915, Gestalt psychologist Wolfgang Köhler advocated the use of *hell* (light) and *dunkel* (dark) to characterize vocalic and consonantal speech sounds. Köhler emphasized that the first two terms were never mere metaphors for him, but rather deeply felt, internalized associations: "If optical examples emerge, then tone and image are not attached to each other through a senseless habit but a light tone appears to be similar to a light optic image. Anything which I'm accustomed to name 'light' on the optical level faces me, even if through mere similarity, in the acoustical field as well." In 1947, Köhler devised a delightful experiment to demonstrate that sound could very elegantly symbolize sensory domains other than just visual brightness. Subjects were asked to match a pair of abstract figures to one of two nonsense words—"maluma" and "takete." Immediately and almost without exception, people matched "maluma" to a soft, round figure, "takete" to a sharply angular figure. The match was based on the "synaesthetic" translation of sound symbolism—the expression by sound of some nonacoustical percept. The long duration, low-pitched vowels and mellifluous "l" and "m" consonants of "maluma" seem intrinsically to express the curvaceous aspect and even haptic texture of the rounded form, while the high-pitched vowels and attacking consonants of "takete" perfectly signify the sharp angles of the other figure.[13]

Köhler's work provided an empirical basis for the philosopher Charles Hartshorne's treatment of synaesthesia. In *The Philosophy and Psychology of Sensation* (1934), Hartshorne opposed a synaesthetic theory of perception to the Helmholtzian dictum of the incompatibility of the sensory modalities. Hartshorne believed that the contents of sensation form "an *affective continuum* of aesthetically meaningful, socially expressive, organically adaptive, and evolving experience functions." At the beginning of the "affective continuum," human perception consisted of pure, undifferentiated affective feeling-tone, which later evolved into discrete sense modalities. But, Hartshorne believed, a common sensory ground was retained both phylogenetically and ontogenetically, and was easily distinguishable in the wide variety of affective experiences where sense modalities converged or crossed. Though he mentioned some of the literature that described cases of idiopathic synaesthesia, Hartshorne did not sharply discriminate between these instances of highly individual perception and the sort of cross-modal ability that Köhler identified as a universal property. Once again, a theory of synaesthesia was put forward with the concomitant imperative that such a theory opposed atomism and materialism. Hartshorne protested that materialism as a philosophy and a worldview engendered "absolute heterogeneity and absolute externality of relationships—the independence of a thing from its context." Synaesthesia, by contrast, which Hartshorne assumed to be a universal human attribute that was only a bit more acute in idiopathic synaesthetes, promised a web of correspondences akin to the Swedenborgian view of the universe. Cross-modal sensory equivalences pointed, it was thought, to the interdependence not only of the sensory realms, but of thought and thing. In his *Phenomenology of Perception* (1962), French phenomenologist Maurice Merleau-Ponty again advanced the idea that synaesthesia is the normal, primordial condition of human perception, which is shattered only "because scientific knowledge shifts the centre of gravity of experience, so that we have unlearned how to see, hear, and generally speaking, to feel, in order to deduce, from our bodily organization and the world as the physicist conceives it, what we are to see, hear and feel." Merleau-Ponty, drawing especially on Heinz Werner's writings, saw synaesthesia as "one more occasion for questioning the concept of sensation and objective thought." Synaesthesia offered a mechanism that, by bridging the gap between the senses, promised to bridge the gap between the feeling subject and the objects of perception and rescue human beings from the behaviorists' conception of them as sensing-reacting machines.[14]

SYNAESTHESIA'S TRUE MEANING

Neither the Romantic visionaries who were so taken with the phantasmagoric aspects of synaesthesia nor philosophers like Hartshorne and Merleau-Ponty who embraced synaesthesia as an alternative to atomistic theories of sensation ever stopped to consider that synaesthetes themselves were from moment to moment totally unaware of their own perceptual idiosyncrasy and, until someone told them differently, assumed that others shared their perceptual style. It seems that it is "invisible" or transparent to those who possess it, just as our own perceptual processes are transparent to us. We never think about them except when we are asked to do so or when our perceptions clash with someone else's. This observation seems to have eluded most of the scientific researchers on synaesthesia, who, after an initial obsession with categorizing synaesthesia as normal or abnormal or with determining just which vowels elicited which colors, largely accepted the view that synaesthesia was an aspect of a perceptual mode that was universally present in children but that usually disappeared as they matured. The work of Osgood, Jakobson, Gombrich, Marks, and others emphasized the persistence of "synaesthetic" expression (meaning intersensory metaphor) in language as evidence of this shift.

All this twentieth-century work that took synaesthesia to be a universal cognitive style, past or present, ignored what was arguably the most significant body of psychological research ever conducted on synaesthesia. In the 1920s Raymond Holder Wheeler and his student, the blind synaesthete Thomas D. Cutsforth, offered a fully elaborated theory of the construction of meaning, based on synaesthesia. Wheeler and Cutsforth were the first psychologists to point out that synaesthetes experienced their photisms (or the other "secondary sensations" stimulated by their synaesthesiae) not as freak sensory data but rather as an essential component of their thought processes. Synaesthetes experienced their own synaesthesiae as a *form of thinking.* Just as most people do not experience language, or their own thought, a sort of "inner speech," as arbitrary or conventional, so synaesthetes do not, either in conversation with others or in thinking to themselves, experience the brightly colored blobs appearing in their visual field as arbitrary. In a series of fourteen papers during the 1920s, Wheeler and Cutsforth showed that synaesthesia is not a phenomenon of perception alone, but of conception, and that synaesthesia is an essential mechanism in the construction of meaning that functions in the same way as certain unattended mental processes in nonsynaesthetes.

Wheeler's first publication, "The Synaesthesia of a Blind Subject" (1920), was largely descriptive, detailing the nature of the photisms experienced by Cutsforth, who had been synaesthetic before he lost his sight in an accident at age eleven. Cutsforth heard a particular voice as "brownish yellow, the color of a ripe English walnut," another as "yellowish, poorly saturated, like old beeswax"; the sound of an organ evoked a photism which was "very rich deep black, [of] bluish cast, [with] spots and streaks of brown, with irradiating flames"; the single consonant "b" produced "a dark, bluish, thick amorphous patch of color, about the size of one's hand." Along with colored photisms for voices and musical tones, Cutsforth experienced color imagery for each of the letters of the alphabet, for proper names and toponyms, for names of the days of the week and months of the year, for numerals, dates, telephone numbers, for the cardinal directions, and colored forms for numbers, weeks, months, centuries, and alphabets. Cutsforth's rich colored imagery for concepts extended to theories he had learned about in college, his own and others' beliefs, and abstract terms like "spirit" or "space"; the photisms for abstract terms were peculiar to the particular concept, and were not merely a product of the colors of the individual letters of the word. Beyond the photisms elicited by sound and thought, Cutsforth experienced color imagery in response to tastes, odors, and tactile and kinaesthetic sensations. Wheeler's Gestalt orientation was apparent in his approach to Cutsforth's synaesthesia; he stressed that a perception carried the "feeling tone" of other modalities, so that a sound, for example, was not just auditory, but such that the part (the sound) was dependent on the whole (the body tonus). Wheeler concluded from his investigation with Cutsforth that the only difference between synaesthetes and nonsynaesthetes was that "it happens that colors, instead of other kinds of processes, may be aspects of the larger whole." Anticipating Heinz Werner's ideas about "syncretic" perception in children, Wheeler hypothesized that early mental life was undifferentiated, and he regarded the multisensory "configurations" of early childhood as the "ground" against which the "figures"—the unimodal qualities of perception—emerged. In synaesthetes, auditory and visual perceptions failed in infancy to emerge as they did in the nonsynaesthetic person. As evidence of the degree to which the synaesthetic photism was "merged" with its stimulus, Wheeler emphasized that if one blocked or removed the visual configuration of its color, form, movement, or position, the entire auditory perception was destroyed. Without their synaesthetic photisms, synaesthetes essentially could not hear, and the same was true for thought: if, during the thought process, the photisms were blocked, further thought was impossible. Wheeler also pointed out how in Cutsforth's process of forgetting things, the last detail to disappear from memory was the color of the associated photism. Finally, Wheeler found that fatigue, nervous excitement, and drugs altered the secondary image—the photism—more than they did the primary experience. It would thus be reasonable to assume that the depleting effects were experienced primarily through the effect they had on the synaesthetic image.[15] To a synaesthete in a state of fatigue or under the influence of drugs, for example, a bell tone sounds lower in volume than the exact same tone heard in a normal state; the diminution in volume is a consequence not of any actual hearing impairment but of reduced vividness in the accompanying photism.

In succeeding papers (1921a, 1921b), Wheeler and Cutsforth investigated Cutsforth's number forms, synaesthetic representations that were substituted for numbers when he did arithmetic, and also explored the role of synaesthesia in learning. In this latter study, they compared Cutsforth's introspections with those of a blind nonsynaesthete. Both were presented with a series of nonsense syllables, first in Braille and then in speech. Cutsforth found that he was completely dependent on his photisms to "learn" the nonsense syllables, and his learning was slower than that of the nonsynaesthetic subject because the nonsense syllables produced detached or dissociated colors that did not "hang together" as did familiar words or concepts, so that they actually overwhelmed his consciousness at times. In 1925, they also explored the role of emotion in synaesthesia. For this study, Cutsforth trained a synaesthetic graduate student to look back consciously into her earliest memories and found that just as it was impossible for him to understand a sound without its associated color, it was impossible for her to describe or know past experiences without reference to their emotional component. The student experienced tactile as well as visual synaesthesia in response to sound and, like Cutsforth, was "utterly helpless" to describe her tactile synaesthesiae in any other terms than those of "meaning." Although her photisms appeared to have some abstract properties of their own, such as intensity and hue, she could not characterize her tactile synaesthesiae abstractly. Cutsforth's conclusion was that the conventional distinction between thinking and feeling failed to hold true in synaesthetes. Wheeler (1920b) also found that Cutsforth experienced synaesthesia in his dreams; schematic forms of persons were identified by their "color" (the color of the associated photism), as were their voices, spatial directions, and other sounds, such as the "croaking" of a singing carp and the barking of a bulldog. In another paper not specifically on synaesthesia, Wheeler took note of the cry from contemporary behaviorists to "do away with" introspection, but he argued that psychology, in order to become an empirical science, must ground its observations in the senses. Wheeler discounted previous behaviorist theories of the will. He proposed instead that all notions of human striving, activity, and force are rooted in kinaesthetic sensations (those related to movement) and even claimed that all mental processes were "nothing more than kinaesthetic sensation."[16]

Wheeler and Cutsforth's fully developed theory of the construction of meaning appeared in two papers in the *American Journal of Psychology* in 1922. In a brief statement of the ideas they would present in their major paper, Wheeler, again reporting on Cutsforth's reflections on words, focused on his kinaesthetic responses. He concluded that "in every stage kinaesthesis is the core of the phenomenon which we call meaning. . . . It is quite probable that pure meanings, so-called, are in reality masses of diffuse muscular sensations, which the reagent has not succeeded in recognizing and describing" (Wheeler, 1922, p. 233). This emphasis on kinaesthesis continued in "Synaesthesia and Meaning," which reported on three sets of introspections performed by Cutsforth and another blind, but nonsynaesthetic, introspector. Reiterating the observations that meanings fail to develop in the absence of synaesthetic colors of the appropriate appearance and behavior and that synaesthetic imagery constitutes the context for meaning, the two concluded that "synaesthesia *is* the act of perceiving, itself" (Wheeler and Cutsforth, 1922, p. 370). Wheeler and Cutsforth also, in declaring that despite a century and a half of scientific investigation of synaesthesia, "the real root of the problem seems never to have been investigated" (1922, p. 361), placed their work within a historical context. Clearly they had demonstrated that rather than being "about" a transcendental set of meanings, the shifting color images of the synaesthete were highly idiosyncratic carriers of their own meaning. The photisms "labeled" or "interpreted" each object of consciousness, whether it was a concrete sensory perception of a sound, odor, taste, or touch or an abstract mental concept, thereby making it meaningful. Wheeler and Cutsforth's detailed research on introspection, totally unlike any previous attempts to understand synaesthesia, demystified the phenomenon, and although they did not identify a mechanism for the production of the images, the two essentially provided a full explanation of synaesthesia's psychological significance. As the first synaesthete who was also a trained introspector, Cutsforth's descriptions of his own mental processes allowed closer scrutiny of the behavior of the images. Cutsforth's imagery was as fantastic as anything the Symbolists could dream up: presented with the incomplete statement by Wheeler of an analogy, "Table is to furniture as dog is to _____?," Cutsforth saw first the colors of Wheeler's voice, then the color of each individual word as it paraded in his mind. Not until after a specific yellow photism appeared for the word "animal" was Cutsforth able to mentally complete the statement (Cutsforth, 1924, p. 95). The observation that without his synaesthetic imagery Cutsforth was unable to do *any* type of thinking, not just creative, aesthetic, or somehow transcendental mental activity, would have gone a long way toward dispelling the Romantic interpretation of synaesthesia as a form of expanded consciousness.

No one, however, who had an interest in synaesthesia either as the next step in human evolution or as a return to a paradisiacal form of perception ever encountered Wheeler and Cutsforth's theories. Even within the professional psychological community, few recognized the significance of the studies; though Wheeler and Cutsforth published seven more articles (Cutsforth, 1924, 1925; Wheeler, 1923, 1932; Wheeler and Cutsforth, 1922, 1925, 1928) over the next six years, their work linking synaesthesia and the construction of meaning had little effect on subsequent thinking about either of the two problems. In a 1933 review in *Human Biology* of 159 articles about synaesthesia, 64 of them published between 1910 and 1933, Otto Ortmann (1933) merely cited another psychologist's summary (Langfeld, 1926) of Wheeler and Cutsforth's 1922 article. He then dismissed their contention that synaesthesia was a "normal type of mental reaction." Two observations, Ortmann maintained, contradicted their claim: 1) until their attention is drawn to their synaesthesia, synaesthetes are unaware of it; 2) if it were a normal process, the complete inability of normal persons to give evidence of it could not be explained. Ortmann had probably not read the articles, though he cites the original publication—"The Synaesthesia of a Blind Subject"—as well as the 1922 article, in his bibliography. In those articles, Wheeler and Cutsforth do not say that synaesthesia is "normal," but that it functions as do certain invisible mental processes in nonsynaesthetes with regard to the construction of meaning. From Ortmann's bibliography it becomes evident that during the period when Wheeler and Cutsforth were active—approximately 1920 to 1935—most of the publications on synaesthesia were in German or French, and very few were in English. Presumably, general interest among American and British psychologists had declined, reflecting the general decline of psychological work on subjective psychological topics. But in a 1934 paper, Dartmouth College psychologists Lorrin Riggs and Theodore Karwoski cited three of Wheeler and Cutsforth's publications, only to conclude that Cutsforth was not a "true" synaesthete (p. 36). The psychologist most responsible for popularizing the idea that synaesthesia was a primitive perceptual style, Heinz Werner, was unfamiliar with Wheeler and Cutsforth's publications, as were the principal scholars investigating how meaning is constructed. Neither C. E. Osgood (Osgood et al., 1951) in psychology, Stephan Ullmann (1951) and Roman Jakobson (Jakobson and Waugh, 1979) in linguistics, nor Charles Hartshorne (1934) and Maurice Merleau-Ponty (1962) in philosophy, all of whom allotted synaesthesia a pivotal role in their ideas about the making of meaning, drew on Wheeler and Cutsforth's work. The first major review of the literature on synaesthesia to appear in almost half a century, Lawrence Marks's *The Unity of the Senses* (1978, p. 94), mentioned Wheeler only to say that he had investigated the synaesthesia of a blind subject, and more recently, neurologist Richard Cytowic's *Synesthesia: A Union of the Senses* (1989, p. 69) completely misinterprets their research. Since Wheeler and Cutsforth's findings were not replicated by any other researchers and their own work generated no interest, their critical insight that photisms (or other secondary sensations) *constituted* meaning for the synaesthete went unnoticed.[17]

The obscurity of Wheeler and Cutsforth's work is directly traceable to the triumph of the modern behaviorist-functionalist approach in experimental psychology, and its rejection of the subjectivist-phenomenological tradition, which sought to study the contents of consciousness. Introspection, the principal technique of subjectivist psychological study, was a tool for describing immediate consciousness "as is," without reference to the "is for" of the world of consensual meanings. This was done by "avoiding the stimulus error"; in essence, experienced introspectors could attend to the qualities of a stimulus in any sensory mode without allowing the mind to recognize the stimulus. When such stimuli as the sound of a bell, the odor of jasmine, or the touch of a feather brushed against the skin were examined introspectively, their normally masked or "unconscious" aspects were brought to awareness, and the mind could actually observe itself in the process of thinking. Within the rich tradition of introspectionist reports from England, Germany, and America, perhaps the most gifted introspector and most vocal advocate of introspection as a scientific method was Edward Bradford Titchener, who developed an extensive experimental research program at Cornell University. Titchener's group, focusing on the most elementary element of consciousness—the recognition of meaning supplied by simple sensory stimuli or associated with single words or letters (the model followed by Wheeler and Cutsforth in their work)—concluded that all higher mental processes were based on imagery. At the same time as Titchener, Otto Külpe and his associates were looking at consciousness, as well, in a lab in Würzburg, Germany, and finding nothing; arguing that thought was "imageless," they objected to Titchener's interpretation. Almost all psychology textbook accounts of the "Würzburg controversy" maintain that the two laboratories used the same methods and ended up with different results, and that this impasse led to the abandonment of introspection as a technique for studying consciousness. The Würzburg researchers, however, rather than using introspective techniques to recognize simple meanings, were actually trying to put those methods to use during episodes of complex problem solving. Asked questions like "Can the atomic theory ever be proved untrue by any discovery?," the Würzburg introspectors, when they arrived at the moment of insight into the given problem, found "imperceptible awareness" (*unanschauliche Bewusstheiten*), an ultrarapid illumination with no specifiable content. The resulting "imperceptibles" were resistant to sensory description only because they had not been sufficiently examined introspectively; on further introspection, these too would have yielded the sort of phenomenological descriptions reported by the Cornell psychologists.[18]

Wheeler and Cutsforth's work, though important to the understanding of synaesthesia, was of much greater import to discussion of the pressing psychological issue of the time—the question whether the "contents" of meaning (and thus of consciousness) were exclusively sensory and imaginal. Wheeler argued strenuously that their work on synaesthesia demonstrated that there was no such thing as imageless or sensationless meanings. Though the representations of meaning differed for synaesthetes and nonsynaesthetes, synaesthetic representations merely being more salient, their function was identical.[19] Images or not, the products of introspection were artificial, disruptive, and ultimately unrelated to efficient cognitive activity, the critics of the introspectionist technique argued. Presented with a simple stimulus, introspectors spun elaborate self-enclosed descriptions; here is Thomas Cutsforth's introspective account of reading the word "good" in Braille:

As the tip of my fingers passed over the word, the first time, I perceived the letter "d." This perception developed as follows: at the outset I was aware only of indefinitely grouped blunt points; these points at once became arranged, spatially, in terms of visual imagery, and at the same time took on the poorly saturated bluish-grey of the "d"; at this juncture the obscure tactual qualities, which had at first appeared, entirely vanished and the color of the letter persisted alone in consciousness as my awareness of the letter itself. The second time I inspected the word, the color of the "d" persisted in consciousness; I failed to add any letters to my consciousness of the word; there only appeared meaningless and confused jumbles of tactile impressions which, as fast as they appeared, shifted to visual, grey imagery—my synaesthetic imagery of the temperature of the paper. [Wheeler and Cutsforth, 1922, p. 379]

Cutsforth's description continues for another page, elaborating synaesthetic colors and tactile qualities of *o*, "double *o*," and *g*, the mixing of these colors, and the alternate contraction and relaxation of various muscle groups in his body, until finally, after five exposures to the Braille word, he recognizes it via the merging of the colored photisms and the attendant vocal-motor imagery. No wonder functionalists questioned whether such solipsistic reveries could disclose the mechanism of human recombinatory, intelligence; introspection was like pouring molasses into the fluid, lightning-like activity of thought. One later critic, Ludwig Wittgenstein, likened introspective accounts to mental doodling. Wheeler and Cutsforth's use of introspection to demonstrate the nature of idiopathic synaesthesia coincided with the virtual disappearance of introspection from experimental psychology, and as a consequence their work fell on deaf ears.

Unlike previous researchers who approached synaesthesia with some preconceived notion that some absolute correspondences might actually exist between sight and sound, Wheeler and Cutsforth had no such assumptions. Interested in studying more than Cutsforth's sound-induced photisms, they made the first detailed experimental study of tactile-visual synaesthesia, replicating the experimental method that Roland Fisher had followed in an earlier study on how nonsynaesthetic subjects developed concepts. Wheeler molded a series of similarly shaped nonsense figures (christened *mipas*) out of clay and then at ten-second intervals placed them on Cutsforth's hand; Cutsforth in turn reported on his process of building a mental image of these figures. The report of this experiment, in which a totally blind person itemizes the visual characteristics of nonsensical lumps of clay, was by far the most intense probing of synaesthetic imagery to appear in the scientific literature. On being presented with the first clay figure, Cutsforth reported:

The instant my fingers came in contact with the body-part of the first mipa, perception developed in terms of a chocolate-brown pressure, mixed with black and dark grey streaks of kinaesthesis from finger movements. At one end of the body there suddenly appeared two grooves perceived in terms of fleeting colorations of chocolate-brown curving around the under surface of thumb and forefinger of the right hand; but these colors gave way at once to a smoky-white, tinged with blue, rapidly assuming the contour and shape of visualized grooves. (The bluish, smoky-white is the synaesthetic quality of the "Mi-" sound of mipa.) Then the perception of the body-part clarified as to shape and size, still in terms of synaesthetic pressure and kinaesthesis. As the inspection continued, the black of the kinaesthesis came more and more to dominate over the chocolate-brown of the pressure. For some time awareness of each mipa was dominated by the body-segment. As the procedure continued, consciousness of other parts took the form of extensions and variations in this chocolate-black mass. My perception of the loop segment developed as a pear-shaped hole of neutral grey at one end. This hole expanded, contracted, or lengthened, as the case might be, when moving my fingers rapidly over the different mipas. Momentarily there would stand out a black-brown visualization of a doughnut-shaped ring, much lighter in color than the body-segment, and this was interpreted to mean that the part under inspection was lighter in weight than the middle part. Irregularities and various types of projections at the other end of the object appeared in terms of deep brown or black rings and ridges. Frequently similar visual projections appeared on the body-part, which latter, by this time, had become more and more of a bluish, smoky, white, at the end opposite the loop. Here the color was more intense at the base of the horn-like projection, where I originally detected the grooves. The only association which I recall, was the appearance, early in the inspection, of a brown, oblong area, surrounding the neutral-grey hole at the ringed end of the mipa. This was a synaesthetic appearance of the meaning, plasticene clay.[20]

At a subsequent sitting, Cutsforth was asked by Wheeler to disclose all he knew about "mipas," and then through introspection to reflect on this recollection. Cutsforth defined the mipa as an object segmented into three parts, its top being a sort of circular loop, its middle section varying a great deal in shape and size, but generally flat on top with occasional ridges and grooves, and having a neck on the left side of the middle section. Introspection on this description revealed to Cutsforth that he was giving a definition by finding a series of words to fit a series of three visual images that made up his "type," or composite, image of the mipa. The first image was of the "neck," which was identified by a "dull, tactual yellow," with a "very little, light, smoky-blue" color at its base; the second of the body, a "sooty black"; and the third of the loop section, which was the same color as the neck, except for the hole, which was "neutral grey." This entire suite of synaesthetic imagery appeared at about arm's length in front of Cutsforth. Describing the synaesthetic imagery that attended his mental recollection of the mipa, Cutsforth said he saw

> horns, ridges and indentations . . . in a mixture of tactual-yellow, brown and kinaesthetic black. This imagery rides upon a curdled dark area hovering about the type image. This area is black with indefinite kinaesthetic imagery of finger-movements of exploration. Occasionally the type image . . . changes in size and shape; but these fluctuations are exceedingly shifty and vague. The quality and brightness of coloration also varies. In all of these shiftings, the type image tends to disintegrate. In its place there appear separated masses of yellow, brown, and black coloration which constitute residual, tactual, and kinaesthetic memory-images of individual mipas. [p. 152]

Wheeler also asked Cutsforth to introspect on his comprehension of the word "mipa" in a sentence; in response to the statement "I reached into a collar-bag and pulled out a mipa," Cutsforth saw the following imagery:

> As the experimenter read the first few words of the sentence, synaesthetic perception of his voice stood out in bright, silvery grey forms hovering in the center of the visual field close to my head. Adjacent to these forms there appeared a circular halo of kinaesthetic black, which was interpreted as a feeling of expectancy—a waiting for something. When he spoke the words, "collar-bag," there was a sudden shift of visual attention to the left where there appeared a visual image of my hand moving downward into the neck of an opened laundry bag hanging from the right handle of the top drawer in my dresser. The hand was colored a tactual-yellow and was visualized no farther than the wrist. . . . In response to the words, "pulled out," the hand began to move upward as if being drawn from the bag. No sooner had the movement commenced, however, when I perceived the word, *mipa,* in terms of synaesthetic coloration chiefly of the light, smoky-blue of the "mi-" sound. Instantly I saw hanging from the fingers of my hand the ringed, third segment of a mipa. This image was rich in tactual-yellow and black, kinaesthetic streakings. (The imagery was so clear that it would have been possible to estimate from it the supposed weight of this segment.) The black streakings were concentrated on the under surface of the ring, next to my fingers. All of this imagery was detached from my actual hand, and localized about two feet in front of me, in about the same position as my hand and the laundry bag would be if I were actually reaching for a collar. [p. 152]

The experiment clearly showed that not only did synaesthetic imagery appear at the very first encounter with an unfamiliar object, but the imagery immediately became the focus of the developing concept for the object as the synaesthete's familiarity with it grew. That attempts to recall an individual mipa rather than the "type" mipa proved difficult for Cutsforth suggests the same economy of representational effort at work in nonsynaesthetes' thought processes. Moving from initial attention to the commonalities in a set of stimuli, through a replication of this commonality to form a mental set, to the seemingly effortless process where the mental set comes to "stand" automatically for its represented object, both synaesthete and nonsynaesthete experience meaning in the exact same way, except for the substitution of the synaesthete's suite of colors for the nonsynaesthete's interiorized kinaesthesis. In the process of neatly elaborating how generic, abstract concepts are formed from specific individual experiences with objects in the physical world, Wheeler and Cutsforth also demystified the puzzling "language" of color hearing. Like the phonemic units of spoken language, the colors were completely fluid in their relation to that which they signified, but once the representational relationship was established, the colors, like the complete phonemic units that constitute words, were understood as fixed and anything but arbitrary. For Cutsforth, in a very short time, the trifling plasticene creations became significant members of his mental world, with their own unique telltale sequence of synaesthetic imagery. Rather than pointing to some transcendental world beyond the sensory, as so many had believed they did, the synaesthete's colors defined the object itself, unmistakably fixing its position. Considered in the light of Wheeler and Cutsforth's findings, the Symbolist and Expressionist interpretation of synaesthetes as aesthetically or spiritually superior to nonsynaesthetes was a grievous error.

Since virtually no one, including professional psychologists, understood the significance of Wheeler and Cutsforth's work, synaesthetes continued to be thought of as special; and the transcendental interpretation of synaesthesia was nowhere so obvious as in the continued aspiration after a sublime form of color music. A. B. Klein, a painter whose early work aimed at abstraction and who had designed a color projector in 1921, was in 1925 still rhapsodic about the possibilities of color music: "Can one imagine anything in the arts which would surpass the visible rendering of sound, which would enable the eyes to partake of all the pleasures which music gives to the ears?" Noting Western civilization's disillusionment about its own future, Klein ranked the dream of a color music with religious and political utopias: "For the singularly few who enjoy loveliness, it might snatch one or two more gems from the chaos before the end." Klein eventually became extremely bitter about "greedy, selfish colour-music idealists" who failed to acknowledge predecessors and who were motivated more by commercial than artistic interests.[21] He felt that the golden age of color music was over and that by 1930, coopted by film, what had begun as a sublime aspiration ended in ridiculous cartoons—Walt Disney's "Silly Symphonies" and then *Fantasia* (1937). Virginia Woolf's satirical treatment in her novel *Jacob's Room* of a color-sound theorist (a minor character) suggests that the aspirations of color musicians were beginning to look farcical to their audience as well. Woolf's character sat all day in a cubicle in the British Museum and wrote pamphlets to promote her philosophy that "colour is sound—or, perhaps, it has something to do with music. She could never quite say, though it was not for lack of trying" (Woolf, 1922, p. 104).

Still, Thomas Wilfred's Clavilux performances remained popular, and Claude Bragdon's synthesis of ideas about color music and the fourth dimension continued to influence artists interested in synaesthesia. Wilfred himself, who went on composing lumia pieces, eventually became trapped in the sort of hubris that afflicted Scriabin; his 1941 "Vertical Sequence No. II" ran for two days, twelve hours, and fifty-nine minutes, while the performance of "Nocturne," opus 148 (1958), was projected to fill five years, 359 days, nineteen hours, twenty minutes and forty-eight seconds (Gage, 1993, p. 246). In the 1940s, the painter Ira Jean Belmont, who claimed to be a synaesthete himself, explained his chromaesthesia by reference to Bragdon's and P. D. Ouspensky's theories of the fourth dimension (Belmont, 1944, pp. 215–216). Some idea of the extent to which color music was identified with synaesthesia, and both with the search for a transcendental language of representation, can be gained from the fact that a performance of "Colour-Light Plays" was given by Bauhaus artists Ludwig Hirschfield-Mack and Kurt Schwertfeger at the 1930 Congress of Psychologists for Colour-Sound Synaesthesia in Hamburg (Gage, 1993, p. 245). If any audience should have been aware of Wheeler and Cutsforth's research, it was this one. In 1938, in a study of the photisms of chromaesthetes in response to music, psychologists T. F. Karwoski and H. S. Odbert included a lengthy review of the attempts to create color music, concluding that eventually someone would produce color music "broad enough in range to satisfy the patterns of practically all synaesthetes" (Karwoski and Odbert, 1938, p. 52). From a survey of more than 250 college students, Karwoski and Odbert identified 9 who possessed strong synaesthetic visual imagery, and tested 8 of these students for their synaesthesia in response to a variety of musical selections. Their focus on the stability of the synaesthetic photisms (the report includes color plates comparing 4 subjects' photisms for their initial listening and another one eight months later) highlights their hope of discovering a generalized color music schema that would be acceptable to a broad range of listeners, both synaesthetic and non-synaesthetic. The intertwining of idiopathic synaesthesia and technological efforts to replicate color hearing is so complete that the *New Oxford Companion to Music,* the *New Grove Dictionary of Music,* and other musical reference works contain lengthy entries on "colour and music" that review the scientific literature on idiopathic synaesthesia as if it were part of the same problem. The journal *Leonardo,* devoted to technological issues in music and visual art, has even, since its debut in 1968, consistently published articles on "visual music," "kinetic art," and "synaesthetic art"—all continuations of the earlier attempts to create color music (Pocock-Williams, 1992).

During the era of Symbolism, the identification of synaesthesia with a form of transcendental knowledge was especially prevalent because the phenomenon of synaesthesia itself was so poorly known. When Scriabin's *Prometheus* was performed in 1915, scientific questions about synaesthesia still largely followed the extrascientific tendency to search for a law of cross-sensory correspondences. That such extravagant interpretations of the meaning of synaesthesia as Wilfred's continue to be proposed is possible because the desire for a truly transcendental form of knowledge has not abated. The particular character, however, of the ideas, images, and metaphors that a culture endows with transcendental meaning changes with dissemination of scientific knowledge. Religion—that which we invest with transcendental meaning and value—is continually bumping up against the reality of empirical knowledge. In the case of synaesthesia, the religious sentiment that transformed the arcane perceptual style into a dream of expanded consciousness should have been tempered by Wheeler and Cutsforth's findings in the 1920s. Had psychological science not been in the process of delegitimizing introspection as a technique for studying consciousness, their work might have received a wider hearing and thus have helped to restrain the Romantic interpretation of synaesthesia. The triumph of behaviorists' view of the human mind and body as reacting machines only served to intensify the Romantic quest for art forms and theories of knowledge that de-emphasized the world of material causes. Romantics held fast to the ideal of the primacy of the imagination, and synaesthetes would continue in their eyes to offer proof positive of the possibility of attaining new ways of knowing.

Chapter 4 Sensory Unity
Before the Fall: Synaesthesia,
Eideticism, and the Loss
of Eden

Wheeler and Cutsforth's research suggested that synaesthesia, by facil-
itating the apprehension of meaning, was of great utility in early
cognitive processes because it could actually accelerate childhood
learning, and that its subsequent disappearance as the new, more
abstract linkages of language were formed was a normal process. By
showing via the technique of introspection that nonsynaesthetes had
an analogous "invisible" locus of meaning in certain kinaesthetic
processes, they demystified synaesthetic imagery. Although they did
not make it explicit themselves, their work implied that in most
individuals, synaesthesia was usually superseded during childhood by
kinaesthesis as the "mechanism" of meaning production. Rather than
conceiving of synaesthesia as a necessary developmental stage that was
transcended as new, higher cognitive modes replaced it, however,
many writers continued to view synaesthesia as being in itself transcendental. For those who saw phylogenetically earlier styles of consciousness as superior to contemporary alienated consciousness, it was
completely possible to visualize synaesthesia as a "next step" in the
evolution of consciousness, even if it seemed characteristic of early

developmental phases (ontogenetically). Championing synaesthesia as a primordial perceptual style that had been eclipsed by modern civilization, such authors, though placing more value on the past than on the future, elevated synaesthesia as a faculty to the top of the human developmental hierarchy.

ROMANTICISM AND RECAPITULATION

From the outset, scientific investigators of synaesthesia had uncovered indications that synaesthesia was prominent in early stages of psychological development, both ontogenetically and phylogenetically. Francis Galton, in his pioneering work, *Inquiries into Human Faculty and Its Development,* had remarked on the tendency of children to experience distinct mental imagery such as number forms and color hearing, and the explosion of research at the turn of the century confirmed Galton's observation. Much of the descriptive literature on synaesthesia was written by college psychology teachers, whose freshmen survey classes were full of young men and women who retained vestiges of childhood forms of mental imagery. Other psychologists, their awareness of synaesthesia heightened by the enormous interest their peers showed in the subject, published intriguing accounts of the synaesthesiae of their own children. In a series of papers in the early 1900s, British psychologist Charles S. Myers (1911, 1914), repeatedly drew attention to the more common occurrence of synaesthesia in children than in adults and speculated that synaesthesia was one among many types of "undifferentiated perception" prevalent among children.[1]

Although the doctrine that ontogeny recapitulates phylogeny goes back to the writings of ancient Greece, the modern idea of recapitulation was born in the last two decades of the eighteenth century. Its extension beyond morphology to consciousness can be detected as early as the writings of Vico, but it gained greater prominence at the turn of the twentieth century. By 1910, American and European psychological journals were full of recapitulationist developmental schemata.[2] Analogies between the undifferentiated thinking of children and that of "primitive" peoples were common at the time, and the literature on synaesthesia reflected this line of thought. Auguste Lemaître, in his 1901 study of color hearing in schoolchildren, had pointed out the prevalence of synaesthesia among children and "primitives," and F. L. Wells (1918, p. 485) compared synaesthesia and "autistic" thinking—automatic, unconscious thinking (as opposed to logical thinking)—and proposed that the symbolism of "savages," "psychotics," and children could be traced to autistic and synaesthetic thought: "Whatever community exists between psychotic and primitive ideas . . . is due to regression in *modes* of thought. There is a regression to modes of thought which more characterize primitive man, but not to special topics of thought. If the topics of thought, the precise ideas associated, do happen, only one of these is in the foreground; the others come to awareness not at all or as synaesthesias." Though Wells was aware that synaesthesiae are highly idiosyncratic, he theorized that certain common symbolic expressions derived from synaesthetic associations; he offered as an example the consistency between Karl Lehmann's observation that his own photism for bitter tastes was dark brown and the expression "dark brown taste." Wells cited anthropologist Robert Lowie's conjecture that synaesthesia accounts for some archaic symbols (Lowie found number forms to be hereditary in certain archaic communities). Just as Lowie believed that the close biological relationship among members of small communities could account for their use of idiosyncratic number forms, Wells hypothesized that "the more strictly synaesthetic phenomena" might similarly evolve into culture-specific symbolisms (Wells, 1918, p. 486).

The speculation about synaesthesia and other relatively "undifferentiated" perceptual modes and their relationship to human development was first summarized and systematized by Heinz Werner, who carried out a wide range of studies at the psychological laboratory at Hamburg. Werner's work focused on the primacy of what he called physiognomic structuring (*physiognomische Wahrnehmungsweisen*)—of the expressive properties communicated by affect and movement—in developmentally earlier forms of experience. Beginning in 1927, Werner argued for a developmental sequence from the global (characterized by a relative fusion of self and world), affective, highly subjective physiognomic mode to delineated, geometrical-technical, objective modes of perceptual structuring. Werner first addressed synaesthesia in a 1934 article and later expanded his ideas about its integral place within a schema of differentiation and hierarchic integration in his *Comparative Psychology of Mental Development* (1940). Werner drew on the study of children, "primitives," and schizophrenics to support his idea that synaesthesia is a primitive condition, reflecting a "primordial unity of the senses." As evidence that "synaesthesia plays a much greater role among *primitive* and *archaic* peoples than it does at our own cultural level," Werner cited the cosmologies of ancient Egypt, Babylonia, Mexico, and China, as well as those of the contemporary "relatively primitive" Zuni Indians, whose systems of symbols equating such elements of the natural world as cardinal directions, colors, animals, weather, and other phenomena he took to be "undoubtedly synaesthetic in nature." Werner interpreted the universality of such symbolic systems as confirmation that synaesthetic perception was once "a fundamental psychological phenomenon" whose basis was "an undifferentiated perceptual experience which permits the linking together of the separate realms of sense that is lacking or in abeyance in the highly differentiated and objectified forms of experience." In citing these multisensory symbolic systems, Werner was making the same error about synaesthesia as the Symbolists had in equating the Gesamtkunstwerk with synaesthesia; he assumed that symbolic systems derived from the actual synaesthetic experiences of archaic peoples and expressed correspondences no longer detectable to moderns. At the same time, Werner's feeling that artists retained or recovered "physiognomic" perception, and his citation of passages from Kandinsky's writings as evidence for it, helped reinforce earlier Romantic views of synaesthesia as an aesthetically superior form of perception.[3]

As further proof of the "syncretic unity of the senses," Werner stated in his *Comparative Psychology* that Western children were generally synaesthetic, asserting that "instances of synaesthesia can be found in almost any carefully written diary of observations on child behavior" (p. 88). He gave examples of children who smelled the colors of various plants, heard colors, and insisted that they could not hear without their eyes open. Werner reviewed scientific studies showing the presence of chromaesthesia in children to be about 50 percent (a percentage that progressively diminished in children more than ten years of age). To the then-popular comparison of the mental constructs of schizophrenics and "primitives," Werner added evidence of synaesthesia among schizophrenic patients. Also, synaesthesia could be experimentally induced via mescaline and other drugs, creating an "abnormal primitivity" (p. 92). Werner argued that synaesthesia was not a "bizarre" or "merely aberrant" mode of perception but a fundamental perceptual faculty. On the basis of his own experimental work, he advanced the idea that a generalized bodily reaction to stimuli accounts for synaesthetic correspondences. Werner's theory stated that any form of sensory stimulation would produce undifferentiated, tonic muscular reactions whose effects could be measured. Both his sensory-tonic theory of perception and his notion of physiognomic perception were rooted in a belief in the fundamental unity of the senses.[4]

MORE INVENTED TRADITIONS: NEW
EXAMPLES OF THE SYNAESTHETIC SUBLIME

Rather than presenting an obstacle to the Romantic conception of synaesthesia as a higher form of consciousness, synaesthesia's supposed prevalence in the mental life of children and archaic peoples actually strengthened this view. Romantic thinkers had long venerated the seeming innocence, spontaneity, and relative egolessness of both children and primitive peoples, so integrating synaesthesia, with its overtones of heightened subjectivity, the unseen, and acute aesthetic sensibility, was easy. In a sense, the archetypal Romantic, Percy Bysshe Shelley, actually anticipated Heinz Werner's ideas about the "syncretic" nature of childhood consciousness. In *Prometheus Unbound,* Shelley observed that in childhood, "we less habitually distinguished all that we saw and felt from ourselves. They seemed as it were to constitute one mass." He also noted the persistence of this type of thinking in some adults like himself who, "in this respect are always children: [They] feel as if their nature were dissolved into the surrounding universe, or as if the surrounding universe were absorbed into their being" (quoted in Gelpi, 1992, p. 91). Partly because they recognized this confluence, literary scholars, from the early interwar years, looked back past the Symbolists to the eighteenth century and tried to show that the Romantics were correspondingly fascinated with synaesthesia, and for much the same reasons. By 1912, when June Downey hunted for synaesthetic expression in the literature of the English and American Romantics—Poe, Swinburne, Shelley, Keats, Blake—students of French Romanticism had fully documented their claim that Baudelaire was not the first French writer with a predilection for synaesthesia. Unlike many of the later writers on Romanticism, Downey made a clear distinction between "true synaesthesia" (idiopathic synaesthesia) and "so-called colored thinking or the employment of sense analogies," which was really more accurately intersensory metaphor: "the man who actually *sees colour* when he hears music must be distinguished from the man who *images colour* or merely *thinks* it" (Downey, 1912, p. 490). Erika von Siebold carried this search for synaesthesia far beyond Downey's and was able to catalogue hundreds of examples of synaesthetic expression in German, English, and French writers. Siebold added most of the remaining leading figures of English Romanticism—Wordsworth, Coleridge, Byron, Tennyson, Browning, and Rosetti—to Downey's original listing. In her study of Percy Bysshe Shelley's writing, Siebold found that he tended to employ intersensory tropes in climactic passages describing states approaching mystical union, such as in the fourth act of *Prometheus Unbound.* Terming such states *Sinnesuniversalismus,* she maintained that the achievement of this unity was the ultimate goal of all Romantic experiments with "synaesthesia" (that is, intersensory metaphor) in writing.[5]

Just as the French had pioneered the interpretation of synaesthesia as an esoteric form of knowledge, German writers were most insistent in their claims for the "primitivist" interpretation. In a series of seven articles between 1930 and 1936 (1930, 1931a, 1931b, 1931c, 1931d, 1935, 1936), Albert Wellek, chair of the psychology department at the University of Breslau, built an argument for an archaic *sensorium commune* on the basis of linguistic evidence. Wellek speculated that synaesthetic perception dated back to at least the third millennium before Christ, and he gave examples from the literature of Japan, China, India, Persia, Arabia, Egypt, Babylonia, and Palestine. In ancient Rome, Wellek pointed to Vitruvius' definition of architecture as "frozen music," and Cicero's cross-sensory combinations (*splendor vocis* and *verborum fulmina*) as examples of the antiquity of the synaesthetic psychological style. During the Middle Ages, Wellek maintained, the synaesthetic outlook suffered as the European mind moved toward rationalism, although he found some synaesthetic sensibilities preserved in the early troubadours and in the Norse Edda. Wellek also documented what he believed to be synaesthetic expressions from literature of the Renaissance and Baroque periods. He contrasted the Baroque characterization of synaesthesia with the "synaesthesia" (again, really cross-sensory metaphor) of Renaissance poets, which, based on Pythagorean ideas of number-harmony, was evident in such passages as this one from Shakespeare's *Merchant of Venice* (V, i): "How sweet the moonlight sleeps upon this bank! / Here will we sit, and let the sounds of music / Creep in our ears: soft stillness and the night / Become the touches of sweet harmony." According to Wellek, the Renaissance poets and dramatists used synaesthesia to express the impression of man and nature as tuned to the divine, while in Baroque synaesthesia individual sensations and sensuousness itself predominated over the sense of reciprocity between microcosm and macrocosm. With the Enlightenment, according to Wellek, synaesthesia was transmuted from a mode of perception into a mere scientific problem, initially pondered by such figures as John Locke, Adam Smith, Samuel Johnson, Anthony Ashley Cooper, Henry Fielding, and Erasmus Darwin. Throughout his work, Wellek used "synaesthesia" to refer to the entire range of cross-sensory metaphoric language and to sensory equivalences, as well as to the idiopathic synaesthesia examined in psychological studies. As with other authors who embraced synaesthesia as an ideal form of consciousness, Wellek had a wide-ranging conception of synaesthesia and a concomitant underlying faith in the transcendental knowledge to which synaesthesia somehow gave access. By turning up evidence of "synaesthesia" throughout premodern literature, Wellek believed he was documenting a long and lonely *Abfall* from the Eden of the sensorium commune.

The continued vitality of the Romantic interpretation of synaesthesia can be seen in the writing of English poet Peter Redgrove. In *The Black Goddess and the Unseen Real* (1989, p. 32), Redgrove calls the ether—which he sees as responsible for a variety of occult phenomena—"a kind of synaesthetic 'cloud of glory.'" In his wide-ranging attempt to validate the "unseen real" and its perception by primal sensory means, Redgrove describes Coleridge's weather sensitivity (a condition Redgrove says he shares) as a form of synaesthesia: "weather and organic nature combined in a synaesthetic multi-media event, and this was the ground of all perception before it was divided up in daily living: the Primary Imagination giving way to the Secondary" (p. 84). Redgrove sees synaesthesia as a fundamental characteristic of black magic, which "is black only in the sense that it is a science of the invisibles" (p. 120). The "cloud of blackness" worked by the magician permits both sensory extension and fusion, "as in Baudelaire's 'Correspondances'" (p. 121). Redgrove firmly believes that the magician's "synaesthetic" (that is, cross-sensory) technique is the principal work also of the poet. On the way to synaesthetic perception, the visionary, whether poet or magician, "must pass through the Cloud of Unknowing, the blackness, the depression where all the senses seem closed, until the conscious senses flower with the unconscious ones, upwards to the known senses, downwards to the unknown ones. The magician will be assisted in his synaesthesia by established vertical and horizontal correspondences, in his temple, resonances between colours, sounds, materials, incenses, planets and god-forms with their attributes which he will learn until they are second nature" (p. 123). Along with more recent magical techniques, Redgrove sees cultivation of synaesthesia as a necessary path to "a state of unknowing which is actually charged with knowledge. . . . This unknowing . . . is the synaesthetic plenum of the unconscious or subliminal senses, responding to a continuum of such complexity and grandeur in nature that it can only be approached by means of ignorance and emptying, with symbolic and imaginative guides" (p. 132). Setting out from a set of premises about the nature of synaesthesia completely distinct from that of more academically inclined writers, Redgrove arrives finally at the same destination—a vision that the fusion of the senses in synaesthesia represents a form of ultimate knowledge.

The "something" about synaesthesia which lends itself to interpretation as a vanished condition of consciousness that modern humanity must again recover is everywhere apparent in a recent literary work that rivals Scriabin's *Mysterium* for its solipsistic hermeticism—José Arguelles's *Earth Ascending: An Illustrated Treatise on the Law Governing Whole Systems* (1988). The book was originally published in 1984 and went out of print within the year, but the huge success of

Arguelles's *The Mayan Factor: Path Beyond Technology,* which in 1987 had caused a worldwide irruption of New Age millennialism, motivated a publishing house in Santa Fe, New Mexico, to reprint *Earth Ascending.* In the Introduction, Arguelles made a utopian promise:

> *Earth Ascending* announces the manifestation of the new paradigm, the *resonant field paradigm.* The first premise of this paradigm asserts that everything is in resonance and that the primary nature of reality is resonance—vibrational frequency—and not matter. Thus, the new paradigm transcends in a stroke the Newtonian atomistic materialistic model. As paradigms go, so do ways of life and whole civilizations. If the Newtonian model helped contribute to a fantastic global civilization of materialism and war, the new paradigm will contribute to an interplanetary civilization of harmony and a multidimensional metaphysical potential undreamed of in the old.[6]

The ubiquity of the word "paradigm" in this paragraph and throughout Arguelles's text testifies to his intent to have it taken as a scientific set of ideas. But in the usage of nonscientists in search of transcendental realms of consciousness, the word "paradigm" had changed from a synonym for "model" to a highly charged code word for "higher knowledge." For Arguelles's audience, "paradigm" or "new paradigm" meant "transcendental paradigm" and signified a form of knowledge that seamlessly merged the hard physical sciences with the softer science of psychology and the even softer realm of religion.

The key to Arguelles's theory of knowledge, and equally a theory of history, was the concept of synaesthesia, which Arguelles defined as "the sense fields mutually interpenetrating and acting in harmony with each other" (p. 60). In Arguelles's view of evolution, humans once existed in a state of "aboriginal synaesthesia," where sight, sound, smell, taste, and touch were fused in blissful unity. The historical process was marked by a progressive falling away from this primal condition, culminating in the present condition of "mechanistic psychosensory alienation," characterized by "the loss of sacred view, the splintering of knowledge, the divorce of art and science, and the general collective confusion" attributable to the absence of a synthetic model of the world and humanity's place in it (p. 62). Arguelles's theory, like the "Harmonic Convergence" he predicted in *The Mayan Factor,* promised an impending "holonomic" stage of history, in which the contemporary alienation would be replaced by "a heightened, posthistoric synaesthesia." Arguelles's predictions for the posthistoric synaesthetic landscape included computer-assisted light and sound art, "synaesthetic baths" for the "masses of humanity now deadened to the living vitality of the natural world," "eco squads purifying and studying the natural harmonies of the terrestrial environment," "psychoatmospheric investigation groups," "geoeconomic resource arbiters," and "therapy theater units" (p. 68).

Arguelles's conception of synaesthesia, like Baudelaire's, Rimbaud's, Kandinsky's and Scriabin's, implicitly linked the fusion of the senses to an experience of transcendence of the world of physical reality. Arguelles's transcendental vision was most akin to Scriabin's in the association between this fusion of the senses and the end of history: "*Earth Ascending* should . . . reveal itself as a primer for the creation of those synthesizing and synaesthetic interdimensional communication bridges between ourselves and the star people" (p. x). The primer was basically a collection of imaginative diagrams constructed by Arguelles, which, though wildly speculative, were accompanied by urgently serious explanations and prefaced with this claim: "*Earth Ascending* is not speculation, but a precise set of keys, a code, a matrix, and ultimately a display of the underlying patterns governing the conscious experience of life on this particular planet" (p. 28). Arguelles's claims of empirical validity (in the obvious absence of any supporting evidence) did not necessarily strike his readers as outrageous. Since the early 1970s, the audience for "new paradigms" had been imbibing a variety of texts that purported to reconcile science and religion. The themes of most of these books revolved around certain other "invisibles" drawn from contemporary scientific knowledge. Like Arguelles's "resonant field," both the "implicate order" of quantum mechanics and the hologram from optical physics were borrowed concepts that were employed at best as suggestive metaphors in such works, but the images were deceptively offered as actual scientific models.

Arguelles's "maps" of the "psi bank matrix," "binary triplet configuration," "resonant field model," " geomantic flow chart," "holonomic brain," "aboriginal attunement templates," and "holonomic model of knowledge" culminated in the "Synaesthetic Field Map or a History of the Senses." The "map" was in fact a chart on which the traditional five senses were plotted out along a vertical axis, with a highly schematized view of human evolution (also divided into five sections—the "primary," "ancient world," "medieval world," "modern," and "holonomic") along the horizontal axis. Along with standard events like "painting/writing/compass/sculptural/craft techniques" crammed into the ancient world or "telegraph/telephone/radio/television/radar/transistor/computer" in the modern column, a strange assortment of landmarks in human history were deployed on the chart. These cumulative stages of psychosensory elaboration dead-ended in Arguelles's "Holonomic," where one of his ubiquitous spheres hung, this one a pentatentacled amoeboid representing the "psychogenetic feedback core" of "primal synaesthesia." Its five pseudopods stretched out to touch a series of "perimeters"—the "synaesthetic aboriginal field," "hieratic stasis," "medieval synthesis," and the contemporary "zone of mechanistic psychosensory alienation," otherwise known as the "communication jam" (p. 61). Though the sensory pseudopods seemed to shrink back from their contact with this zone, Arguelles's diagram assured the patient cryptographer that this horrible zone of the present condition of alienation was also the "holonomic perimeter of radiosonic synaesthesia"; and the next map in the series, the "Psychogenetic Feedback Loop," simplified and reoriented Arguelles's synaesthetic model of history, reconfiguring time as a twining loop about to break through the holonomic horizon into the "electromagnetic sky of posthistoric synaesthesia" (p. 83). According to Arguelles, who claimed the Mayan calendar as his authority, this era would dawn in December of the year 2012.

In the accompanying explanation, Arguelles stated that "history is the loop between the two stages of synaesthetic unity—the aboriginal and posthistoric." Arguelles embraced a recapitulation model of history, in which ontogenetic history was symmetrical with phylogenetic history: "Through the process of growth each of us emerges from a condition of synaesthetic unity—the womb and early childhood—into a stage of expansion, growth, and experimentation, in which we are tested and formed only to return at last to a more highly synthesized condition of fulfillment and realization" (p. 18). In later maps, Arguelles reinforced his vision by mixing in musical and chromatic symbolization, designating civilizational "pulses" with the notes of the musical scale and the seven colors of the rainbow. Arguelles envisioned a "planetary rainbow, a celestial guardian being" stretching across the violet sky of the imminent "holonomic posthistoric future," this rainbow symbolizing "a complete synaesthesia, a condition of complete planetary synthesis almost unthinkable today" (p. 29). Arguelles's illustrations of evolution's endpoints—the prehistoric synaesthetic sea from which human consciousness was supposed to emerge and the posthistoric synaesthetic sky into which it was supposed to erupt—were archetypal images of fusion. Arguelles used sea, sky, and synaesthesia as powerful metaphors to express his belief that human consciousness had once been cradled by some all-encompassing invisible power—and would be again. Preferring the typhonic states of childhood and prehistory over the "zone of mechanistic psychosensory alienation" imposed by contemporary rational consciousness, Arguelles's visionary timeline represented his choice of an oceanic merger over true transcendence.[7]

Independently of Arguelles, other contemporary celebrants of an impending shift in consciousness have chosen synaesthesia as a central metaphor. In *Dreaming with Open Eyes: The Shamanic Spirit in Twentieth-Century Art and Culture* (1992, p. xxiii), Michael Tucker recasts as "shamans" the entire constellation of modern Western artists and poets who shared Romantic ideals. He, too, anticipates a shift in consciousness, "from mechanistic, rationalist modes of thought to what has been called a sense of *participation mystique* in life." Tucker's invocation of Lucien Lévy-Bruhl's *participation mystique*—the unconscious, nearly dreamlike state that Tucker imagines premodern peoples to have enjoyed—as a desirable alternative to rationalism indicates that he shares Arguelles's view of the future as bringing a return to past stages of consciousness. Though he uses the term loosely, Tucker employs "synaesthesia" as if it were a synonymn for participation mystique, envisions synaesthesia as characteristic of the "shamanic" state enjoyed already by certain modern artists, and in store for Western consciousness as a whole as it advances toward the Primitive. Tucker calls Henri Matisse a shaman, and says that "the synaesthetic grace" of Matisse's collection of primitivist cutouts and writings entitled *Jazz* (1947) "suggests that, ultimately, the search for Paradise is the self-transformative development of the wonder-struck heart, in endless, creative search of the transmutative harmony which lies at the core of life" (p. xxiii). Using the word at first to describe cross-sensory artistic endeavors, Tucker links synaesthesia with "the original interplay of the elements of creative expression in shamanism," and points to Wassily Kandinsky and Paul Klee as exemplars (p. 122). But Tucker interprets synaesthesia as more than just an aesthetic technique, and he weaves Baudelaire's "Correspondances" and Rimbaud's "Voyelles" into his thesis that artist-shamans see the nature of reality more clearly than the mass of mortals.

Robert Lawlor ascribes synaesthesia to "Dreamtime," the English translation of the aboriginal name for an altered state of consciousness experienced by the aboriginal people of Australia, the late twentieth century's archetypal primitive culture. "The second stage of the Dreamtime awareness is marked by a state of perception called synesthesia, the mingling of the senses. . . . Aborigines frequently make synaesthetic statements. . . . The synaesthetic experience, which occurs in the deep neural system, marks our entrance into the blending, merging world of the Dreamtime. Aboriginal society allows shamanistic and psychedelic experience to blend with, enhance, and uphold the full expression of life." (Lawlor, 1989, p. 381) Lawlor, suggesting that the experience of synaesthesia is available to all of us, not just aboriginal shamans, turns synaesthesia into an expression of an oceanic merger:

One universally important revelation that anyone can experience in the blending of sensory experience that occurs in a synesthetic state is this: there is no *single* thing. Nothing exists in the world isolated from everything else. Each object, each process, is more than it appears to be. . . . The perceivable world is a magic symbol turning our sense of reality to another world more powerful, more awesome, more wonderful than we have allowed ourselves to believe. The network of correspondences that flood our vision as the sense perceptions merge is not a neural malfunction, a psychic illusion, or a device of poetry and romanticism. It is the experience of a crucial, long-ignored mode of intelligence founded in a deep neural physiological base and essential to the full manifestation of our conscious being. [Lawlor, 1989, p. 383]

Though he apparently derives his inspiration from a completely different source than did previous Romantic writers, Lawlor sings the same song of synaesthesia as an indicator of a higher reality. Each of his statements, rather than delineate the experience of synaesthesia, instead outlines a desire for evidence that the pedestrian physical world hides a magical invisible world behind it. By rejecting interpretations of synaesthesia as either a pathological symptom or a literary device and in their place positing synaesthesia as a biological foundation of "intelligence," Lawlor elevates synaesthesia. Lawlor's citation of Rimbaud and Baudelaire as his authorities on synaesthesia indicates that his understanding of synaesthesia has been shaped by the popular view of the faculty as a transcendental visionary state. The dream state has long been idealized by Romantics as a source of transcendental truths; the existence of a culture where dreams still appear to have a hieratic function has proved to be as powerfully attractive to Romantics as has synaesthesia.

THE EIDETIC IMAGE: ANOTHER FORM
OF TRANSCENDENTAL TRUTH?

The idea that synaesthesia was a primitive faculty was given support by research early in the twentieth century on eidetic images. In the psychological literature a variety of characteristics have been employed to define the eidetic image, but most contemporary researchers (see, for example, Ahsen, 1977a) accept the following criteria as diagnostic: in eideticism a normal, subjective visual image is experienced with particular vividness; although not dependent on the experience of an actual external object, the eidetic image is "seen" inside the mind and is accompanied by bodily engagement with the image (including a sense of its "felt meaning"); experience of the eidetic image is a healthy, not pathological, structure; like the photisms of color hearing and other synaesthetic percepts, the eidetic image is noteworthy for its vividness and memorability, and for the subjective sense on the part of the viewer that it is being projected; like synaesthetes, eidetics believe their images to be real, even though so few people share their perception of such images. A significant number of eidetics are also synaesthetes, but a lesser proportion of synaesthetes possess eidetic perception.[8] Finally, as with synaesthesia, eideticism has repeatedly been taken as an extraordinary sensory endowment, one that could belong only to particularly gifted individuals. Many of the people who are thought of as having "photographic memory" are in fact eidetics; the vast majority of eidetic images originate in scenes remembered from their own experience. Though the word "images" suggests that these subjective sensations are always of a visual nature, they can, as in synaesthesia, occur in nonvisual sensory modalities—hearing, taste, smell, and touch. As in synaesthesia, when the eidetic images are visual, they seem to appear on a "screen" hovering before the face; when tactile, the images feel as if they are on or in the skin; when auditory, eidetic images are heard as if they were real sounds; and olfactory and gustatory eidetic images are similarly experienced as if they are "real."[9]

A 1936 study by psychologist D. M. Purdy of the University of California at Berkeley, of an eidetic (and synaesthetic) woman, gives an excellent phenomenological description of the mental world of the eidetic. The woman, "R," a senior in college at the time of the study, had experienced eidetic imagery as long as she could remember and had never suspected that such imagery was unusual. Among early memories of her eideticism, she gave the example of how, when confined to a hospital bed at age ten, she had entertained herself by dressing dolls in imaginary garments. Asked to form a mental image of the sun, she reported a glaringly bright image which lasted several minutes, so that it became painful for her eyes, which began to water. As the image faded, it turned into a purple disk with a white corona, identical to an afterimage of the actual sun. R could briefly study all manner of pictorial images and then report on them with prodigious detail and accuracy. Colored pictures gave better eidetic images than black and white, and the more meaningful and interesting a picture was to her, the more completely she could recall it onto her eidetic "screen." Often, the images were slightly modified versions of the original, with the individual elements of the picture—trees or rivers in a landscape, for example—animated and more naturalistic in appearance than in the original. In fact, the entire eidetic image almost invariably appeared to her as much more vivid than the original image and the colors more saturated and glossier. Usually, she could see through the eidetic image to her real surroundings, but occasionally, the images were so vivid as form an opaque screen, and she could not see beyond them.

In addition to her visual imagery, R. experienced eidetic auditory, olfactory, and tactual imagery. If she imagined the roar of the sea, the auditory impression was so intense that it muffled or even completely masked the actual sounds of her surroundings, including peoples' voices. When R imagined an insect crawling on her skin, the thought caused the same visceral reaction as if it were really present. Her tactual eidetic imagery included temperature. Olfactory imagery was comparably vivid. Often, the various modalities were experienced together during an episode of eidetic imagery: shown a drawing of a hunter aiming his gun at a rabbit, R reported hearing the gun go off and seeing smoke issue from the muzzle. Imagining a rose, she smelled its perfume as clearly as she saw its deep red color, and she had the kinaesthetic sensation of its velvety texture. When she formed a picture of ocean waves breaking on the shore, the accompanying eidetic imagery included the sound and smell of the sea. Imagining a visit to the doctor, she could smell the ether in the examination room (Purdy, 1936).

Although V. J. Purkinje (1819), Johannes Müller (1826), Gustav Theodor Fechner (1860), Francis Galton (1886), and Alfred Binet (1892; 1894) had studied eidetic phenomena in the nineteenth century, V. Urbantschitsch in 1907 was the first to associate eideticism (which he called *Anschauungsbild*) with childhood, and in 1909 Erich Jaensch, whose work dominated the field for the next two decades, coined the word *eidetische.* Jaensch extended the idea of eideticism as a primitive cognitive function in a series of publications that appeared between 1911 and 1930. Jaensch, who with the assistance of his brother Walther and a number of assistants conducted most of his studies with schoolchildren in Marburg, Germany, had two principal working theories; that eidetics were special, and that their images were the Ur-form from which all mental imagery arose. Jaensch assumed that in infancy and early childhood, perception and memory did not exist as distinct faculties and that in some unique individuals this condition persisted into adulthood. Jaensch defended the idea that this undifferentiated archaic perception is the root of all perception by means of three types of evidence: 1) studies, principally those carried out at Marburg, concerning the nature and extent of eideticism in children of various ages; 2) studies of "eidetic disposition" in adults; and 3) studies of primitive tribes and cultures.[10]

In Jaensch's studies, and in most of the work in eideticism up until around 1935, most young children were considered to be at least partially eidetic. (Since

1964, most empirical studies with elementary-age school children have reported incidences of eideticism ranging from 2 percent to 15 percent.) For Jaensch, the building up of the perceptual world for all humans was initially dependent on eidetic phenomena, and so he expected that given the right test at the right time, *all* children would display some form of eidetic perception. Jaensch maintained that eideticism persisted into adulthood in the "T-type" (for "tetanoid" condition, caused by underactivity of the parathyroid gland) and "B-type" (for "basedowoid," caused by a hyperactive thyroid), both of which were supposedly distinguishable on the basis of certain somatic characteristics. The B-type most frequently exhibited eidetic images that were visualizations of ideas—that is, B-type subjects could literally "see" whatever they thought about. They could call up eidetic images and then banish them at will and even mentally manipulate the color, form, and location of the images if such manipulation was carried out as part of a particular mental inquiry. B-type eidetics could literally set their mental images in motion, as Nikola Tesla would do to check the performance of his inventions before they were actually turned into material creations.

T-type eidetics were much more limited in their capacities for visualization, and their eidetic images assumed more the character of after-images. The image could not be produced or erased at will, and the manipulation of the image, if it was possible at all, proceeded slowly and with great effort. While B-type eidetic images were rich in detail, the T-type eidetic image was indistinct and often seen in the complementary color. Jaensch owed his biological classification of the types to his brother Walther, who combined physiology with Lombroso-style characterology in an effort to "read" types of eidetics by their facial physiognomies. Erich Jaensch later switched to a typology of "integrate" (for "B-type") and "disintegrate" (for "T-type") individuals. The integrate subjects were the key to his ontogenetic theory of eideticism, for they displayed the unity of eidetic perceptions and images that Jaensch considered primordial. "The integrate type is an earlier one from the evolutionary point of view. The younger children are, the more fully do they show this characteristic integration. Integration also dominates the behavior of primitive peoples." According to Jaensch, the rationalized environment of school tended to destroy childhood eideticism, just as contact with modern Western societies caused primitives to lose their eidetic abilities. Despite the glaringly ideologically driven findings, Jaensch's work won wide support among European psychologists. In America, though G. W. Allport early on discounted the speculative method of the Marburg school, others found it at least partially appealing, although not

necessarily for scientific reasons. D. M. Purdy combined fin de siècle degeneration theory with Jaensch's typology in her 1936 study when she labeled the
American businessman a disintegrate. According to Purdy, because of the
disintegrating effect of modern civilization on personality, disintegrates were
"especially common in America."[11]

Although the Marburg school studies furnished extensive evidence of eidetic
imagery in children, few of the studies provided detailed phenomenological
descriptions, given the difficulty of working with young subjects. Almost all the
case studies were of eidetic imagery in adults. Jaensch repeatedly stressed his
"integrative" interpretation of eidetic ability, and his major papers were heavily
laden with language aimed at elevating the status of eidetic perception. In his
major book-length review of eidetic imagery, *Eidetic Imagery and Typological
Methods of Investigation* (1930a), Jaensch emphasized that eidetic images were
regarded as "something belonging to the self; not as an annoyance . . . but as a
gift, often as an intimate, loved possession that one wants to retain" (p. 28).
Jaensch's fixation on typology polarized eidetic "integrates" and noneidetic
"disintegrates"; he likened the integrate to an organism, while comparing
disintegrates to machines (p. 106). He claimed that Henri Bergson's philosophy
defined the integrate, and that integrates could escape the "disintegration
induced by civilization" (p. 108) and return to "organic modes of Being"
(p. 109).

Just as writers enamored of synaesthesia endowed certain esteemed historical
personalities with synaesthesia, Jaensch attributed eidetic ability to a select
group of individuals in accordance with his interpretation of eidetic capacity as
a preferred perceptual style. German psychologist Wilhelm Wundt was assumed to be eidetic, as was Jean-Jacques Rousseau, whose pedagogic philosophy was akin to Jaensch's own. The premier eidetic for Jaensch and other
German students of eidetic imagery, however, was Johann Wolfgang von
Goethe. Albert Wellek, who had given synaesthesia such an august heritage,
joined his colleague Jaensch in categorizing Goethe as "Eidetiker und Syn-
ästhetiker," and in surrounding that avatar of German intellect and art with a
halo of primordial perception. Wellek also gave the designation *Augen-
mensch*—visually oriented person—to Goethe, whom his mentor Herder had
chastised for his obsession with vision. (Herder preferred the ear's revelations to
the eye's.) Wellek and Jaensch set the "artistic" outlook of the child and such
personalities as Goethe over against the "logical" outlook instilled by contemporary culture and schooling. In a footnote, Jaensch defended the Jugend-
bewegung (Youth Movement) from charges of anti-intellectualism, and im-

plied that many of its ideals were consistent with his own goal of revitalizing education (pp. 45–46).

A "subform" of the integrate type was the "S-type" (for synaesthetic). Jaensch valued integrate subjects for their high degree of *Einfühlung* (empathy), which showed up in their tendency to "surrender themselves lovingly to the impressions from outside" (p. 113). But the synaesthete's *Zufühlung* (propathy) was even more demonstrative of a union between the perceptual subject and object. While "the emotional tone (*Stimmung*) of the I$_1$ [integrate] type depends upon external circumstances; that of the synaesthetic is due to his inner circumstances, and he impresses his emotional tone on external circumstances and objects" (pp. 113–114). Though Jaensch valued the synaesthete's high degree of subjectivism, he warned that the S-type was liable to estrangement from reality and noted that many schizophrenics were also synaesthetic (p. 115).

Other eidetic researchers echoed Jaensch's reservation about the danger of the solipsism to which synaesthetes and eidetics were sometimes prone; according to Helena O'Neill and J. Edward Rauth, "No lotus-land was ever more alluring than the realm of eidetic imagery. Here [the eidetic] can find escape from the harshness of everyday life and build up a sphere of lovely unreality out of which personality difficulties and even insanities are born. Here is a magic carpet on which he can ride away from the ridicule of companions and the scolding of superiors" (O'Neill and Rauth, 1934, p. 17). Still, Jaensch considered synaesthesia, like eideticism, to be a healthy, desirable mental phenomenon, and along with his associate at the Marburg Institute of Psychology Otto Kroh, Jaensch believed that synaesthesia and eideticism were typical of a roster of some of Germany's finest intellectuals and artists—Otto Ludwig, Ludwig Tieck, E. T. A. Hoffman, J. V. von Scheffel, and Goethe. Jaensch pointed out that the philosopher Riehl considered himself eidetic (Klüver, 1928, pp. 78, 91–92). He allied himself with Johann Gottfried von Herder, who in *Abhandlung über den Ursprung der Sprache* attributed the sensory unity experienced by the synaesthete to Aristotle's explanation of the sensorium commune. Like Herder, Jaensch saw synaesthesia as a necessary precursor for the development of language, "since it is the first and primary mediator between the described perceptual complexes of objects and the descriptive sound complexes of language" (p. 108). Jaensch also gave credit to the S-type for much of the abstract geometric thought that was fundamental to the development of modern science.[12]

Jaensch also asserted that eidetic ability was much more common in archaic cultures, and in addition to publishing theoretical articles developing this view, he encouraged ethnographers to attend to it in their field work. Jaensch drew heavily on the work of Lucien Lévy-Bruhl; according to Jaensch, "Lévy-Bruhl's material leads almost convincingly to the conclusion that the perceptual and conceptual worlds of tribal peoples are close to the eidetic world of children" (p. 91). Francis Galton was the first to suggest the occurrence of eidetic imagery among archaic peoples, noting the ability of South African Bushmen and Australian and Tasmanian aborigines to draw from memory the exact outline of landscape objects. Galton, who ascribed eidetic ability to Paleolithic European peoples as well, suggested that some of the earliest known artistic representations had been produced not from life but from eidetically recalled images. In the early 1900s, when Haeckelian recapitulation theory was still popular, many writers on Paleolithic art compared the graphic representations of children and "primitives," and the Marburg eidetic studies were cited in support of this work. Recently, a number of psychohistorians have reworked Jaensch's ideas to explain certain features of Paleolithic cave art. In 1979, Julian Jaynes surmised that the hundred or so paintings in any particular Paleolithic cave were done by only a few Cro-Magnons over a few decades, "a unique few whose strong eidetic imagery may have been more similar to the extreme of Luria's adult mnemonist than to the usual eidetic child."[13]

Behind the Marburg group's idealization of both synaesthetic and eidetic perception lay the German psychological school known as *Ganzheitspsychologie* and its philosophical parent, *Lebensphilosophie*. Both the unity of the senses displayed in synaesthetic perception and the "integration" displayed by eidetics were powerful expressions of *Ganzheit* (totality), and they lent themselves to satisfaction of the Romantic hunger for wholeness. The biologization and psychologization of human character and personality of Jaensch's typology meshed well with the prefascist irrationalism of Ludwig Klages's vitalistic psychology of expression, in which the intellect was seen as the destroyer of life. Klages and others used vitalism to attack reason and "rationalistic" culture; after vitalism degenerated into Nazi totalitarianism, Jaensch added anti-Semitism to his typology of perception, wedding eidetic theory to Nazi racial doctrine. There was a distinct hiatus in psychological research on eidetic imagery between 1935 and 1964; though most attribute this hiatus to the behaviorists' distaste for so introspective a subject, it may also be due to the association of eidetic research with the National Socialist scientific program.[14]

Despite being a "primitive" form of perception, eideticism was seen as a perceptual mode preferable to the modern mechanistic, intellectualistic outlook. Part of the reason for Jaensch's and other German psychologists' enthusiasm for eideticism was their intimation that the eidetic had tapped into a

Platonic realm of pure, "higher" mental imagery. Partly because eidetics, like synaesthetes, were more likely to experience paranormal events than the average person, Jaensch's (and the other Marburg psychologists') papers were laced with speculations about various parapsychological phenomena and their relation to the perceptual style of the "integrate." The ability of the eidetic to bring back detailed mental pictures unavailable to most people was seen as synonymous with the ability of Theosophical initiates to read the Akashic Record, the transcendental inscription of all of earth history. According to Rudolf Steiner (1975, p. 30), the twentieth century's most indefatigable investigator of the Akashic Record, it was "no ordinary script":

> Think of the course of events, just as they happened, presented to your spiritual vision; think, let us say, of the Emperor Augustus and all his deeds standing before you in a cloudlike picture. The picture stands there before the spiritual-scientific investigator and he can at any time evoke the experience anew. He requires no external evidence. He need only direct his gaze to a definite point in cosmic or human happenings and the events will present themselves to him in a spiritual picture.

Statements like this about images voluntarily called forth were interpreted as describing a sort of eidetic imagery. Both eidetic images and the images recovered from the Akashic Record were seen by many, including some of the Marburg psychologists, as *objective* recordings of events, untainted by the vagaries of normal perception and memory. In almost the same fashion as had happened with synaesthetic photisms, eidetic images were given greater authority than the seemingly subjective images of normal memory. These speculations, which helped to reinforce the interpretation of eideticism as a higher form of consciousness, survive in many "New Age" works, including those of Arguelles and Lawlor. As with the Romantic interpretation of synaesthesia, they spring from a tendency to categorize any uncommon subjective visual phenomenon as indicative of an invisible world, attainable only by the highest initiates or the most "uninitiated," the children, primitives, and artists whose perceptual freshness has not been corrupted by modern civilization.[15]

THINKING IN PICTURES

Time
I never see what I am looking at
I see what I think. [Barnstone, 1968, p. 50]

In the 1960s, nine-year-old Aliki Barnstone was one of a number of child "poets" lauded by such well-known adult poets as Anne Sexton, who wrote the foreword to a collection of Barnstone's poems. Among these poems was this matter-of-fact declaration of eidetic perception, along with a number of others whose charm came from their frank expression of other syncretic forms of consciousness—synaesthesia, personification of colors and words, and various types of physiognomic thinking. The idealization of these children's faithful descriptions of their mental worlds as "poetry" again suggests how adults, prisoners of their own rationalized thought, have idealized synaesthesia and other syncretic modes of perception. Kenneth Koch, another poet who saw continuities between adult creativity and the syncretistic perception of childhood, wrote:

> One reason that people are so grateful to the arts and poetry is that it takes one back a bit to that paradise that we are forced to live without most of the time in order to take care of ourselves, in order to be reasonable, in order to be nice to people, in order to stay warm, to get enough to eat and so on. But that state of mind . . . in which you could hear the color of a sound is, I think, a state that people are in when they are infants, before the senses are differentiated. It's a state also that can be induced by taking certain drugs. It's also a state that poets are often in when they write. [Koch, 1972, p. 209]

Koch's Eden, like that of the many authors who saw synaesthesia and eideticism as higher states, was a fall into a developmentally early, immature form of perception and cognition. Identifying the Fall in individual and collective history with the triumph of the ego, Romantic interpreters of syncretic perception wished to recover a prelapsarian state of oceanic oneness.

The desire to interpret synaesthetic photisms and eidetic images as transcendental representations from an invisible world prevented these authors from incorporating a body of psychological research on individuals who were unlikely to pass for avatars of heightened consciousness. Occasionally in the early twentieth century, but more frequently in recent research, eidetic imagery (and secondarily, synaesthesia) has been shown to be common in autistic individuals. Although used in the early twentieth century by psychologists (such as F. L. Wells; see Chapter 2) to refer to a variety of pronounced degrees of withdrawal from social interaction, "autism" has, since its clinical description in the early 1940s, come to have a much more narrowly circumscribed domain of reference. An often incapacitating lifelong developmental disability that typically appears during the first three years of life, autism involves some combination of the following diagnostic criteria: qualitative impairment in social interaction (as evidenced by poorly developed or absent nonverbal behaviors such as eye contact, facial expression, and gestures; absence or paucity of peer relationships; lack of social or emotional reciprocity); problems in communication, including a delay in or total absence of acquisition of spoken language or, when speech is present, impaired ability to initiate or sustain conversations, and frequently stereotyped and repetitive or idiosyncratic use of language; repetitive and stereotyped behavioral patterns, such as intense preoccupation with particular interests, strict adherence to specific, nonfunctional routines or rituals, and stereotyped and repetitive movements. Although the severity of autism varies widely, the naive observer will be struck by the sense of the autistic person as tragically walled off from the rest of the world, as evidenced by the lack of speech, lack of interaction with others, seemingly nonempathic treatment of others, preoccupation with his or her own body, and shrinking from being touched. In the early literature on autism frequent but fleeting references are made in case histories to the extraordinary ability of autistic children to retain visual images. The psychologist Leo Kanner, who is considered to have established infantile autism as a diagnostic entity (independently from but at the same time as Hans Asperger in Austria), noted in one of his early papers that "the [autistic] child's memory is phenomenal. . . . After the lapse of several days, a multitude of blocks could be re-arranged, most astonishingly—in precisely the same unorganized pattern, with the same color of each block facing in the same direction as before. The absence of a block or the presence of a super-numerary block was noticed immediately, and there was an imperative demand on the restoration of the missing piece" (Kanner, 1951, p. 25).

Observers were usually more interested in commenting on the ritualistic behavior of recreating past visual patterns than they were on the occurrence of the imagery itself, and even since the renascence of interest in eidetic imagery in the late 1960s, little specific attention has been paid to this dimension of autism.[16]

Part of the reason that the salience of visual imagery in autistic persons was not recognized earlier was of course the limited possibility they had to communicate their experience. Recently, with enhanced understanding of the disorder and its alleviation through new drugs and therapeutic techniques, the eidetic dimension of autism has become ever more apparent. The most striking example is the recent writings of Dr. Temple Grandin, whose *Emergence: Labeled Autistic* (1986) was perhaps the first full self-report of autism by an autistic individual. A professor of animal science at Colorado State University, she is the world's leading authority on the design and construction of livestock handling equipment. In her second book, *Thinking in Pictures: And Other Reports from My Life with Autism* (1995), the importance of eidetic imagery in her own and other autistic persons' mental life emerges full-blown. Her book opens with the declaration:

> I think in pictures. Words are like a second language to me. I translate both spoken and written words into full-color movies, complete with sound, which run like a VCR tape in my head. . . . Visual thinking has enabled me to build entire systems in my imagination. . . . Before I attempt any construction, I test run the equipment in my imagination, I visualize the designs being used in every possible situation, with different sizes and breeds of cattle in different weather conditions. Doing this enables me to correct mistakes prior to construction. . . . I create new images all the time by taking many little parts of images I have in the video library in my imagination and piecing them together. I have video memories of every item I've ever worked with— steel gates, fences, latches, concrete walls, and so forth. [Grandin, 1995, pp. 20–22]

Like the typical synaesthete, even into adulthood Temple Grandin believed that everyone thought in pictures, just the way she did. She eventually devised a way to find out whether someone else was also an eidetic imager.

> I have conducted an informal little cognitive test on many people. They are asked to access their memory of church steeples or cats. An object that is not in the person's immediate surroundings should be used for this visualization procedure. When I do this, I see in my imagination a series of "videos" of different churches or cats I have seen or known. Many "normal" people will see a visual image of a cat, but it is a sort of generalized generic cat image. They usually don't see a series of vivid cat or church "videos" unless they are an artist, parent of an autistic child, or an engineer. My "cat" concept consists of a series of "videos" of cats I have known. There is no generalized cat. If I keep thinking about cats or churches I can manipulate the "video" images. I can put snow on the church roof and imagine what the church grounds look like during the different seasons. [Grandin, 1995, p. 57]

The most spectacular evidence of eideticism among both autistic children and adults has come from the study of people who formerly were unkindly labeled idiots savants and who more recently have come to be called "autistic savants" or "retarded savants." One researcher (Rimland, 1978) found in a survey of 5,400 autistic children that more than 500 were savants, although other studies have found the incidence to be lower. In such individuals, low overall intellectual ability as measured by normative tests is combined with striking, frequently extraordinary ability in one or more discrete fields of endeavor. Many autistic savants are extremely talented musicians. Harriet, who as an infant showed classic signs of autism—withdrawal from social contact, rocking and head-banging, hyperaesthesia—also displayed special musical abilities by the time she was eight months old. Lying on her back in her crib, Harriet could hum in perfect pitch, tempo, and phrasing various arias she had heard rehearsed by voice students of her music teacher–mother. She could also sing with proper accents, phrasing and pitch all their vocal exercises. Even Harriet's banging and rocking followed rhythmic tempos, and she had absolute pitch, as was often demonstrated when her mother's pupils sang off pitch and Harriet responded by yelping in pain. Once Harriet tried to push a student out of the house when he repeatedly failed to sing a high note on pitch. At age three, after watching her sister play the piano, she took it up, and soon learned to play every instrument in her parents' home—violin, trumpet, clarinet, and French horn. By the age of seven she could accompany all the pupils, and her perfect pitch allowed her to name instantly the component notes of any four-note chord sounded on the piano. Playing orchestral works on the piano, she frequently filled in parts from the orchestra which were not in her own score. If she played a transcription of some other instrumental part, she exactly matched the instrument's tone and phrasing. Though her musical language was expressive, imaginative, spontaneous, and playful, she had only rudimentary verbal skills, and her life outside music was flat and affectless, alternating between the counterpoint of passivity and the ritualized fixed behaviors so typical of autism.[17]

Much less common but equally striking, because of the conjunction they reveal of brilliant artistic expressiveness with overall muted intelligence and affect, are autistic individuals who excel at drawing or painting. Nadia, who like Harriet at an early age showed all the symptoms of autism, was similarly precocious in her artistic development. From the age of three and a half, she used perspective and foreshortening, techniques usually acquired only in early adolescence. Her drawings were not lifeless copies of scenes, but vibrantly idiosyncratic. They stood in absolute contrast to her narrow personal life, where she was hemmed in by her autism (Selfe, 1977). In the 1930s two French psychologists reported on a sixteen-year-old boy who could not read or write but who drew fabulously detailed drawings of village life (Stern and Maire, 1937). Among the several gifted Japanese autistic artists is Kiyoshi Yamashita, who has been called the Van Gogh of Japan. Despite his gift, he is a homeless wanderer who begs for food and sleeps in railway stations (Morishima, 1974; Morishima and Brown, 1976).

For at least two centuries, one other group of autistic prodigies—lightning calculators—have captured the attention of both scientists and the general public. These individuals are able to perform extremely difficult arithmetic problems mentally at immense speed; a young autistic man who lived in a French mental asylum could furnish the cube root for any six-digit number in less than six seconds, or the square root of any four-digit number in four seconds. Asked to calculate the number of grains of corn in each of sixty-four boxes, assuming that each box contained twice the number in the preceding box, this same man correctly calculated the number (which had already reached 140,737,355,328 by only the forty-eighth box) of corn kernels in just forty-five seconds. In the eighteenth and nineteenth centuries, when lightning calculators were a favorite public entertainment, wonderfully challenging problems were posed to the autistic performers: How many times would a coach wheel five feet ten inches in circumference revolve in eight hundred million miles? What is the distance from a star to the earth if its light takes six years and four months to get here? How many cubic inches are there in a block of stone measuring 23,145,789 yards by 5,642,732 wide by 54,965 yards?[18]

A seemingly related but more specialized autistic savant ability (although it occurs in fully a third of all autistic savants who have been studied) is the strange feat of calendar calculation. Unlike music, art, and mathematical calculation, arenas in which nonautistic people can achieve great prowess, calendar calculation is a skill that appears to be restricted to persons with fairly severe mental retardation, due in most or all of them to autism. Given a date removed by time spans ranging from a few years to many centuries, these savants can rapidly give the day of the week for that date. In 1926, H. E. Jones described the case of a twenty-six-year-old man who could give the correct day of the week for any date between A.D. 1,000 and A.D. 2,000 (Jones, 1926). Harriet, the musically talented autistic girl, could provide the correct day of the week for any date between 1925 and 1970. But Harriet also had the ability to remember every single weather report she had ever heard on the radio and was able to recite the report for a particular date when asked. She could also automatically recall any phone number from among the three hundred or so given her by people she had met, and for years after her father read her the first three pages of the Boston area phonebook, Harriet could remember any of the numbers at will. Her talent for memorization, not surprisingly, extended to musical knowledge. In addition to being able to identify an enormous range of symphonic music, Harriet could give information about the composer of any piece of music, along with the date of the first performance, the opus number, and the key in which it was written. For any of the evening concerts of the Boston Symphony Orchestra that she had attended over twenty years, Harriet could name the music performed, the conductor, the details of the performance, and biographical details about each member of the orchestra.

A survey of other autistic savants' abilities turns up a curiously circumscribed catalogue of skills—mastery of exhaustive lists of addresses, zip codes, area codes, and telephone numbers, geographical information, transportation time-tables, license numbers, locomotive engine and freight train car numbers, and sporting events and statistics. Harriet's strange habit of memorizing weather reports is just a particular instance of the wide-ranging feats of verbal memor-ization by autistic savants, who variously have been known to recite from memory entire television and film scripts, news reports, collections of poetry, and stories read by or to them, word for word. One autistic man who knew the population of every town in the United States could recite both the population for any given town and, when a population figure was cited, the name of the town or city with that number of inhabitants. The same man could recite the names of about two thousand American hotels, along with their locations and the number of rooms in them. He knew the distance from New York to every other American city, the distances between the principal city and other towns in the same state, and the name of every county seat in the United States. All these mnemonic feats (among which one can reasonably include the musical, artistic, and calculating skills, heavily dependent on memory) depend on the faculty of eidetic imaging. Despite the reluctance of many researchers to attribute all the memory feats of autistic savants to eideticism, the growing scientific literature on savants would seem to support such an interpretation. It may be possible that *all* autistic persons are eidetic, and that this faculty of "conjuring" (a term that appears surprisingly often, given its suggestion of a magical dimension, even in the scientific literature on savantism) detailed mental images has es-caped notice in many cases. If so, it would mean that eidetic imagery is at least one hundred times more common in autistic persons than in the general population.

Despite their feats of hypermnesis, arithmetical calculation, and musical and artistic prowess, autistic savants are incapable of performing most higher men-tal functions, particularly even the most rudimentary forms of abstract reason-ing. For theorists who would identify synaesthesia and eideticism as part of a past Eden, and potentially as the perceptual style for a new Eden that would replace the fragmentation of modernity, the coincidence of these two sup-posedly transcendental modes of seeing with autism is hard to reconcile with the mythic circle they hope to build. The coincidence of autism, eideticism, and synaesthesia should instead suggest that our conception of the human being is conspicuously incomplete, and that we must imagine more complicated developmental hierarchies, both ontogenetic and phylogenetic, than we have constructed in the course of the century that has elapsed since we first began to apply evolutionary theory to our own consciousness. Eidetic imagery is an elegant indication that there is more to consciousness, and its expected transformations, than meets the eye.

Chapter 5 The Gift: Vladimir Nabokov's Eidetic Technique

Perhaps the most famous synaesthete and eidetic of the modern era was Vladimir Nabokov, who in the course of a literary career spanning half a century left an elaborate record of his case of alphabetic chromaesthesia and eideticism. In Nabokov's own ingenious exploitation of his perceptual idiosyncracies and in the critical and popular response to his work can be seen much of the same enthusiasm for syncretic modes of perception documented in the previous chapter. Nabokov's subjective synaesthetic and eidetic visions have repeatedly been read as intimations of the sacred. Many of his readers believe that his "gift" was a divine one, that his perceptual acuity rendered him capable of seeing that which is hidden from the rest of us. The scholars and visionaries discussed in the previous chapter were aware of the nature of the conditions of consciousness that they advocated. In the case of Vladimir Nabokov, however, most of those who interpreted his writing as evidence that he had an ability to see worlds unseen by others were totally unaware of his eidetic ability, even when they were aware he was a synaesthete. There is a curious symmetry to the enchantment with Nabokov's *ars memoria* and the "otherworldly" appeal of poetic and other uses of synaesthesia. Like Symbolist poetry, Kandinsky's abstract canvases, or Scriabin's phantasmagoria, Nabokov's verbal art employs synaesthesia to challenge materialism and privilege individual perception; but instead of pointing to the spiritual world, his art points only to itself, and to Nabokov's subjective inner world. The misinterpretation of Nabokov as having had access to transcendental knowledge is yet another instance of the tendency to mistake the syncretic perceptions of synaesthesia and eideticism as intimations of the sublime.

NABOKOV AS SYNAESTHETE

In addition to employing his chromaesthesia as a stylistic device in his novels and poems, Nabokov endowed many of his fictional heroes—Cincinnatus in *Invitation to a Beheading,* Fyodor in *The Gift,* Van in *Ada or Ardor: A Family Chronicle,* and Adam Krug in *Bend Sinister*—with some form of synaesthesia. In *Bend Sinister,* Nabokov's first American novel, the philosopher Adam Krug tells an uncomprehending listener that "the word 'loyalty' phonetically and visually reminds me of a golden fork lying in the sun on a smooth spread of yellow silk" (Nabokov, 1974, p. 76). In *Ada,* Van has a synaesthetic feeling for time: "I delight sensually in time, in its stuff and spread, in the fall of its folds, in the very impalpability of its grayish gauze, in the coolness of its continuum" (Nabokov, 1969, p. 537). Recalling a series of lectures he gave on the subject of time, Van uses the language of synaesthesia to describe what are essentially numerical or calendrical forms, mental images common to synaesthetes: "I happen to remember in terms of color (grayish blue, purple, reddish gray) my three farewell university lectures . . . on Mr. Bergson's Time . . . I recall less clearly, and indeed am able to suppress in my mind completely, the six-day intervals . . . between blue and purple and between purple and gray. . . . The two intervals are seen by me as twin dimples, each brimming with a kind of smooth grayish mist, and a faint suggestion of shed confetti (which, maybe, might leap into color if I allowed some casual memory to form in between the diagnostic limits)" (pp. 583–584). Van admits that his feel for time and memory is aided by his synaesthesia: "Synesthesia, to which I am inordinately prone, proves to be of great help in this type of task" (584).

In *The Gift,* the young poet Fyodor Godunov-Cherdyntsev repeatedly displays synaesthetic tendencies, and Nabokov brings these out in the open in a scene during which Fyodor and the poet and critic Koncheyev are discussing Russian literature. When they begin to speak of various Russian authors' "feeling" for certain colors, Koncheyev asks Fyodor, "How did it begin with you?" Fyodor replies, "When my eyes opened to the alphabet. Sorry, that sounds pretentious, but the fact is, since childhood I have been afflicted with the most intense and elaborate *audition colorée.*" Koncheyev begins: "So that you too, like Rimbaud, could have—" and Fyodor finishes his thought:

> Written not a mere sonnet but a fat opus, with auditive hues he never dreamt of. For instance, the various numerous "a's" of the four languages which I speak differ for me in tinge, going from lacquered-black to splintery-gray-like different sorts of wood. I recommend to you my pink flannel 'm.' I don't know if you remember the insulating cotton wool which was removed with the storm windows in spring? Well, that is my Russian "y," or rather 'ugh', so grubby and dull that words are ashamed to begin with it. If I had some paints handy I would mix burnt-sienna and sepia for you so as to match the color of a gutta-percha "ch" sound; and you would appreciate my radiant "s" if I could pour into your cupped hands some of those luminous sapphires that I touched as a child . . . when my mother . . . allowed her perfectly celestial treasures to flow out of their abyss into her palm, out of their cases onto black velvet . . . and if one turned the curtain slightly . . . , one could see, along the receding riverfront, facades in the blue-blackness of the night, the motionless magic of an imperial illumination, the ominous blaze of diamond monograms, colored bulbs in coronal designs . . .
>
> *Buchstaben von Feuer,* in short. [Nabokov, 1963, p. 84]

Cincinnatus, the hero of *Invitation to a Beheading,* is also blessed with the perceptual idiosyncrasies of synaesthesia. This perceptual uniqueness has landed him in jail for the crime of "gnostical turpitude," because in the dystopian state where he resides, all things are already known and named. Synaesthetic perception, which is forever inventing the world anew, militates against conventionalism, and Nabokov, through Cincinnatus, pits his own mental vivacity against the stale transparency of his fellow humans. "I am not an ordinary—I am the one among you who is alive—Not only are my eyes different, and my hearing and my sense of taste—not only is my sense of smell like a deer's, my sense of touch like a bat's—but most important, I have the capacity to conjoin all this in one point" (Nabokov, 1959, p. 52). Though elsewhere Nabokov seemingly belittles his synaesthesia ("The confessions of a synaesthete must sound tedious and pretentious" to nonsynaesthetes), Cincinnatus voices his creator's true assessment of his ability, the belief that the capacity to "conjoin" the senses is a superior trait, one that sets him apart.[1] Nabokov is notorious for the degree to which his novels are autobiographical, so it is no surprise that he should endow his principal characters, many of whom are literary artists like himself, with synaesthesia. He gives a detailed description of his own syn-aesthesia in his cryptic autobiography, *Speak, Memory:*

> I present a fine case of colored hearing. Perhaps "hearing" is not quite accurate, since the color sensation seems to be produced by the very act of my orally forming a given letter while I imagine its outline. The long *a* of the English alphabet (and it is this alphabet I have in mind farther on unless otherwise stated) has for me the tint of weathered wood, but a French *a* evokes polished ebony. This black group also includes hard *g* (vulcanized rubber) and *r* (a sooty rag being ripped). Oatmeal *n,* noodle-limp *l,* and the ivory-backed hand mirror of *o* take care of the whites. I am puzzled by my French *on* which I see as the brimming tension-surface of alcohol in a small glass. Passing on to the blue group, there is steely *x,* thundercloud *z,* and huckleberry *h.* Since a subtle interaction exists between sound and shape, I see *q* as browner than *k,* while *s* is not the light blue of *c,* but a curious mixture of azure and mother-of-pearl. Adjacent tints do not merge, and diphthongs do not have special colors of their own, unless represented by a single character in some other language (thus the fluffy-gray, three-stemmed Russian letter that stands for *sh,* a letter as old as the rushes of the Nile, influences its English representation).
>
> I hasten to complete my list before I am interrupted. In the green group, there are alder-leaf *f,* the unripe apple of *p,* and pistachio *t.* Dull green, combined somehow with violet, is the best I can do for *w.* The yellows comprise various *e*'s and *i*'s, creamy *d,* bright-golden *y* and *u,* whose alphabetical value I can express only by "brassy with an olive sheen." In the brown group, there are the rich rubbery tone of soft *g,* paler *j,* and the drab shoelace of *h.* Finally, among the reds, *b* has the tone called burnt sienna by painters, *m* is a fold of pink flannel, and today I have at last perfectly matched *v* with "Rose Quartz" in Maerz and Paul's Dictionary of Color. The word for rainbow, a primary, but decidedly muddy, rainbow, is in my private language the hardly pronounceable: *kzspygv.* [pp. 34–35]

Nabokov's chromaesthesia had a Russian variant as well. In *Drugie berega,* the Russian version of *Speak, Memory,* Russian letters representing sounds roughly similar to their Latin counterparts are usually duller, though of the same hue. For example, the Latin *p*—"unripe apple"—is brighter than the Cyrillic П, which is experienced by Nabokov as a "gouache" green. In his native tongue, alphabetic sensory crossovers other than the visual mode are even more pronounced than in English, Nabokov saying that his Cyrillic characters' "color sensation is formed by palpable, labial, almost gustatory means. In order to determine thoroughly the hue of a letter, I have to savor the letter, let it swell and radiate in my mouth while I imagine its visual design." His Russian letters include such synaesthetic delights as a "hard rubber" *g* sound, smooth *r,* "bitter chocolate" *zh,* "dry roll" *kh,* "fluffy gray" *sh,* and a "moist sky-blue" *s* (Nabokov, 1978, pp. 27–27, quoted/translated in Johnson, 1985, p. 14). Though he does not discuss it in either version of his autobiography, his poetry and fiction suggest that at least occasionally his synaesthesia approached that of the five-point synaesthete. In 1918, a young Nabokov composed his first long poem, "Svetloi Osenyu" (In radiant autumn), which began with a discussion of color hearing and then described both his photisms (colors elicited by sound) and phonisms—sounds, particularly vocalic, elicited by colors (Boyd, 1990b, p. 144).

Nabokov's commentary on his synaesthesia gives ample evidence that he is a true idiopathic synaesthete. He discovered his synaesthesia at age seven, the age when most children are beginning to lose their primarily physiognomic conceptualization of the world (I use the word "physiognomic" here in Werner's psychological sense, as discussed in Chapter 4). The young Nabokov's discovery came when he disagreed with his mother as to the appropriate colors for a set of alphabet blocks; ironically, such blocks were believed by many nineteenth-century researchers to be the source of the colors for alphabetic chromaesthetes. That Nabokov's synaesthesia is allied with a fuller suite of physiognomic perceptions is evidenced by the adjectives he uses to characterize his alphabet; letters possess not merely hue and luster, but "personality." So do numbers; in the foreword, Nabokov reveals that while the number three is "sharp," four is "as square and resilient as a rubber pillow." Though seemingly the product of Nabokov's poetic word use, the characterizations are very similar to the ones offered by nonliterary synaesthetes. Such descriptive language is common among children. As with most color hearers, Nabokov's alphabetic chromaesthesia does not depend on hearing, but on mentally configuring the letters. The critical diagnostic of idiopathic synaesthesia—that the images be projected—is suggested by Nabokov's statement that he "matched" the letter v with a color plate in a reference work on color classification. "Matched" for an idiopathic synaesthete means visually placing the projected mentally imaged patch of color, formed by thinking (or, as Nabokov points out, shaping his mouth to form) the letter, alongside a physical color.[2]

Compared with most synaesthetes, Nabokov was well read on the scientific study of synaesthesia. In his autobiography he notes Sachs's 1812 dissertation as the earliest work on the subject, and he was aware that within a few months after his reflections on his synaesthesia appeared in the *New Yorker* (in "Portrait of My Mother," an article that would become the basis of chapter 2 of *Speak, Memory*), they were cited in another scientific article, "Language and Synaesthesia," Gladys Reichard and Roman Jakobson's collaboration with synaesthete Elizabeth Werth. In that article, Nabokov found that his descriptions of his colored alphabet were interpreted as "a concession to literature" (Boyd, 1990a, pp. 136–137). Nabokov objected strenuously in a letter to Gladys Reichard that these were empirical phenomenological descriptions, not fanciful metaphors. In interviews, Nabokov was always asked about his visual acuity. On one occasion he included a remark about his "rather freakish gift of seeing letters in color." His answer suggests that he had queried scientific authorities about the phenomenon: "Perhaps one in a thousand has [colored hearing]. . . . But I'm told by psychologists that most children have it, that later they lose that aptitude when they are told by stupid parents that it's all nonsense, an *A* isn't black, a *B* isn't brown—now don't be absurd" (Nabokov, 1973, p. 17). Since synaesthesia is a wholly *subjective* perceptual oddity, Nabokov not surprisingly makes his own synaesthesia the centerpiece of a chapter whose subject is hallucinations, to which, he confesses, he has been subject for as long as he can recall. He surveys his experience of hypnagogic aural and visual imagery and afterimages, and even mentions the muscae volitans, the threadlike dancing shadows upon the retina that so intrigued Rimbaud. "On top of all this" introduces Nabokov's synaesthesia, clearly placing it midway on a spectrum that concludes with a childhood out-of-body experience, whose accompanying episode of clairvoyance is a sort of "true hallucination."[3]

Nabokov does not give the kind of authority to hallucinations that Rimbaud and the Symbolists did. At best, he regards them "with interest, with amusement, seldom with admiration or disgust," and at worst, they are an annoying and unwanted distraction from his conscious mental life. In *Speak, Memory,* when Nabokov says that "by none [of these hallucinations] have I profited much," he seems to be tossing out a double entendre, for though his primary meaning is clear enough, "profited" seems intended also to be heard as "propheted," that is to say, "prophesied," for his next sentence alludes to the "fatidic accents" of Socrates and Joan of Arc. Whereas their subjective visions were of personal and social consequence, Nabokov likens his own visions (and auditory hallucinations) to the gibberish one hears on a busy telephone party line. He is careful to distinguish the unbidden mental images from those he himself has called forth: "What I mean is not the bright mental image . . . conjured up by a wing-stroke of the will; that is one of the bravest movements a human spirit can make" (p. 33). Even the fever-induced clairvoyant episode that concludes the chapter, though potentially more meaningful than the other hallucinations, pales when compared to the shimmering poignancy of Nabokov's normal waking consciousness. Speaking of his mother's casual acceptance of her son's unusual visual sensations and her reluctance to explain them, Nabokov finally sides with her fatalistic faith in the physical: "All one could do was to glimpse, amid the haze and the chimeras, something real ahead, just as persons endowed with an unusual persistence of diurnal cerebration are able to perceive in their deepest sleep, somewhere beyond the throes of an entangled and inept nightmare, the ordered reality of the waking hour" (p. 39). In his waking hours, the nightmare- and hallucination-prone Nabokov controlled the images.

NABOKOV AS EIDETIC

Nabokov's most characteristic subjective visual experience, a type of "hallucination" that endlessly recurs in his writing, is not discussed in this or any other chapter of *Speak, Memory*. Instead, it hides in plain sight, like so much of Nabokov's artistry. Nabokov, the alphabetic chromaesthete and fancier of letters and numbers, possessed one other form of syncretic perception—eidetic imagery. Eidetic imaging is the "method" of his autobiography and of his fiction, a method he discloses at the outset of *Speak, Memory*, but which has gone undetected. Speaking of his revision of earlier versions of the chapters in *Speak, Memory*, he makes no mention of stylistic errors but complains only about their "amnesic defects"—that is, the failure of his memory to provide specific details of his biography. Nabokov admitted that he was repeatedly troubled by the points in his narrative where he had placed randomly chosen, "dummy" objects, preferring to restore if he could the minutiae of the actual event. The "arbitrary spectacles" mentioned in one chapter, for example, "were metamorphosed into a clearly recalled oystershell-shaped cigarette case, gleaming in the wet grass at the foot of the aspen on the Chemin du Pendu, where I found on that June day in 1907 a hawkmoth rarely met with so far west." The acutely visual nature of this act of recollection is obvious; describing how he corrected the "blank spots, blurry areas, domains of dimness" of his autobiography, Nabokov says that he "discovered that sometimes, by means of intense concentration, the neutral smudge might be forced to come into beautiful focus so that the sudden view could be identified and the anonymous servant named." Whether "anonymous servant" of his parents or cigarette case dropped in the grass, Nabokov had the ability to recall the image eidetically so that it literally stood before him as clearly as it had four or five decades previously. When Nabokov states in the foreword that all our memories should be microfilmed, the metaphor is not chosen loosely. When he says that the willed mental image "is one of the bravest movements a human spirit can make," he is covertly praising his eidetic ability (p. 12).

Fittingly, given eideticism's association with the syncretic perceptual style of childhood, the first eidetic image to appear in *Speak, Memory* coincides with Nabokov's account of his first childhood memory. Like noneidetics, Nabokov has no memory previous to the formation of his own self-consciousness, and since individual human self-consciousness is not formed overnight but rather emerges episodically between the ages of two and four, memory, too, is episodic. Nabokov's conception of the development of self-consciousness is completely consistent with that accepted in contemporary psychology: "I see the awakening of consciousness as a series of spaced flashes, with the intervals between them gradually diminishing until bright blocks are formed, affording memory a slippery hold" (p. 21). He describes the earliest "flash," the moment at which he distinguishes himself as a being separate from his parents, as occurring when he realizes that his mother and father are not the same age as he is. He calls this moment his second baptism:

> At this instant, I became acutely aware that the twenty-seven-year-old being, in soft white and pink, holding my left hand, was my mother, and that the thirty-three-year-old being, in hard white and gold, holding my right hand, was my father. Between them, as they evenly progressed, I strutted, and trotted, and strutted again, from sun fleck to sun fleck, along the middle of a path, which I easily identify today with an alley of ornamental oaklings in the park of our country estate, Vyra, in the former Province of St. Petersburg, Russia. Indeed, from my present ridge of remote, isolated, almost uninhabited time, I see my diminutive self as celebrating on that August day 1903, the birth of sentient life. (p. 22)

As Nabokov's memories go, this one is rather unimpressive, lacking the sensual details that move so many of his readers to describe passages of his writing as "hallucinatory." But once his self-consciousness is firmly established, the eidetic images begin to cascade, each one besting the last in evocative power. He playfully begins with his childhood "primordial cave"—a sofa that was used to fashion a make-believe cave:

> A big cretonne-covered divan, white with black trefoils, in one of the big drawing rooms at Vyra rises in my mind, like some massive product of a geological upheaval before the beginning of history. History begins . . . not far from one end of this divan, where a large potted hydrangea shrub, with pale blue blossoms and some greenish ones, half conceals, in a corner of the room, the pedestal of a marble bust of Diana. On the wall against which the divan stands, another phase of history is marked by an engraving in an ebony frame—one of those Napoleonic-battle pictures in which the episodic and the allegoric are the real adversaries and where one sees, all grouped together on the same plane of vision, a wounded drummer, a dead

horse, trophies, one soldier about to bayonet another, and the invulnerable emperor posing with his generals amid the frozen fray. (p. 23)

Nabokov's nostalgic lens is here only slightly focused, for the four-year-old who looked out upon the scene in the drawing room was still just barely emerging from the dark cave of selflessness and timelessness. No sensory details stand out, other than visual ones, and these are common enough that they might have been recalled even by a non-eidetic. But the reader's pronounced sense of a fixed point of view, as if the adult Nabokov were looking at a photograph of the scene, reveals that this is indeed an eidetic image; and his choice to bring into closer focus the engraving of the battle scene, or more exactly, the language he uses to describe it, reinforces the interpretation that Nabokov is beginning to put his eidetic capacity to work. The details of the engraving—the wounded drummer, the dead horse, and so forth—are gathered together by the artist within the same frame, just as Nabokov has gathered together the divan, the hydrangea, the bust of Diana, and the engraving in its ebony frame. Here Nabokov is not so much dazzling us with his picture-making ability as he is simultaneously calling attention to and concealing the origins of that ability.

Slowly, nonvisual details are recalled—the "singing" in the ears "so familiar to small boys in dusty hiding places"—that is, the white noise heard in enclosed spaces; "thudding" hands and knees; the taste of the sheet in his crib. With them come stunning visual images—"a mesh of sunshine on the parquet under the canework of a Viennese chair and two gamesome flies settling by turns," "lateral net of fluffy cotton cords" of his crib—that explicitly reveal that this four-year-old, or at least his fifty-year-old memoirist, is a discoverer of optical patterns (p. 23). Perhaps the recurring reticulations are not recoverable exclusively through the process of eidetic recall, but the pair of gamesome flies seems too minor a detail to appear to anyone but an eidetic. None of these images could be refreshed by revisiting the scenes of his childhood, for the Nabokovs had gone into exile late in 1917, never again to return to Vyra. Nabokov's memory allowed him to overcome this exile, easily collapsing the half-century that stood between him and his emergence from his divan-cave: "How small the cosmos (a kangaroo's pouch would hold it), how paltry and puny in comparison to human consciousness, to a single individual recollection, and its expression in words!" (p. 24).

From the epicenter at Vyra, Nabokov's eidetic images spread out like ripples to encompass his memory's hinterlands.

I see myself, for instance, clambering over wet black rocks at the seaside while Miss Norcott, a languid and melancholy governess, who thinks I am following her, strolls away along the curved beach with Sergey, my youngest brother. I am wearing a toy bracelet. As I crawl over those rocks, I keep repeating, in a kind of zestful, copious, and deeply gratifying incantation, the English word "childhood," which sounds mysterious and new, and becomes stranger and stranger as it gets mixed up in my small, overstocked, hectic mind, with Robin Hood and Little Red Riding Hood, and the brown hoods of old hunch-backed fairies. There are dimples in the rocks, full of tepid seawater, and my magic muttering accompanies certain spells I am weaving over the tiny sapphire pools. [pp. 25–26]

"I see myself," a recurring phrase in Nabokov's autobiography, marks each time the careful consideration of an eidetic image, and here on the Adriatic shore the feeling again surfaces of painterly three-point perspective, the scene spilling away into the distance. Up close, between the boy and the black rocks, a new form of consciousness emerges, distanced slightly from the paratactic, magical, nearly purely body-self of the divan cave dweller. The five-year-old tidepool sorcerer who delights in the world of primary processes—of wordplay and the recitation of spells—is poised on the edge of syntactical thinking and the secondary process. That shoreline of the self is where most children lose their ability to form eidetic images, as they move onto the terra firma of what Piaget terms "operational" thought, around the age of seven.

Other eidetic details follow from the tidepool reverie. The toy bracelet comes into sharper focus and is identified as the fruit of a Christmas tree, "made of semitranslucent, pale-green and pink, celluloidish stuff" (p. 26), which when it begins to dry out and change its appearance, creates a sort of magical dread in the boy. This recollection leads to the eidetic image of a hasty departure that same day from a waterside café, and Nabokov's memory of the ache of a scoop of lemon sherbet in his mouth. The images are still chronologically sequential, seeming to come via the familiar process of association. The next image, however, of a Russian general on the divan at Vyra, showing young Nabokov a trick with matches, is juxtaposed with one of the same general asking his father for a light, fifteen years later. The match, rather than the Russian general, generates the second memory, which is not an eidetic image at all, since it is known to Nabokov not from experience but from his father's narration of the incident. This "evolution of the match theme" pleases Nabokov, and he declares that "the following of such thematic designs through one's life should be . . . the true purpose of autobiography" (p. 27). Recalling and juxtaposing such incidents is facilitated for Nabokov by his eidetic capacity, the "gift" that, when matched with his incomparable gift for language, gives his writing its hallucinatory power.

Just as Nabokov's synaesthesia colors both the sensibility present in his own prose and the perceptual style of some of his protagonists, his eidetic ability forms both the constant backdrop and an intermittent foreground in many of his novels. *The Gift* is punctuated with auditory eidetic images ("mingling their uproar with exaggerated 'whoas,' the droshky drivers called to the early arrivals"; "the roar of the motor with the muffler bypass opened") and tactile eidetic images ("the first sensation immediately upon walking out of the station: the softness of the ground, its kindred proximity to your foot, and around your head the totally unrestrained flow of air"), as well as visual ones. The long sentence that contains these eidetic images ends with the casual remark that there was "only the tiniest aperture left for the song of a skylark," playfully suggesting that even Nabokov's prodigious capacity for recall had its limits. But he immediately stretches those limits: "Perhaps one day . . . I shall again come out of that station and without visible companions walk along the footpath that accompanies the highway the ten or so versts to Leshino. One after another the telephone poles will hum at my approach. A crow will settle on a boulder— settle and straighten a wing that has folded wrong. The day will probably be on the grayish side. Changes in the appearance of the surrounding landscape that I cannot imagine, as well as some of the oldest landmarks that somehow I have forgotten, will greet me alternately, even mingling from time to time. I think that as I walk I shall utter something like a moan, in tune with the poles" (Nabokov, 1963, p. 37). Imagining a future return to a childhood landscape, he can speak with confidence of its ambience, for he has carried a faithful picture of it with him always. He even carries his childhood companions, who though invisible to others, are fully visible to him through his eidetic images of them. Temple Grandin said about her "thinking in pictures" that "the first memory that any single word triggers is almost always a childhood memory" (Grandin, 1995, p. 30). Nabokov's eideticism repeatedly led him back to his childhood with similar ease.

When Fyodor, eidetic poet extraordinaire, assesses his own artistry, he highlights the eidetic quality of his poetry: "What about his poems from the point of view of form? These, of course, are miniatures, but they are executed with a phenomenally delicate mastery that brings out clearly every hair, not because everything is delineated with an excessively selective touch, but because the presence of the smallest features is involuntarily conveyed to the reader by the integrity and reliability of a talent that assures the author's observance of all the articles of the artistic covenant" (Nabokov, 1963, p. 39). Fyodor seems to intuit some relationship between his synaesthesia and eideticism. As he reveals to Koncheyev his gift of color hearing, his description moves seamlessly from his colored letters to his mother's jewels and then, "turn[ing] the curtain slightly" to the jewel-like lights outside in the night. That these are eidetic images is suggested once again by the implied visual perspective; the riverfront where the lights are displayed is described as "receding." But Nabokov provides another clue when he has Koncheyev respond to Fyodor's imagery by uttering, "Buchstaben von Feuer, in short." These images are indeed "letters on the wall," projected, as are the colored photisms of his color hearing. John Shade, another Nabokov double with regard to perceptual ability, delineates his eidetic ability at the outset of his poem "Pale Fire" in the novel of the same name:

> All colors made me happy: even gray.
> My eyes were such that literally they
> Took photographs. Whenever I'd permit,
> Or, with a silent shiver, order it,
> Whatever in my field of vision dwelt—
> An indoor scene, hickory leaves, the svelte
> Stilettos of a frozen stillicide—
> Was printed on my eyelids' nether side
> Where it would tarry for an hour or two,
> And while this lasted all I had to do
> Was close my eyes to reproduce the leaves,
> Or indoor scene, or trophies of the eaves. [Nabokov, 1962, p. 34]

Nabokov here suggests that he could "order" the "photographs" to be taken, and that these eidetic images would last for a few hours. He testifies to the exactness of his image by saying that he can "reproduce" any of its features. (A little later in the poem, when Shade says "I had a brain, five senses (one unique)" (p. 37), he may be referring to his eideticism, his synaesthesia, or both combined.) When elsewhere Shade seems to evoke a common optical illusion—the superimposition of a room's interior reflected in a glass window upon the landscape outside—he may instead be describing the uncommon optical effect of eidetic superimposition.

> And from the inside, too, I'd duplicate
> Myself, my lamp, an apple on a plate.
> Uncurtaining the night, I'd let dark glass
> Hang all the furniture above the grass,
> And how delightful when a fall of snow

Covered my glimpse of lawn and reached up so
As to make chair and bed exactly stand
Upon that snow, out in that crystal land! [p. 33]

This "trick photography," a sort of double exposure, was exactly the method that Nabokov frequently used to create jarring juxtapositions in his fiction. It is not something that occurs by accident, for he states that it is he who uncurtains the night to let the dark glass of his mind project the eidetic image out onto the surrounding scene. This is the "combinational delight" he alludes to near the end of the poem.

Shade goes on to recall vivid images from his youth, all of them probably Nabokov's own eidetic images. The white butterflies that pass through the shade of his favorite shagbark "turn lavender"—a chromatic detail possible for only the most observant artist, or an eidetic projectionist. The "trivia" of his Aunt Maud's room are easily enough recalled by a noneidetic—a glass paperweight, a guitar, a skull—and yet, that Shade recites the entries from a verse book ("Moon, Moonrise, Moor, Moral") and a headline from a newspaper clipping ("Red Sox Beat Yanks 5–4 On Chapman's Homer") suggest once again that Nabokov is using his eidetic ability to create Shade's poem. Later in the poem, Shade recalls his girlfriend during a high school field trip. His recovery of images of her "slender back and . . . neat small head" are common enough, but not what follows: "One palm with fingers spread, / Between a star of trillium and a stone, / Pressed on the turf. A little phalange of bone / Kept twitching . . ." (Nabokov, 1962, p. 42). The poem closes with a series of visual and aural eidetic images:

Where are you? In the garden. I can see
Part of your shadow near the shagbark tree
Somewhere horseshoes are being tossed. Click. Clunk.
(Leaning against its lamppost like a drunk.)
A dark Vanessa with a crimson band
Wheels in the low sun, settles on the sand
And shows its ink-blue wingtips flecked with white.
And through the flowing shade and ebbing light
A man, unheedful of the butterfly—
Some neighbor's gardener, I guess, goes by
Trundling an empty barrow up the lane. [1962, p. 69]

Prosaic, commonplace memory, the sort no doubt possessed by philistines like the barrow-trundling gardener who fails to note the resplendent Vanessa, would never register shadows, yet Nabokov/Shade is supremely attentive to them. "Shadow" or "shade" is an apt term for the eidetic image—a noncorporeal reflection cast by corporeal objects. Additional hints at Shade's eideticism appear in the commentary on the poem by Charles Kinbote (a character in *Pale Fire*); the annotation for the paperweight in Aunt Maud's room offers another of Shade's poems, in which he compares himself to such a glass paperweight: in both of them visual images are "reproduced and glassed" (1962, p. 115).

Even when a Nabokov protagonist is not explicitly endowed with Nabokov's perceptual prowess, he usually perceives eidetically. The entire plot of *Despair* depends on the unreliability of the narrator's perceptions; Hermann mistakes as his physical double a man who does not in any way resemble him. Still, this gross error of visual perception does not alter the reader's recognition that Hermann's perceptual ability is nearly as acute as that of Nabokov's other protagonists. The vagabond Felix, whom Hermann meets and later murders, is undoubtedly drawn from Nabokov's own stock of eidetic images: "He was a man of my age, lank, dirty, with a three days['] stubble on his chin, there was a narrow glimpse of pink flesh between the lower edge of his collar (soft, with two round slits meant for an absent pin) and the upper end of his shirt. His thin-knitted tie dangled sideways, and there was not a button to his shirt front. A few pale violets were fading in his buttonhole; one of them had got loose and hung head downward" (Nabokov, 1966a, p. 19).

The eidetic nature of the image does not call attention to itself, since it is narratively framed as Hermann's portrait of Felix at the time of their first meeting; still, it is drawn from memory, and hence its detail must say something about Hermann's visual recall. The sartorial details he gives mark him as another consummate observer and visualizer. Hermann's mock ironic and prophetic comment that he has "come to know the partiality and fallaciousness of human eyesight" (he has mistaken Felix for his double), cannot be assumed to apply to the narrator Hermann. Immediately after his remark about his eyesight, Hermann paints an eidetic picture: "Anyhow, here is the picture: two men kneeling on a patch of sickly grass; one, a smartly dressed fellow, slashing his knee with a yellow glove; the other, a vague-eyed vagabond, lying full length and voicing his grievances against life. Crisp rustle of neighboring thornbush. Flying clouds. A windy day in May with little shivers like those that run along the coat of a horse. Rattle of a motor lorry from the high road. A lark's small voice in the sky" (p. 19).

Nabokov's abortive writing projects also relied on the eidetic device. While working on *Camera Obscura,* Nabokov outlined another novel in which he would grapple with the issue of whether and in what manner consciousness might survive personal death. The protagonist was to prepare for an examination on his knowledge of his city's geography; because spatial-geographic memory is highly acute in most eidetics, this would have afforded Nabokov an opportunity to display his encyclopedic knowledge of a past landscape. But when the hero arrived at the exam, he would find that he had actually died, and he was to be examined about his life by people he had once known—again, a perfect vehicle for the replay of old eidetic images.

Despite the overwhelming evidence of Nabokov's eideticism, none of his biographers or critics comment on it. D. Barton Johnson, who has written perceptively on the role of Nabokov's alphabetic chromaesthesia, explores the relationship between synaesthesia and memory and in a footnote cites A. R. Luria's *Mind of a Mnemonist* and G. S. Blum's *A Model of the Mind,* both of which described cases of eidetic synaesthetes, without clearly identifying Nabokov as one. Johnson accepts Luria's explanation of the role played by synaesthesia in hypermnesis: that the redundant information provided by the overlap of the senses makes it possible to remember more accurately. He cites a passage from *Speak, Memory* as echoing Luria's explanation: "I witness with pleasure the supreme achievement of memory, which is the masterly use it makes of innate harmonies when gathering to its fold the suspended and wandering tonalities of the past" (Johnson, 1985, p. 26). And yet this passage, which Johnson says shows Nabokov's "almost magical power of conjuring up the minutiae of the past" (p. 26), is clearly an eidetic image, not a vague visual image whose accuracy is ensured by synaesthesia. Nabokov describes a birthday gathering on a summer afternoon with what can only be described as "photographic" detail:

> I like to imagine, in consummation and resolution of those jangling chords, something as enduring, in retrospect, as the long table that on summer birthdays and namedays used to be laid for afternoon chocolate out of doors, in an alley of birches, limes and maples at its debouchement on the smooth-sanded space of the garden proper that separated the park and the house. I see the tablecloth and the faces of seated people sharing in the animation of light and shade beneath a moving, a fabulous foliage, exaggerated, no doubt, by the same faculty of impassioned commemoration, of ceaseless return, that makes me always approach that banquet table from the outside, from the depth of the park—not from the house—as if the mind, in order to go back thither, had to do so with the silent steps of a prodigal faint with excitement. Through a tremulous prism, I distinguish the features of relatives and familiars, mute lips serenely moving in forgotten speech. I see the stream of chocolate

and the plates of blueberry tarts. I note the small helicopter of a revolving samara that gently descends upon the tablecloth, and, lying across the table, an adolescent girl's bare arm indolently extended as far as it will go, with its turquoise-veined underside turned up to the flaky sunlight, the palm open in lazy expectancy of something— perhaps the nutcracker. [1966b, pp. 170–171]

When Nabokov says "I see," "I note," "I distinguish," and when he notes the direction from which he approaches the scene, he does so because he literally sees (and to a lesser degree hears, feels, tastes, and smells) this past event as if it were once more present before him in all its indolent and sumptuous glory. Another clue to the method of Nabokov's ars memoria is that he uses "reconstruct" and "reproduce" as synonyms for "remember." The multisensory quality of eidetic recall, that is, the tendency of the visual image to be accompanied by other sensory memories, is due to eidetic images' carrying with them the related somatic state as well as the "meaning" attached to the image.[4]

Recalling in *Speak, Memory* his first English primer, Nabokov describes how its four protagonists "now drift with a slow-motion slouch across the remotest backdrop of memory; and akin to the mad alphabet of an optician's chart, the grammar-book lettering looms again before me." While D. Barton Johnson points this out as indicative of Nabokov's sensitivity to the physical shape of letters, it actually attests to Nabokov's being a "typographic" eidetic, the form of childhood eidetic ability most intensively studied by psychologists. In *Nabokov's Art of Memory and European Modernism* (1993), John Burt Foster, Jr., exploring the role of memory and visual images in Nabokov's work, stresses Nabokov's preoccupation with reflexivity and time as concurrent with certain modernist literary trends. Like Johnson, Foster identifies synaesthesia as the basis for Nabokov's mnemonic virtuosity: "Colored hearing in the child [of *Speak, Memory*], with its relatively simple and spontaneous verbal-visual correspondences, leads ultimately to the mnemonic image as the crowning achievement of the mature writer who intentionally strives for hallucinatory recall" (Foster, 1988, p. 23). Throughout Foster's book, the passages in Nabokov's writing examined as "mnemonic images" can be interpreted instead as eidetic images. He deconstructs, for example, the following passage from *Speak, Memory*:

I see with utmost clarity the sun-spangled river; the bridge, the dazzling tin of a can left by a fisherman on its wooden railing; the linden-treed hill with its rosy-red church and marble mausoleum where my mother's dead reposed; the dusty road to the village; the strip of short, pastel-green grass, with bald patches of sandy soil, between the road and the lilac bushes behind which walleyed, mossy log cabins stood in a rickety row; the stone building of the new schoolhouse near the wooden old one; and, as we swiftly drove by, the little black dog with very white teeth that dashed out from among the cottages at a terrific pace but in absolute silence, saving his voice for a brief outburst he would enjoy when his muted sprint would at last bring him close to the speeding carriage. [quoted in Foster, 1993, p. 195]

Foster points out the steady accumulation of detail in the multiclausal sentence as representative of Nabokov's control of linguistic focus and pacing, but it is also a direct reflection of the quality of the eidetic image. In recalling this scene, Nabokov sees before him all its elements in the same perspectival arrangement as when he physically experienced it.

A number of critics have correctly identified Nabokov's conjuring up of the past as distinct from Proustian "involuntary memory." Robert Alter (1991, p. 620), for example, says that Nabokov's ability to revisit the past is chiefly a consequence of the "imaginative concentration afforded by artful prose. It is only a little overstated to say that for Nabokov the apt manipulation of language makes the past come back." But this mistakes the result for the cause; the past comes back to Nabokov via his eidetic perception and then is captured thanks to his gift for language. A magnificent gift was still being exercised, but Nabokov may have feared that it would be diminished in the eyes of others if they should ever fully understand its origin in his eideticism. Nabokov repeatedly dismissed any comparisons between his form of memory and that of Proust, saying in one interview that "I see no resemblance whatever. Proust imagined a person . . . who had a Bergsonian concept of past time. . . . I am not an imaginary person and my memories are direct rays deliberately trained, not sparks and spangles" (Nabokov quoted in Green, 1988, p. 23). "Direct rays deliberately trained" is an apt metaphor for a naturalist, which is what Nabokov always claimed to be, to use for the projected visual imagery which was captured afterward with language.[5]

Is there evidence of Nabokov's eideticism outside his literary work? Nabokov's biographer Brian Boyd notes that more than thirty years after viewing American comic films while living in Berlin, Nabokov could "reel off scene after scene in sharp-focus detail" (Boyd, 1990b, p. 363). A friend of Nabokov's, Eugenia Zalkind, has left this telling anecdote about Nabokov from their years as fellow members of the émigré Poets Club in Berlin in the 1920s: "Sometimes he liked to think up games. 'Look for two minutes at this picture, then close your eyes and describe all you've retained.' Of course he was the only one who could recreate the whole picture from memory, not forgetting the least detail. His memory, especially his visual memory, was exceptional. He even complained at times that it overburdened his consciousness" (quoted in Boyd, 1990b, p. 278). In *Speak, Memory*, Nabokov makes a different kind of game of his eidetic ability. Chapter Eight begins, "I am going to show a few slides" (p. 154), and Nabokov does just that, choosing as his subject the series of tutors he and his brother had while growing up. From the unnamed spelling master to Ordo, the black-cloaked cleric's son, to a Ukrainian mathematician, a Polish medical student, and the "large, formidable Lett, who walked on his hands" (and thus came back to Nabokov's mind as an upside-down slide), "the images of those tutors appear within memory's luminous disc as so many magic-lantern projections" (p. 157). But the tutor who demands the most attention is one "Lenski," a pun name that Nabokov provides for his old tutor, Filip Zelenski. Nabokov describes how one winter Lenski staged "magic-lantern projections" every other week at the Nabokov home in St. Petersburg. While Nabokov runs his own projector, dazzling the reader with minute descriptions of everything and everyone in the room, Lenski's paltry show consists of but four slides, which are supposed to illustrate a Lermontov poem of some seven hundred and fifty lines.

In case his visual wizardry has not been enough of a demonstration for us, Nabokov finishes off the magic lantern chapter with what may be his most virtuoso display of eidetic imagery—the passage quoted earlier, cited by D. Barton Johnson as an example of Nabokov's synaesthesia. Without so much as a paragraph break, Nabokov moves from the girl's open palm to the place at the table reserved for the tutor, and finds there "a changeful image, a succession of fade-ins and fade-outs . . . [turning] Ordo into Max and Max into Lenski and Lenski into the schoolmaster" (p. 171). This tendency of an image to meta-morphose into a series of related images is characteristic of the most "gifted" eidetics. Temple Grandin uses the example of dogs rather than butterflies or tutors to illustrate her magic lantern mental process.

It's as if I have a card catalog of dogs I have seen, complete with pictures, which continually grows as I add more samples to my video library. If I think about Great Danes, the first memory that pops into my head is Dansk, owned by the headmaster at my high school. The next Great Dane I visualize is Helga, who was Dansk's replacement. The next is my aunt's dog in Arizona, and my final image comes from an advertisement for Fitwell seat covers that featured that kind of dog. My memories usually appear in my imagination in strict chronological order, and the images I visualize are always specific. There is no generic, generalized Great Dane. [Grandin, 1995, p. 25]

She also demonstrates her ability to train her mental lens on related phenomena in the same fashion that Nabokov does:

If I let my mind wander, the video jumps in a kind of free association from fence construction to a particular welding shop where I've seen posts cut and Old John, the welder, making gates. If I continue thinking about Old John welding a gate, the video image changes to a series of short scenes of building gates on several projects I've worked on. Each video memory triggers another in this associative fashion, and my daydreams may wander far from the design problem. The next image may be of having a good time listening to John and the construction crew tell war stories, such as the time the backhoe dug into a nest of rattlesnakes and the machine was abandoned for two weeks because everybody was afraid to go near it. [Grandin, 1995, p. 28]

Input from the other senses, the invariable accompaniment to Nabokov's eidetic imagery, pours in on his consciousness as he concludes the chapter: "And then, suddenly, just when the colors and outlines settle at last to their various duties—some knob is touched and a torrent of sounds comes to life: voices speaking all together, a walnut cracked, the click of a nutcracker carelessly passed, thirty human hearts drowning mine with their regular beats; the sough and sigh of a thousand trees, the local concord of loud summer birds, and, beyond the river, behind the rhythmic trees, the confused and enthusiastic hullabaloo of bathing young villagers, like a background of wild applause" (1966b, p. 172). While Lenski marveled at the technology of the magic lantern, Nabokov effortlessly produces the motion picture, complete with sound track. For this feat, perhaps, the young villagers projected by Nabokov's consciousness applaud. In *Ada,* Nabokov provides his own applause on the last page of the novel, when the omniscient authorial voice gives its satisfied assessment of his eidetic artistry: "Not the least adornment of the chronicle is the delicacy of pictorial detail: a latticed gallery; a painted ceiling; a pretty plaything stranded among the forget-me-nots of a brook; butterflies and butterfly orchids in the margin of a romance; a misty view described from marble steps; a doe at graze in the ancestral park; and more, much more" (1969, p. 589).

The game of chess, which figures in almost all of Nabokov's novels, was an arena where both Nabokov and his protagonists put their magic lanterns into glorious play. Just as Lenski was at a distinct disadvantage with his crude projection device, Nabokov's opponents cannot match his and his fictional alter egos' visual lucidity in strategizing about chess moves. Humbert Humbert in *Lolita* sees the chess board as "a square pool of limped water with rare shells and stratagems rosily visible upon the smooth tesselated bottom," while his "confused adversary" sees only "ooze and squid-cloud" (Nabokov, 1958, p. 235). Actually, Nabokov himself was only a fair chess player, though he was widely admired in the chess-playing community as a highly original and whimsical composer of chess problems. "Chess problems," Nabokov declared, "demand from the composer the same virtues that characterize all worthwhile art: originality, invention, conciseness, harmony, complexity, and splendid insincerity" (1971, pp. 14–15). In composing chess problems as in writing fiction, Nabokov played with his eideticism by conjuring up a static image, putting it into motion, and then effecting a series of substitutions to dazzle the onlooker.

In Nabokov's fiction, chess-playing prowess is inseparable from eidetic prowess. In *The Defense,* before he becomes a chess prodigy, the young boy Luzhin first displays his eidetic abilities in the equally abstract realm of mathematics. Luzhin, who finds a "mysterious sweetness in the realization that a long number, arrived at with difficulty, would at the decisive moment, after many adventures, be divided by nineteen without any remainder," reflects Nabokov's own childhood predilection for math (Nabokov, 1970a, p. 17). "As a little boy," Nabokov reminisced in *Speak, Memory,* "I showed an abnormal aptitude for mathematics. . . . I felt enormous spheres and huge numbers swell relentlessly in my aching brain. A foolish tutor had explained logarithms to me much too early, and I had read . . . about a certain Hindu calculator who in exactly two seconds could find the seventeenth root of, say, 3529471145760275132301897342055866171392 (I am not sure I have got this right; anyway, the root was 212)" (1966b, pp. 36–37). The striking ability to animate eidetic images is part of the key to Luzhin's chess technique; he can lay out a chessboard in his mind and then set it in motion in order to visualize the outcomes of various stratagems. Luzhin's synaesthesia, less obvious than his eideticism, appears occasionally, as in an episode of hypnagogic reverie where "limpid sounds" were "strangely transformed . . . and assumed the shape of bright intricate patterns on a dark background" (Nabokov, 1970b, p. 60). Young Luzhin, who also memorizes taxicab numbers and delights in working jigsaw puzzles, replaces these obsessions with another—chess. The boy is blind to the world around him, but in the "celestial dimension" where his chess moves are calculated, he sees all. He prefers the mentally projected chessboard and pieces over the real ones to the point that he prefers playing blindfolded; then "he did not have to deal with the visible, audible, palpable pieces whose

. . . materiality always . . . seemed to him but the crude mortal shell of exquisite, invisible chess forces" (p. 91). Here is Nabokov's covert profession of his own attitude toward the physical world, which pales in the face of his "exquisite" (perhaps Nabokov's favorite word) cerebrations.[6]

One hears in Nabokov's work the familiar echoes of autistic savants' abilities. Luzhin's list of taxicab numbers is a classic example of the fetishistic knowledge possessed by the autistic, as is the delight in jigsaw puzzles (the pieces can be rapidly arranged mentally), and Nabokov's own calculating prowess resembled that of autistic lightning calculators. Indeed, Nabokov and Luzhin seem, although obviously far from autistic, to share some of the predisposition to self-absorption that characterizes autism.

POTUSTORONNOST: THE "OTHERWORLD"

Fyodor, the hero of *The Gift,* bears a greater resemblance than Luzhin to Nabokov in that he is a middling player of chess but a gifted chess problematist. Fyodor, whose name means "gift of God," declares that instead of wasting his time giving language lessons, he should be teaching the "mysterious and refined thing" that out of "a million men," he alone knows. This mysterious thing must be more than his ability to write poems or play chess. "Where shall I put all these gifts with which the summer morning rewards me—and only me?" Fyodor asks. "Save them up for future books? . . . one wants to offer thanks but there is no one to thank. The list of donations already made: 10,000 days— from Person Unknown" (Nabokov, 1963, 340). Ten thousand days is the length of Fyodor's life, as well as Nabokov's at the time he wrote the novel, and each and every one of these days has been "saved," stored as eidetic images inside his consciousness. Eidetic imagery, though generally evoked through a fully conscious act of willed cognition, is still a gift, an endowment that comes "out of the blue"; it is not won or developed by its possessor. Eidetics frequently have the impression that their images come from somewhere, or someone, else— hence Fyodor's ascription of them to "Person Unknown." Fyodor's sense of being a shadow of a better, more gifted writer, derives from the feeling of otherness attendant on the recovery of the eidetic image.[7]

Fyodor is not the only Nabokov character to wrestle with the "mysterious and refined thing" that seems indigenous to his own consciousness but alien to others'. Throughout the mirror worlds of Nabokov's fiction this theme is insistently echoed. After Cincinnatus writes in his diary of his ability to "conjoin" the senses, he ends his boast in a dare: "No, the secret is not revealed yet—

even this is but the flint—and I have not even begun to speak of the kindling, of the fire itself" (Nabokov, 1959, p. 52). Elsewhere in the novel he declares that "in spite of everything, I am chained to this table like a cup to a drinking fountain, and will not rise till I have said what I want. I repeat (gathering new momentum in the rhythm of repetitive incantations), I repeat: There is something I know, there is something." (p. 95). The intimation of a secret calls out from Nabokov's poetry too, for example the long poem *Slava* (Fame):

I'm happy that Conscience, the pimp
of my sleepy reflections and projects,
did not get at the critical secret. Today
I am really remarkably happy.

That main secret tra-tá-ta tra-tá-ta tra-tá—
and I must not be overexplicit;
this is why I find laughable the empty dream
about readers, and body, and glory.

Without body I've spread, without echo I thrive,
and with me all along is my secret.
A book's death can't affect me since even the break
between me and my land is a trifle.

I admit that the night has been ciphered right well
but in place of the stars I put letters,
and I've read in myself how the self to transcend—
and I must not be overexplicit.
. . .

But one day while disrupting the strata of sense
and descending deep down to my wellspring
I saw mirrored besides my own self and the world,
something else, something else, something else. [Nabokov, 1970b, p. 111]

This passage from Nabokov's poem was used by Vladimir Alexandrov as the opening epigraph to his study of Nabokov's preoccupation with the "other-world." Impressed by Nabokov's ability to escape time in his sensual relivings of the past, Alexandrov interprets them, using Nabokov's own phrase, as instances of "cosmic synchronization." Alexandrov cites, as a particularly beautiful illustration, this passage from *Speak, Memory* where Nabokov recalls meeting the village schoolmaster:

While politely discussing with him my father's sudden journey to town, I registered simultaneously and with equal clarity not only his wilting flowers, his flowing tie and the blackheads on the fleshy volutes of his nostrils, but also the dull little voice of the cuckoo coming from afar, and the flash of a Queen of Spain settling on the road, and the remembered impression of the pictures (enlarged agricultural pests and bearded Russian writers) in the well-aerated classrooms of the village school which I had once or twice visited; and—to continue a tabulation that hardly does justice to the ethereal simplicity of the whole process—the throb of some utterly irrelevant recollection (a pedometer I had lost) was released from a neighboring brain cell, and the savor of the grass stalk I was chewing mingled with the cuckoo's note and the fritillary's takeoff, and all the while I was richly, serenely aware of my own manifold awareness. [pp. 218–219]

The eidetic nature of the original image is striking; the visual details of the schoolmaster's appearance (the registering of the blackheads adds a virtuoso touch), observed simultaneously with the alighting of the butterfly, combine with the aural element of the cuckoo's call. The image of the schoolmaster himself calls forth another set of eidetic images, of the didactic displays hanging in the schoolroom, which Nabokov has photographically recollected, despite his having been only an occasional visitor to the school. With seeming serendipity, other eidetic images—both visual (the pedometer) and gustatory (the taste of the grass stalk)—tumble out as the scene before him is eidetically remembered. Alexandrov, however, rather than examining this passage as a perfect microcosm of Nabokov's mental process in garnering imagery for his fiction, sees it as an example of "multidimensional metaphoric thinking or cognition," in which time and space are transcended by Nabokov.

The sense of "worlds in regression" that Nabokov gives personal voice to in his autobiography is the basis for the appealing alterity that Nabokov repeatedly creates in his novels. It is also frequently commented upon by Nabokov's characters, but perhaps nowhere as extensively as in *Ada*. The novel, whose title was originally intended to be *The Texture of Time,* contains Nabokov's most explicit statements about the relation between consciousness and the cosmos, in which memory is the go-between. The section of the novel in which the nature of time is most closely examined is interwoven with observations of and questions about eidetic imagery, as well as a string of spectacular eidetic images. The psychologist (a professional title he earns by virtue of studying his own mind, as did Nabokov) Van Veen rejects the view that the past is "changeless, intangible, and 'never-to-be-revisited'" and immediately offers proof to the contrary by reproducing an eidetic image from the "section of Space which I see": "a white villa and its whiter (newer) garage with seven cypresses of unequal height, tall Sunday and short Monday, watching over the private road that loops past scrub oak and briar down to the public one connecting Sorcière with the highway to Mont Roux." Van dismisses the metaphor of dissolution that is usually applied to time and prefers the metaphor of agglomeration, "an accumulation of sensa." It is space that dissolves, and he neatly reinforces this feeling by framing the entire discussion of the "texture of time" within his account of the images seen from a moving automobile. Again, his "proof" that the past is a "constant accumulation of images" is exactly that—a litany of Nabokov's own eidetic images, distributed like the diamonds that head the list over a parquet of invented dates:

> diamonds scattered all over the parquet in 1888; a russet black-hatted beauty at a Parisian bar in 1901; a humid red rose among artificial ones in 1883; the pensive half-smile of a young English governess, in 1880, neatly reclosing her charge's prepuce after the bedtime treat; a little girl, in 1884, licking the breakfast honey off the badly bitten nails of her spread fingers; the same, at thirty-three, confessing, rather late in the day, that she did not like flowers in vases; the awful pain striking him in the side while two children with a basket of mushrooms looked on in the merrily burning pine forest; and the startled quonk of a Belgian car, which he had overtaken and passed yesterday on a blind bend of the alpine highway. [Nabokov, 1969, pp. 545–546]

Van then poses a series of questions that Nabokov must surely have answered over the years of testing his own eidetic capacity, such as whether the color or other visual aspect of objects changes from image to image or whether there was any way of discerning from the image itself the date of its occurrence. Confirmation that Van Veen is examining eidetic images during his research "in the laboratories of psychology" (that is, in the observation of his own mental imagery) comes from his declaration that "it is impossible . . . to avoid the intrusion not only of different characteristics but of different emotional circumstances" when considering two different "objects" (1969, p. 546). What makes the eidetic image so powerful is that the original *affect* is also restored to the viewer, who re-experiences the emotional quality that infused the earlier perception of the scene, person, or object.

As Van ruminates on his "experiments," he performs one of them before our very eyes:

> Therefore we can assume that the experiment can be performed—and how tantalizing, then, the discovery of certain exact levels of decreasing saturation or deepening brilliance—so exact that the "something" which I vaguely perceive in the image of a remembered but unidentifiable person, and which assigns it "somehow" to my early

boyhood rather than to my adolescence, can be labeled if not with a name, at least with a definite date, e.g., January 1, 1908 (eureka, the "e.g." worked—*he* was my father's former house tutor, who brought me *Alice in the Camera Obscura* for my eighth birthday). [1969, p. 547]

Here the very act of writing about the process of remembering produces the "eureka" reaction, by bringing with it the exact date of a particular memory. Van's use of a date different from that of Nabokov's actual eighth birthday hardly obscures the nature of the recollection: this is not an invented description but a specific eidetic image from Nabokov's boyhood. (Whether by accident or design, Nabokov clearly lets slip that this is *his* memory, not "Van's": calendrical arithmetic places the boy's date of birth in 1899, the year of Nabokov's birth, not 1870, the birth date assigned by Nabokov to Van Veen.) The vaguely perceived image of an unidentified person is focused into an entirely identifiable character through the very act of writing "e.g." and the date. It is as if when the magician claps his hands, a person in all his corporeality—a childhood tutor—suddenly appears before him. As he shows in *Speak, Memory,* his tutors occupy a memorable place in his slide show carousel from that period of his life. Nabokov slyly points to the eidetic nature of his experiment by altering the gift book's title from *Alice in Wonderland* to *Alice in the Camera Obscura.* The camera obscura is perhaps Nabokov's favorite metaphor for his own mind, for both are apparatuses that form an exact image of objects.

Continuing his soliloquy on time, Van systematically identifies the diagnostic characteristics of the eidetic image. He notes that the eidetic image is accompanied by aural imagery: "Memory-images include afterimages of sound, regurgitated, as it were, by the ear which recorded them a moment ago while the mind was engaged in avoiding hitting schoolchildren, so that actually we can replay the message of the church clock after we have left Turtsen and its hushed but still-echoing steeple behind" (p. 547). Since Van/Nabokov was driving a car while he first recorded this image inside his camera obscura consciousness, the experience returns with the original quality of sound; the church clock's chime still bears the Doppler effect caused by his speedy passage in the automobile. Uncannily, while his attention was focused on the road, where he had to be mindful of children walking, his subconscious recorded the striking of the steeple clock. The remembered clock provides a convenient entry point for the familiar metaphor of "beats" of time, which Van notes can either be dim or dark—that is, noneidetic or eidetic mental images. His synaesthesia is also in evidence at this juncture, for in the example he gives, the lectures in the series evoke particular colors, whereas no such imagery is associated with intervals of time between lectures. This pulse of significance-insignificance is the very thing that most of the experimental psychological research on eidetic imagery has tended to overlook. Subjects are typically asked to form eidetic images based on unfamiliar drawings or photographs, and in those circumstances, even people with some degree of eideticism often fail to reproduce the pictures eidetically. The most vivid eidetic images are of memories that are personally meaningful to the observer. Thus, in Van's eidetic recall, the circumstances surrounding the lectures he gave are brightly painted punctuation marks in a neutral stretch of time. Time that was initially experienced as without affect is unrecoverable eidetically.

> But I visualize with perfect clarity the circumstances attending the actual lectures. I was a little late for the first (dealing with the Past) and observed with a not-unpleasant thrill, as if arriving at my own funeral, the brilliantly lighted shadows of Counterstone Hall and the small figure of a Japanese student who, being also late, overtook me at a wild scurry, and disappeared in the doorway long before I reached its semicircular steps. At the second lecture—the one on the Present—during the five seconds of silence and "inward attention" which I requested from the audience in order to provide an illustration for the point I, or rather the speaking jewel in my waistcoat pocket, was about to make regarding the true perception of time, the behemoth snores of a white-bearded sleeper filled the house—which, of course, collapsed. [1969, p. 583]

These "ludicrous but salient details"—eidetic images—no doubt chosen by Nabokov from his years of lecturing at Cornell, mark the synaesthetically recalled (grayish blue, purple, and reddish gray) lecture days, while the intervening stretches of time are synaesthetically and physiognomically perceived as "twin dimples, each brimming with a kind of smooth, grayish mist, and a faint suggestion of shed confetti" (p. 584). Just as the resolution and clarity of eidetic images depends on the degree of felt meaning that accompanies them, the associated synaesthetic photisms are either brightly colored or gray, depending on the significance of the mental image at their source.

Van also comments on the possibility of adding his own pictorial elements to the recollected image: "Here they are, the two rocky-crowned hills that I have retained for seventeen years in my mind with decalcomaniac romantic vividness—though not quite exactly, I confess; memory likes the *otsebyatina* ("what one contributes oneself"); but the slight discrepancy is now corrected and the act of artistic correction enhances the pang of the Present. The sharpest feeling of nowness, in visual terms, is the deliberate possession of a segment of Space collected by the eye" (p. 551). "Decalcomania," the art of transferring designs from one surface to another, exactly denotes (though his scientific exactness forces him to qualify the metaphor slightly) what Nabokov does with his eidetic images, lifting them from their origin in the past and applying them like decals onto the surface of the present. This decalcomaniacal consciousness, which gives Nabokov the ability to live, at any present moment, the fullness of the past, to the point that the experiences of nearly every day of his life are retrievable in an instant, effectively obliterates Time, ends its tyranny, and gives the individual consciousness seemingly unlimited scope. The result for the reader of Nabokov is a powerful sense that Nabokov's characters have achieved a sort of immortality by escaping time. That sense wholly depends on the convincing vividness with which Nabokov and his characters seem to see and feel events and objects from the past that nonsynaesthetes are unable to see.

Vladimir Alexandrov regards this sort of visual clarity as an epiphany akin to those of Wordsworth or Joyce. It is by way of just such moments of privileged perception that Alexandrov believes Nabokov both experiences and communicates to the reader *potustoronnost,* the "otherworld" beyond the physical realm. Indeed, Alexandrov dismisses the widespread critical view of Nabokov as a metaliterary writer, instead seeing his writing as "rooted in his intuition of a transcendent realm" (Alexandrov, 1991, p.3). He argues that "the characteristic features of Nabokov's epiphanies are a sudden fusion of varied sensory data and memories, a feeling of timelessness, and intuitions of immortality" (p. 7). Alexandrov quotes a passage in which Nabokov expresses an aversion to Plato ("I am afraid to get mixed up with Plato, whom I do not care for, but I do think that in my case it is true that the entire book, before it is written, seems to be ready ideally in some other, now transparent, now dimming, dimension" (p. 29), Alexandrov interprets Nabokov's metaphysics as Platonic. Alexandrov is so convinced of Nabokov's transcendentalism that in the conclusion to his study he sets him squarely within the tradition of Russian Silver Age mysticism and of Andrei Bely, Nikolai Gumilev, and Peter Ouspensky.[8]

Many other Nabokov critics have had a similar reaction to his oeuvre. John Burt Foster repeatedly points out the backward-looking "Nabokovian ecstasy" that is the basis of his ability to outwit time. Jonathan Sisson compared Nabokov's "cosmic synchronization" to Ezra Pound's and T. S. Eliot's poetic evocations of "holistic experiences" and even compared the Nabokovian ecstasy with the sorts of experiences of "universal noetic awareness" that William James gathered together in *The Varieties of Religious Experience* (Sisson, 1979, pp. 3–5). W. W. Rowe (1985) inventoried the "ghosts" in Nabokov's fiction in order to emphasize Nabokov's "spectral dimension, . . . [his] persistent attempt to push beyond the boundaries of human consciousness." Brian Boyd, though characterizing himself as a rationalist "disinclined to believe in any unseen spiritual realms," finds his rationalism and materialism challenged by Nabokov's spectral speculations (Boyd, 1990b, p. 304). In both of his recent biographies of Nabokov, Boyd highlights Nabokov's "metaphysical" orientation, through his choice of epigraphs. The volume on Nabokov's Russian years is prefaced with Nabokov's answer to an interviewer's question about what surprises him in life: "The marvel of consciousness—that sudden window swinging open on a sunlit landscape amidst the night of non-being." The epigraphs for the other volume, which treats Nabokov's American years, allude more pointedly to Nabokov's intuition of an afterlife: the statement "Life is a great surprise. I do not see why death should not be an even greater one" is paired with Nabokov's comment in *Speak, Memory* about being overwhelmed by "the sense of something much vaster." Boyd casts Nabokov as a "maximalist" in an era of minimalist artistry, one who "explored human nature at the upper reaches of consciousness." He explains the imperial outlook of Nabokov's main characters by claiming that "Nabokov wants to test thought at its highest and most diverse." Nabokov's artist-protagonists act the way they do because they are "at the last ramparts of consciousness, ready to jump the moat to total freedom if anyone can" (Boyd, 1990b, p. 308). D. Barton Johnson likened Nabokov's metaphysics to that of Neoplatonism, assuming that because both acknowledged an invisible world hidden beyond the visible one, they might be referring to the same world. Johnson calls Nabokov's otherworldly speculations those of a "gnostic seeker" and points out that the potustoronnost theme first identified by Nabokov's widow in 1979 is evident as early as 1919, in one of his early poems. Johnson suggests that Nabokov's view of art as a route to transcendence was nurtured by Russian Symbolism, the artistic and cultural milieu in which he matured. Despite native Russian readers' objection to the absence of spirituality in Nabokov's work, Johnson attempts to offer Nabokov's "otherworld" theme as a substitute for more conventional Russian ideas about a transcendental world (Johnson, 1981, p. 379).

For many of Nabokov's readers, a great deal of the appeal of his writing, apart from the beauty and force of his use of language, has consisted in this intimation of unseen worlds. Cherished by both Nabokov and his characters as a secret gift to them alone, this intimation of another world is a direct result of their eidetic perception. Epiphany is indeed the effect that Nabokov's stunning prose has on the reader, and yet it can be attributed, not as the typical reader does, to a brush with transcendence, but to the vertigo induced by visual eideticism. In the face of descriptive images that capture the past so faithfully, the reader is left reeling, unsure of his or her location in the imaginary narrative world. The various fictional characters who have these experiences probably, like their creator, whose perceptual states they mimic, do feel them as encounters with potustoronnost. Once more, lacking a clear map of the spiritual world, a very personal and altogether vague substitute, simply by virtue of its suggestion of "something more," is widely embraced. Nabokov himself played with the tentative nature of his knowledge of potustoronnost; in Canto 3 of his poem "Pale Fire," Nabokov's skepticism about an afterlife is revealed in John Shade's narration of his own near-death experience. The vision "reeked with truth," consoling Shade with the knowledge that consciousness survives death. He later reads a story about a woman who had a similar near-death experience: she saw a white fountain as she seemed to "cross over," a detail that matched his own vision. But upon investigating further, Shade discovers that the article contained a typographical error; the woman had seen not a fountain but a mountain (Nabokov, 1962, p. 60). Nabokov's visionary abilities brought him a cornucopia of gnostic treasures, but they were his and only his. Shade's disappointment may have been Nabokov's way of discounting the possibility of an absolute, objective language of representation for describing a spiritual world.[9]

Virginia Woolf's fictional expressions of this "numinous" world, rooted in her tendency to lose her consciousness of self during manic states, has frequently been interpreted as synaesthesia. The same sensations often accompany the dissociative states caused by temporal-lobe epilepsy. Fyodor Dostoevsky's reaction to these states mirrors Woolf's: "For several instants," Dostoevsky told his official biographer, "I experience a happiness that is impossible in an ordinary state, and of which other people have no conception. I feel full harmony in myself and in the whole world, and the feeling is so strong and sweet that for a few seconds of such bliss one could give up ten years of life, perhaps all of life" (Rice, 1985, pp. 83–84). In *Speak, Memory,* Nabokov, after drawing a set of eidetic portraits that take him from a bog near his St. Petersburg home in 1910 to a ponderosa pine forest in California many years later, declares that he does not believe in time. The sense of timelessness induced by recalling a series of eidetic images resembles the suspension of time experienced during an epileptic fit. Nabokov's description of the bliss synaesthetes can experience is eerily reminiscent of Dostoevsky's: "This is ecstasy, and behind the ecstasy is something else, which is hard to explain. It is like a momentary vacuum into which rushes all that I love. A sense of oneness with sun and stone" (p. 139).

The testimony given by these authors about the effect their eidetic episodes have on them finds unexpected corroboration. In his memoirs, Francis Galton, the pioneer investigator of mental imagery, concluded his discussion of his studies of hallucinations in sane persons with a remarkable affirmation: his own memories were so vivid as to seem present. "In short, this experience has given me an occasional feeling that there are no realities corresponding to Past, Present, and Future, but that the entire Cosmos is one perpetual Now. Philosophers have often held this creed intellectually, but I suspect that few have felt the possible truth of it so vividly as it has occasionally appeared to my imagination through dwelling on these 'Memories'" (Galton, 1909, pp. 277–278). That so sober and scientific an observer as Galton should be driven to philosophical reflection by his eideticism testifies to the power of the eidetic image. As in Nabokov's case, Galton's visual imagery prompted him to adopt a gnostic attitude to the phenomenal world.

In "Fame," the poem that according to Vera Nabokov most clearly embodies her husband's sense of potustoronnost, can also be found the most explicit link drawn between his sense of another world and the melting away of the physical world perceived through the senses. In the verse "Without body I've spread, without echo I thrive," Nabokov announces the transcendence of time and space that he achieves thanks to his engagement with his eidetic imagery. He exults in his exemption from the constraints of the physical world: "A book's death can't affect me since even the break/between me and my land is a trifle." His exile from Russia is overcome by his power to be there at any moment through his eidetic recall of the most precious moments of his youth. He reveals his method of transcendence—"disrupting the strata of sense and descending deep down to my wellspring"—but cloaks it in wordplay. Diving to the source of his identity by consciously recalling eidetic images, Nabokov disrupts, indeed dispenses with, the five senses, since eidetic images require no present sensory input. (His three allusions to his "secret," backed by the petulant childish rhythm—"tra-tá-ta tra-tá-ta tra-tá"—constitute a cryptic admission that he still wishes to hide his gift of eideticism.) Besides seeing his "own self and the world" via the eidetic image, he sees "something else, something else." He is not just being coy; though it sounds as if he knows what Other lies beyond the material world, he really can't say any more than he does. Like Dostoevsky, Nabokov, though regarding his epiphanic moments as paramount in his emotional life, was never quite certain of the ultimate meaning of those moments.

In addition to conducting "experiments" with his images such as those outlined by Van Veen, Nabokov stepped outside his own consciousness to investigate the experience of others who had a sense of contact with an unseen world. In *Speak, Memory* he relates that he endured visits with elderly believers in Spiritualism who regaled him with their tales of past lives and that he "ransacked" his dreams for clues about personal immortality, with no success whatsoever.

As a boy, Nabokov was told by his father that it wasn't necessary to believe in God. The young Vladimir grew up heeding his father's advice "to stay godless . . . in a world that is swarming with godheads" (Nabokov, 1970b, p. III). Nabokov does not need God, for the transcendent consistently appears to issue from inside himself, not from some outer source. Nabokov's other term for these momentary gnoses—"inspiration"—rather than conveying the usual sense that the individual is filled with the divine, implies instead that the individual fills the cosmos. The person best able to fill the world is of course the literary artist, the "genius" who, to the commonplace fusion of present phenomena with past memories, "adds a third ingredient: it is the past and the present and the future (your book) that come together in a sudden flash; thus the entire circle of time is perceived, which is another way of saying that time ceases to exist" (Nabokov, 1981, p. 378). Not only time but the physical body seem to evaporate at these moments. In *Invitation to a Beheading*, Cincinnatus appears "as if one side of his being [had] slid into another dimension," "as though at any moment . . . [he] would step in such a way as to slip naturally and effortlessly through some chink of the air into its unknown coulisses to disappear there" (Nabokov, 1959, pp. 120–121). In one of Nabokov's early short stories, "Torpid Smoke," the protagonist, Grisha, has the ability to visualize several scenes simultaneously, which seems a form of clairvoyance. As he lies in a darkened room and hallucinates, he feels transformed: "Everything traversed his inner being, and that sense of fluidity became transfigured into something like second sight" (Nabokov, 1973a, p. 28).

By so artfully capturing in words the protean capabilities that eideticism confers, Nabokov too appears to his admirers, to possess such clairvoyance. Fyodor clearly describes its "mechanism":

> You look at a person and you see him as clearly as if he were fashioned of glass and you were the glass blower, while at the same time without in the least impinging upon that clarity you notice some trifle on the side—such as the similarity of the telephone receiver's shadow to a huge, slightly crushed ant, and (all of this simultaneously) the convergence is joined by a third thought—the memory of a sunny evening at a Russian small railway station; i.e., images having no rational connection with the

conversation you are carrying on while your mind runs around the outside of your own words and along the inside of those of your interlocutor. [Nabokov, 1963, pp. 175–176]

Each time one tumbles with Nabokov's characters into one of these eidetic vortices, space and time appear to collapse. When Nabokov describes in *Speak, Memory* the capture of his first butterfly, the passage begins at the swallowtail's perch on a honeysuckle on his family's summer estate in 1906 and ends on a dandelion under an aspen in Colorado forty years later. This is what memory does for all of us, but rarely with the overpowering displacement that the "virtuality" of eideticism causes. In *The Gift,* perhaps the most transparent fictional embodiment of Nabokov's perceptual style, an eidetic image opens the novel—a yellow moving van with the company name on the side in blue letters. The classically Nabokovian reflexivity of the opening scene ("Someday, he thought, I must use such a scene to start a good, old-fashioned novel") gives way to phenomenological dissection of the perception: "The fleeting thought was touched with a careless irony; an irony, however, that was quite unnecessary, because somebody within him, on his behalf, independently from him, had absorbed all this, recorded it, and filed it away" (Nabokov, 1963, p. 1). The sense that his eidetic capacity is actually an independent entity inside him is voiced in Nabokov's poem "An Evening of Russian Poetry," where in a talk on Russian poetry to an American women's group, the magic lantern device makes another appearance: "My little helper at the magic lantern, / insert that slide and let the colored beam / project my name or any such-like phantom / in Slavic characters upon the screen. / The other way, the other way. I thank you" (quoted in Johnson, 1985, p. 14).

But sometimes the magic lantern projections could get out of hand. Nabokov complained that at times his extraordinary visual gift "overburdened his consciousness," and the same lament surfaces in his fiction. He does this most explicitly through Dementia, the psychotic alter ego of the distinguished Anglo-Russian writer Vadim Vadimovich N. (aka "Mr. N., a Russian noble-man," aka "Mr. V. S.," aka "McNab," aka "Vivian," all pseudonyms for Nabokov himself), whose autobiography appears in *Look at the Harlequins!* Dementia is the dark side of eidetic consciousness and is described as a "con-fined madman"—just what Nabokov considered his all-seeing double to be (Nabokov, 1974, p. 8). Dementia is troubled by "abstract and trite anxieties (problems of infinity, eternity, identity, and so forth)" (p. 7)—in other words, the abysses that the gift of eideticism constantly opens up for its possessor.

When Vadim Vadimovich describes his mental condition as "a nervous complaint that skirted insanity" (p. 5) or as "flayed consciousness" (p. 31), Nabokov is revealing the price he pays for eidetic memory. The various mental and physical paralyses to which Vadim Vadimovich is prey—from headaches and dizziness to a more frightening existential affliction, the inability to distinguish past from present or future (symbolized in the novel in Vadim Vadimovich's inability to visualize left/right reversals)—are drawn from Nabokov's own condition. Another sort of paralysis is suggested in "Torpid Smoke." In the middle of his episode of clairvoyance, Grisha finds that "to move was, however, incredibly difficult, because the very form of his being had now lost all distinctive marks, all fixed boundaries" (Nabokov, 1973a, p. 29).

Just how much can eidetic imagery intrude on an eidetic's normal consciousness? Psychologist D. M. Purdy described the case of a woman who was both eidetic and synaesthetic:

> For R, the world of actual perception is readily annihilated, as a whole or in part, and replaced by eidetic imagery. Thus, she can abolish the perception of a person who is standing before her open eyes, and in his place see an eidetic vision of some absent person. Through eidetic imagery she can transport herself to some remembered or fantastic scene—a ballroom in Quebec or an island in the South Seas; her real surroundings are sometimes completely blotted out, and sometimes she sees only the marginal part of her "real" visual field. . . .
>
> R can often remove particular real objects from her field of vision; for instance, it is easy for her to see a human being as devoid of a head. She can also add many kinds of eidetic details to the things in the real world, e.g., she can place green leaves upon barren winter trees, or supply a smooth-shaven man with a full beard.
>
> Eidetic imagery often appears when R does not expect it. Once when she was in a lecture hall filled with students, she suddenly, for no apparent reason, acquired the impression that all the students were wearing black goggles over their eyes. . . .
>
> R seldom mistakes her eidetic images for reality, but this does happen occasionally. Thus, when riding in an automobile, she has sometimes warned the driver against objects in the road which, as she soon discovered, were figments of her eidetic vision. [Purdy, 1936, pp. 444–445]

Ernest, a polymodal synaesthete who was studied by Alfred Ulrich in 1903, experienced colored photisms for letters of the alphabet, animal sounds, music, temperature, taste, and smells. He also had sensations of color, sound, and temperature in conjunction with geometric figures. Sometimes Ernest's "couleurs magiques," as he called his photisms, played with him, telling him stories.

He said that sometimes they were so overwhelming as to "bewitch" him, an effect that disturbed him terribly (Ulrich, 1903, p. 184). In *Speak, Memory,* Nabokov reveals that he too was occasionally at the mercy of his eidetic faculty. Chapter 11, which describes the composition of Nabokov's first poem, alternates between narrative and metanarrative. The metanarrative gives some idea of the tension that lay behind the apparent ease with which both the young Nabokov's poem and the middle-aged memoirist's memory of it were produced. Random images and sounds intrude while he is in the process of composing, almost like stray radio signals interrupting the channel: "I would suddenly become aware that a plate of something I could not even remember having sampled was being removed and that my mother, her left cheek twitching as it did whenever she worried, was narrowly observing from her place at the top of the long table my moodiness and lack of appetite. I would lift my head to explain—but the table had gone, and I was sitting on a roadside stump, the stick of my butterfly net, in metronomic motion, drawing arc after arc on the brownish sand; earthen rainbows, with variations in depth of stroke rendering the different colors" (p. 222). Sounds make the same capricious demands on his consciousness: "It might be the dinner gong, or something less usual, such as the foul music of a barrel organ" (p. 223). The "contest" between visual and auditory eideticisms intrudes on Nabokov's consciousness in a good many other places in *Speak, Memory.* In one passage, as he recounts in meticulous visual detail a meeting with his lover, "the ancient limes crowding close to the house drown Mnemosyne's monologue with their creaking and heaving in the restless night. Their sigh would subside. The rain pipe at one side of the porch, a small busybody of water, could be heard steadily bubbling" (p. 226). This cacophony of past sounds comes not at Nabokov's behest, but as unavoidable accompanist to the visual images he wishes to savor and describe. In describing his audition colorée, Nabokov chooses a metaphor that reflects the involuntary nature of his synaesthesia and eideticism: "The confessions of a synesthete must sound tedious and pretentious to those who are protected from such leakings and drafts by more solid walls than mine are." Though he cherished his porous perceptual walls, occasionally they let through too much of the past.

And there was another, less terrifying side effect of his gift. As the newly fledged poet anxiously approaches his mother to recite his first encounter with his Muse, he encounters another obstacle. "An armchair stood by the sofa, but I always avoided it because of its golden satin, the mere sight of which caused a laciniate shiver to branch from my spine like nocturnal lightning" (p. 226). It seems that Nabokov was "gifted" with color-induced pain, a rare form of visual-tactile synaesthesia. In *Ada,* Nabokov alludes to this condition: Van relates the story of Spencer Muldoon, a "chromesthesiac" whose eyebrows go up "slightly at red, higher at orange, still higher at the shrill scream of yellow and then stepped down through the rest of the prismatic spectrum" (Nabokov, 1969, p. 469).

Though young Vladimir wins his mother's complete approval of his poem ("She was smiling ecstatically through the tears that streamed down her face. 'How wonderful, how beautiful,' she said"), the memory ends in a disquieting scene of self-dissolution. Nabokov's mother holds up a mirror to his face to show him that he has unconsciously crushed a mosquito against his cheek. "But I saw more than that. Looking into my own eyes, I had the shocking sensation of finding the mere dregs of my usual self, odds and ends of an evaporated identity which it took my reason quite an effort to gather again in the glass" (1966b, p. 227). As obsessed as he was with his own image, Nabokov could barely hold a self-image together, embattled as it was by the relentless demands of Dementia.

When, in *Speak, Memory,* Nabokov says that he has not profited much from his hallucinatory states, he is referring to these unwanted intrusions on consciousness, not the willed eidetic images. The only thing that Nabokov detested more than uninvited visions was the thought of having no visions at all. "Over and over again, my mind has made colossal efforts to distinguish the faintest of personal glimmers in the impersonal darkness on both sides of my life. . . . Short of suicide, I have tried everything" (p. 20). Because he constituted himself from the eidetic images of his past, he was frustrated that in looking back he eventually reached a point (his first childhood memory from the age of four) beyond which no more images came. The same blank screen confronted him when he tried to look forward from the present, beyond death. In *The Eye,* his first novel written in the first person, Nabokov intimates that nothing more lies on the other side of death than the images reconstituted from a person's life. The narrator, Smurov, a lonely, disoriented young man who has shot himself and mistakenly believes he is dead, thinks of a hospital, "and at once obedient to my will, a spectral hospital materialized around me. . . . What a mighty thing was human thought, that it could hurtle on beyond death! Heaven knows how much longer it could pulsate and create images after my defunct brain had long since ceased to be of any use" (Nabokov, 1965, p. 31). In Smurov's description of himself as "a cold, insistent, tireless eye" observing self-generated images, Nabokov is assessing himself. No new visions lie over the wall of death; all that remains to Smurov is the prospect of the continued tyranny of his visual apparatus. Smurov acts as Nabokov's mouthpiece when he declares: "I have realized that the only happiness in the world is to observe, to spy, to watch, to scrutinize oneself and others, to be nothing but a big, slightly vitreous, somewhat bloodshot, unblinking eye" (pp. 113–114). This is hardly the credo of a Neoplatonist convinced of a transcendent otherworld in the face of which the physical world is but a transitory shadow. Nabokov not only venerated the shadows over the real entities that produced them; he wished to produce all the shadows himself, and to continue to provide the illumination in the cave after his own flickering light had been extinguished.

Between birth and death, those two dark endpoints of consciousness, Nabokov faced the daily darkness of sleep. Nabokov was a chronic insomniac. Worshipful biographers have accepted this as the curse of an overly active artistic imagination, but it seems that it may have had more to do with Nabokov's abhorrence of losing consciousness. In *Speak, Memory* he says: "Sleep . . . is a mental torture I find debasing. . . . No matter how great my weariness, the wrench of parting with consciousness is unspeakably repulsive to me. I loathe Somnus, that black-masked headsman binding me to the block" (Nabokov, 1966b, p. 20). At age seventy-four (in 1973), Nabokov noted in his diary: "For the first time in *years,* (since 1955? 1960?) had this night a six-hour stretch of uninterrupted sleep (12–6). My usual extent of sleep (apart from periodical insomnias), even if induced by more or less potent pills (at least thrice daily) is a $3 + 2 + 1$ or at best $4 + 2 + 2$ or at frequent worst $2 + 1 + 1 + 2 + 1$–hour affair with intervals $(+)$ of hopelessness and nervous urination" (quoted in Boyd, 1990a, p. 627).

Episodes where the body image shatters, which Nabokov fictionalized in his novels, are usually simultaneously frightening and exhilarating. In *Pale Fire,* John Shade's reminiscences of the "thread of subtle pain" that haunted him as a boy are linked to experiences of dissociation.

> I felt distributed through space and time
> One foot upon a mountaintop, one hand
> Under the pebbles of a painting strand,
> One ear in Italy, one eye in Spain,
> In caves, my blood, and in the stars, my brain.
> There were dull throbs in my Triassic; green
> Optical spots in Upper Pleistocene,
> An icy shiver down my Age of Stone,
> And all tomorrow in my funnybone. [p. 38]

These lines evoke the intimation of immortality that frequently accompanies dissociation. Though every afternoon for an entire winter (when he is eleven years old) Shade falls into that "momentary swoon," eventually he escapes it, but not without a twinge of regret ("The wonder lingers and the shame remains," Nabokov, 1962, p. 38). He obviously feels that the signs the family doctor has attributed to growing pains are actually a link to the transcendent. The color hearing chapter in *Speak, Memory* ends with a description of perfusing space itself during an out-of-body experience caused by a childhood fever:

One day, after a long illness, as I lay in bed still very weak, I found myself basking in an unusual euphoria of lightness and repose. I knew my mother had gone to buy me the daily present that made those convalescences so delightful. What it would be this time I could not guess, but through the crystal of my strangely translucent state I vividly visualized her driving away down Morskaya Street toward Nevski Avenue. I distinguished the light sleigh drawn by a chestnut courser. I heard his snorting breath, the rhythmic clacking of his scrotum, and the lumps of frozen earth and snow thudding against the front of the sleigh. Before my eyes and before those of my mother loomed the hind part of the coachman, in his heavily padded blue robe, and the leather-encased watch (twenty minutes past two) strapped to the back of his belt, from under which curved the pumpkin-like folds of his huge stuffed rump. I saw my mother's seal furs and, as the icy speed increased, the muff she raised to her face— that graceful, winter-ride gesture of a St. Petersburg lady. Two corners of the voluminous spread of bearskin that covered her up to the waist were attached by loops to the two side knobs of the low back of her seat. And behind her, holding on to these knobs, a footman in a cockaded hat stood on his narrow support above the rear extremities of the runners.

Still watching the sleigh, I saw it stop at Treumann's (writing implements, bronze baubles, playing cards). Presently, my mother came out of this shop followed by the footman. He carried her purchase, which looked to me like a pencil. I was astonished that she did not carry so small an object herself, and this disagreeable question of dimensions caused a faint renewal, fortunately very brief, of the "mind dilation effect" which I hoped had gone with the fever. As she was being tucked up again in the sleigh, I watched the vapor exhaled by all, horse included. I watched, too, the familiar pouting movement she made to distend the network of her close-fitting veil drawn too tight over her face, and as I write this, the touch of reticulated tenderness that my lips used to feel when I kissed her veiled cheek comes back to me—flies back to me with a shout of joy out of the snow-blue, blue-windowed (the curtains are not yet drawn) past.

A few minutes later, she entered my room. In her arms she held a big parcel. It had been, in my vision, greatly reduced in size—perhaps, because I subliminally corrected what logic warned me might still be the dreaded remnants of delirium's dilating world. Now the object proved to be a giant polygonal Faber pencil, four feet long and correspondingly thick. It had been hanging as a showpiece in the shop's window, and she presumed I had coveted it, as I coveted all things that were not quite purchasable. The shopman had been obliged to ring up an agent, a "Doctor" Libner (as if the transaction possessed indeed some pathological import). For an awful moment, I wondered whether the point was made of real graphite. It was. And some years later I satisfied myself, by drilling a hole in the side, that the lead went right through the whole length—a perfect case of art for art's sake on the part of Faber and Dr. Libner since the pencil was far too big for use and, indeed, was not meant to be used. [pp. 37–39]

Remarkably, Nabokov retains his sensory acuity when his consciousness leaves his body; the exacting details of the horse's movements, the coachman's clothing (including the crowning image of the time on his watch), his mother's face, the footman's placement on the sleigh all attest that, as in his eidetic reveries, "without body [he has] spread." His high fever has brought about a state of spatial consciousness that is symmetrical with his familiar feeling of having become "unstuck in time," like Vonnegut's Billy Pilgrim. The telepathic transport through space replicates the temporal telepathy Nabokov and his characters routinely experience as a result of their eidetic perception. The sensory details and the eventual appearance of his mother with the telepathically viewed toy pencil appear to confirm that he was seeing a real event and moreover place the entire experience in the same category as his eidetic imagery, as distinguished from the capricious hallucinations with which he opens the chapter.

This discovery that consciousness is not fixed, but movable in space as well as time, is the cornerstone of Nabokov's sense of potustoronnost. As with his color hearing, Nabokov discovered that his mother also had experienced such alterations of consciousness: "'Oh yes,' she would say as I mentioned this or that unusual sensation. 'Yes, I know all that,' and with a somewhat eerie ingenuousness she would discuss such things as double sight, and little raps in the woodwork of tripod tables, and premonitions, and the feeling of déja vu" (p. 39). Her response reveals that she placed her son's "remote viewing" experience in the same category as other instances of the paranormal, all of which are intrusions of the unseen upon the seen. Unlike in the case of the "hallucination" of alphabetic chromaesthesia—for which Nabokov possessed, if not explanation, at least some scientific description—he seems baffled by his vision, unable to either explain or make use of it. As he transmits it to us, it has an aura of the otherworldly.

The fictionalized version of this incident that appears in *The Gift* reinforces the feeling that this distortion of the boundaries of the self has important implications for Nabokov's perceptual (and literary) style. Fyodor's fever comes on during a severe case of pneumonia:

> The fever had ebbed away during the night and I had finally scrambled ashore. I was, let me tell you, weak, capricious and transparent—as transparent as a cut-glass egg. Mother had gone to buy me—I did not know what exactly—one of those freakish things that from time to time I coveted with the greed of a pregnant woman, afterwards forgetting them completely; but my mother made lists of these desiderata. As I lay flat in bed among bluish layers of indoor twilight I felt myself evolving an incredible lucidity, as when a distant stripe of radiantly pale sky stretches between long vesperal clouds and you can make out the cape and shallows of God knows what far-off islands—and it seems that if you release your volatile glance just a little further you will discern a shining boat drawn up on the damp sand and receding footsteps filled with bright water. In that minute, I think, I attained the highest limit of human health: my mind had been dipped and rinsed only recently in a dangerous, super-naturally clean blackness. [Nabokov, 1963, pp. 34–35]

Both the account of the original experience and its fictional retelling stress Nabokov's desire for this escape of consciousness from the body and the consequent episode of clairvoyance. "Transparent as a cut-glass egg," Fyodor/Nabokov's "incredible lucidity" is experienced as the "highest limit of human health." Nabokov uses the same language of ecstasy for this momentary flight of consciousness from the body as he uses for his eidetically inspired flights.

NABOKOV AS NARCISSUS

Nabokov could not leave this world for the "otherworld" without confessing his secret. To a 1988 issue of *Antaeus* devoted to the journals of various celebrated writers, Nabokov's son Dmitry contributed the following diary entry: "July 2, 1977, Lausanne: I have returned from Munich in time to be with Father when he dies. He expires with a triple moan of descending pitch, just like Boris Christoff on his *Boris* recording. . . . He has had time to tell me, one sunny day on a Swiss mountain, that his creative process was simple: writing was like developing an exposed film stored in one's mind. And he was happy, for almost all of the film had been developed." (D. Nabokov, 1988, p. 320). Nabokov waited until he was dying to reveal to his son the secret of his gift, a gift which, it seems, Dmitry shared to some extent. Vladimir Nabokov records in his own diary a list of his son's color-vowel associations at age six. And at age seventeen, Dmitry, then a student at Harvard, writes: "When I am not too exhausted from daily track practice, it is enough to focus briefly on a page for it to register photographically. But the image fades quickly, alas" (1988, p. 321).

For Vladimir Nabokov, the images of his past perennially ready to be recalled for his artistic purposes, never did lose any of their luster. In conjunction with his remarkable linguistic gifts, his synaesthesia and eideticism kept him in the green garden of childhood, forever returning to the halcyon days when the world was still largely of his own making. We all display vestiges of the narcissistic self, but very few of us can truly re-create the omnipotent glories of narcissistic perception. We must content ourselves with the drabness of unimodal sensory perception and the monotony of the present moment, while the synaesthetically and eidetically endowed Narcissus, forever young, forever gazing into the pool at his own reflection, lives in a sensory and temporal phantasmagoria. For Narcissus, time is frozen; empathic love is impossible; nothing ever really happens. No growth, no maturation; no death, but no life. Vladimir Nabokov embodies the paradoxes of both narcissism and synaesthesia. We envy his whimsically sensual chromaesthesia, his mnemonic capacity, and their translation into art, just as we envy his unshakable self-confidence. We may also share his desire for union with the otherworld, but we do not envy his characters the solipsistic prisons they inhabit, the result of the very idiosyncrasies that so captivate us readers. Obsessed by the world that might lie on the other side of death, Nabokov banished death from his world through his eternal return to past images.

That Nabokov's work has consistently been read as pointing to a transcendent otherworld suggests again the degree to which the modern world has lost its knowledge of the noumenal realm. Like its sister syncretic perceptual style, synaesthesia, Nabokov's eideticism has spawned elaborate transcendental readings that elevate an "unseen" realm that hardly deserves such idealization. With great pictorial variation through dozens of tales, Nabokov artfully metamorphosed his eidetic imagery to create ethereal otherworlds. But what are these worlds? They are never anything more than that ideal world envisioned by Cincinnatus from his prison cell, nostalgic glances back to eidetically luminescent moments. The supposedly all-knowing Cincinnatus sees no higher, transcendent realm, but only eidetic memory images of the Tamara Gardens, the municipal park where he once walked happily with his fiancé. Many of his readers may believe, as his biographer Brian Boyd does, that Nabokov's artist-protagonists act the way they do because they are "at the last ramparts of consciousness, ready to jump the moat to total freedom if anyone can" (Boyd,

1966b, p. 308). But the "something more" to which they might leap is only more thought, more reflection, more self-generated imagery. Nabokov had no metaphysics, as he had no personal experiences with "higher" worlds. With his superlative observational powers and his extraordinary literary gifts, Nabokov made magnificent prose from his eidetically recalled past, but its images brought him and his readers no closer to any transcendental truth than did the synaesthete's photisms.

AFTERWORD: SHERESHEVSKY'S SYNCRETIC PRISON

About two hundred miles southeast of St. Petersburg, in the town of Torzhok, another Russian man, born around the same time as Vladimir Nabokov, also bore the gifts of eideticism and synaesthesia. He left no legacy of inventive fiction or superbly crafted autobiography—and indeed would have been unable to understand the most transparent of Nabokov's works. But the memoir left by psychologist A. R. Luria about the man he called S. suggests that he too was a prisoner of childhood, an eidetic synaesthete whose gifts kept him in a cognitive Eden that was far from paradisiacal. S. (later identified by Luria as a Mr. Shereshevsky) was sent to Luria's laboratory in Moscow in the late 1920s, when he was twenty-nine years old. He had been sent by his boss, a newspaper editor who was astonished at Shereshevsky's prodigious memory, which he learned of after questioning Shereshevsky about why he never wrote down any of the verbal instruction the editor gave him about daily assignments. Luria conducted a series of examinations that showed that Shereshevsky could remember any number of figures or words from long random lists—reciting them either forwards, backwards, or in any other requested sequence—weeks, months, even years later. Shereshevsky could repeat all the details of any conversation he had ever heard. His memory for what he saw matched his recollection of what he heard. He could form from memory an exact mental duplicate of scenes, faces, and other visual images from memory. Luria, who had intended at the outset of his investigation to measure Shereshevsky's memory, quickly discerned that both the capacity and durability of Shereshevsky's memory were essentially immeasurable. He thereupon began what became a twenty-year qualitative study, which he summarized in *The Mind of a Mnemonist* (Luria, 1968).

Luria discovered that along with having eidetic recall, Shereshevsky was a synaesthete, and that his synaesthesia aided his remarkable memory. Like other synaesthetes, Shereshevsky could draw on the secondary sensations (such as colors associated with words) that he experienced to help him recognize and remember things. Luria noted that Shereshevsky displayed the usual characteristics of synaesthesia—its early onset, primarily visual modality (he experienced colored or shaded photisms as the most dramatic synaesthesiae), and fixity over time—but that he was exceptional in that he was a multiple, or "five-point," synaesthete; that is, he experienced secondary sensations in all of his five primary sensory modalities. In addition to color hearing, Shereshevsky had both tactile and gustatory hearing—he experienced sensations of taste and touch in response to sounds. A particular tone might be heard by him as "sweet and sour borscht" or "a briny pickle," a voice as "crumbly yellow" (Luria, 1968, p. 84). Luria thought that Shereshevsky's descriptions of his synaesthesiae had "the authentic ring of childhood" about them: "Take the word *mama,* or *ma-me,* as we used to say when I was a child. It's a bright haze. *Ma-me* and all women—they're something bright. . . . So is milk in a glass, and a white milk jug, and a white cup. They're all like a white cloud." He could describe his early memories of how such associations initiated: "When I was about two or three years old I was taught the words of a Hebrew prayer. I didn't understand them, and what happened was that the words settled in my mind as puffs of steam or splashes. . . . Even now I *see* these puffs or splashes when I hear certain sounds" (p. 22). Though he could recall distinct images from childhood, such as his mother taking him in her arms, these images tended to be superseded by diffuse, syncretic sensations that were midway between perceptions and emotions, and that were difficult to put into words. Shereshevsky shared at least some of the irrecoverability of childhood experienced by nonsynaesthetes.

Shereshevsky's mental world had a distinctly hallucinatory quality to it: in a restaurant, the taste of the food would change with the music he heard; he could not eat when he read, because the taste of the food spilled over into his perception of the words he was reading. His eideticism heightened this quality, and he often became caught up in purely mental actions. He recalled the experience common to most children in which their imaginary world takes on the aura of reality:

> This is the way things tended to work when I was a boy and going to Hebrew school. I'd wake up and see that it was morning and that I had to get up. . . . I'd look at the clock and think: "No, there's still time, I can stay in bed for a while." And I'd continue to see the hands of the clock pointing at 7:30, which meant it was still early. Suddenly my mother would come in and say: "What you haven't left yet: Why, it'll

soon be nine." Well, how was I to know that: I saw the big hand pointing down—according to the clock, it was 7:30. [Luria, 1968, p. 144]

But in Shereshevsky such vivid mental images continued to play an important role even in adulthood. "To me there's no great difference between the things I imagine and what exists in reality," Shereshevsky declared (Luria, 1968, p. 146). He gave numerous instances of his magical thinking, from curing himself and others of illness by mentally picturing the disappearance of its cause to willing a store clerk to give him too much change. He could also affect his own physiological functions by visualizing the appropriate images, such as sending his resting pulse rate from 70 to 100 by imagining himself running after a train, or raising the temperature of the left hand by imagining it to be placed on a stove, while simultaneously lowering the temperature of the right by visualizing it in a bath of ice water.

Many previous investigators of synaesthesia had commented on synaesthetes' propensity for daydreaming and imaginative activities in general, Luria's study was the first to devote serious consideration to the personality of the synaesthete. By interviewing Shereshevsky over a period of many years, Luria came to intimately know how synaesthesia affected his overall worldview. A good deal of research had represented synaesthesia and eideticism as remnants of childhood syncretic perception, but none of this research had the anecdotal richness of Luria's case study. In addition to documenting the strengths conferred by Shereshevsky's synaesthesia—his vivid imagination, acute observational powers, and practical problem-solving ability, Luria was the first to highlight certain handicaps that synaesthetic perception entailed. Luria noted that when Shereshevsky read, each word produced such vivid photisms that he often became so deeply involved with them rather than the text that the overall meaning of a passage was lost. The same thing happened to him in conversation, and he was rarely able to speak to people without falling into long digressions. Luria found that Shereshevsky was extremely conservative in his use of words and that he was routinely confused by homonyms and synonyms. Because they sounded alike, and hence had the identical secondary associations, homonyms were experienced as exactly the same; Shereshevsky could not distinguish between them. Synonyms were confusing for a similar reason; Shereshevsky found it difficult to conceive how two words with such different sounds (and hence associated taste, color, touch or smell) as, say, "similar" and "alike," could possibly have the same meaning. Worst of all were metaphors, which were virtually impenetrable. In fact, Shereshevsky seemed to have no ability for abstraction. All words were concrete objects to him, usually with a host of synaesthetic associations to give them even further "weight." For example, the concepts of "nothing" and "infinity" were both impossible for Shereshevsky, since both these words evoked real, material entities for him. Shereshevsky was not alone in this perception. Temple Grandin notes her difficulty learning things that cannot be thought about in pictures; philosophy is incomprehensible to her; even the verb conjugation "to be," strikes her as meaningless. In order to understand the Lord's Prayer, she had to work consciously with concrete pictures: " 'The power and the glory' were high-tension electric towers and a blazing rainbow sun. I visualize the word 'trespass' as a 'No Trespassing' sign on the neighbor's tree" (Grandin, 1995, p. 31). Neil Smith and Ianthi-Maria Tsimpli (1995) note how their subject Christopher, an autistic savant who has a genius for languages (he is fluent in sixteen), is, like Shereshevsky, absolutely unable to handle irony and metaphor or understand jokes.[10]

Here was a great paradox: synaesthesia, the perceptual style that the Symbolists had imitated in their effort to dematerialize the world of the senses, was, in its most highly developed form, an actual barrier to the ability to conceive of anything beyond the material. It also impeded the capacity for symbolization: once a concept had taken on a particular significance for Shereshevsky, it could not be metaphorically transferred to new arenas of meaning. In concluding that "a person who has 'seen' and experienced life synaesthetically cannot have the same grasp of things the rest of us have, nor is he likely to experience himself or other people as we might," Luria (1968, p. 151) was not suggesting that the synaesthete possessed a uniquely desirable gift. From his long relationship with Shereshevsky, Luria understood that Shereshevsky, with a memory crammed full of concrete sensory images without the ability to convert those sensory details into general concepts, was a conceptual cripple. Although Shereshevsky always sensed that "something particularly fine was about to happen" to him, he ended up incapacitated by his synaesthesia and eideticism and was eventually forced to make his living as a stage mnemonist. His limited ability for communication with others prohibited him from full participation in the linguistically and conceptually fluid world of normal social interaction.

If Nabokov and Shereshevsky are considered along with Temple Grandin and her fellow autistic savants, the hierarchical suppositions harbored by scientists and Romantics alike about synaesthesia and eideticism begin to break down. Eideticism and synaesthesia exist in individuals at either end of the intellectual spectrum. Occasionally they also appear in people of middling intelligence, undistinguished by either the pyrotechnic linguistic abilities of a Nabokov, the bottomless memory of a Shereshevsky, or the spectacular skills and concomitant social limitations of autistic savants. If these syncretic forms of perception do indeed signal something about the evolution of human consciousness, we have not as yet fathomed what that is.

Chapter 6 Conclusion:

The Redemption of Thinking

French Symbolists' mythologization of synaesthesia as a form of transcendental perception had spread in a groundswell of enthusiasm for an imminent revolution in consciousness; in the 1960s, promoters of a revolution in consciousness seized on synaesthesia once again. Old myths were retrieved and new ones added; in North America in particular, synaesthesia was rediscovered as an impending advance in human evolution. Though there had been a thirty-year hiatus in scientific research on synaesthesia and eideticism and nonscientific interest had largely abated, when the word "synaesthesia" began to appear again on the lips of a new generation of Romantics, a desire for transcendence attached to it, as it had in Paris in the 1890s. Synaesthesia was offered as an antidote to the same poisons—rationalism, materialism, and positivism—that had vexed the late nineteenth century. Synaesthesia fit neatly into the metaphorical and ideological mixture of the sixties counterculture. Thought to be rooted in the body rather than the mind, synaesthetic awareness seemingly defied limitations and conventions and offered a path to unity and transcendence. The modern renascence of synaesthesia did not take its inspiration from scientific study. Interest in the subject was rekindled when non-synaesthetes encountered synaesthesia experientially through the use of hallucinogenic drugs and championed its mythic reconfiguration as a holistic and participatory cognitive style.

"SYNAESTHETIC" AS A SYNONYM FOR "PSYCHEDELIC"

In the 1960s, "synaesthetic" became a synonym for, or perhaps a subset of, "psychedelic." One of the most characteristic features of the ingestion of LSD is the confusion of sensory channels, particularly vision and hearing. In October of 1977, a decade after the Summer of Love and the popularization of LSD, Dr. Albert Hoffman, the inventor of LSD, told a crowd gathered at the University of California at Santa Cruz of how he had first discovered the effects of the drug. The no-nonsense Swiss research chemist read his diary entry for April 16, 1943, relating how in his laboratory, after accidentally absorbing LSD through his skin, he went into a sort of synaesthetic swoon, in which sounds created optical effects and visual images generated sounds. The audience laughed knowingly (Lee and Shlain, 1985, p. xv). As knowledge of LSD grew both within the scientific community and among recreational users, the synaesthetic effects of LSD intoxication became almost a cliché. Humphry Osmond, the doctor who first gave mescaline to Aldous Huxley, and who, along with the ex-spy Alfred Hubbard, administered LSD to prime ministers, United Nations representatives, and British parliament members in an attempt to "expand" their consciousnesses and thereby change the world, noted in the early 1960s that the cause of synaesthesia during LSD intoxication remained a mystery. The other cliché about LSD was that it was an agent of consciousness expansion. Osmond spoke for thousands of seekers of transcendence when he said: "For myself, my experiences with these substances have been the most strange, most awesome, and among the most beautiful things in a varied and fortunate life. These are not escapes from but enlargements, burgeonings of reality."[1]

Much of American popular culture in the late 1960s reflected the attempt to externalize the LSD experience, and synaesthetic dreams became as ubiquitous as they had been in fin de siècle Paris. The widespread use of LSD allowed an enormous number of nonsynaesthetes to experience the bright colors and other anomalous sensations of synaesthesia. As psychedelic culture spread from Haight-Ashbury to Wall Street and Madison Avenue, apologists for and explicators of LSD culture like Robert Masters and Jean Houston emerged to "make sense" of the synaesthetic experience for the uninitiated. In a series of books, Masters and Houston described the synaesthetic experience and even presented an exercise for cultivating synaesthetic perception. Readers were instructed to select some music, lie down on the floor in loose clothing, relax, and allow the music to flow over them. "After this has been fully experienced and the music has become a part of you, allow yourself to feel the colors and textures of the music . . . its smells and tastes . . . heat and chill . . . its light and darkness . . . so that the music sweeps through your senses . . . blending them together in a full orchestration of the sensorium [and] . . . carrying you into and beyond the hearing of the music." Masters and Houston promised that by repeating the exercise, anyone could "begin to experience synesthesia, or a crossing of the senses, to 'see' sound, to 'taste' texture" (1978, pp. 47–48). As one of their "mind games," which Masters and Houston characterized as "education, ecstasy, entertainment, self-exploration, powerful instruments of growth," the syn-aesthesia exercise was intended to alter consciousness. In particular, it would afford access to unused capacities—"images, accelerated mental processes, more acute sensory impressions, access to other places of the mind, subjective realities, new space-time orientations" (Masters and Houston, 1972, pp. 7–8). All of these "capacities" were believed to be enhanced by LSD, and the mind games, like Ken Kesey's Dome and Stewart Brand's Trips Festival, were in-tended to replicate the LSD experience.

Because they interpreted synaesthesia as a transcendental experience, Mas-ters and Houston were awed by the powers of Shereshevsky, the mnemonist studied by Luria, and were particularly impressed by his use of his mental imagery to alter his body temperature. Such feats, Masters and Houston de-clared, "usually can only be achieved by yogis and adepts in similar disciplines after huge and arduous training" (1978, p. 49). Shereshevsky became a minor cult figure in the 1960s; his life was regarded within the psychedelic subculture as the ultimate acid trip, a state of permanent sensory hallucination. Masters and Houston saw Shereshevsky as naturally endowed with the sort of advanced consciousness to which their audience aspired. Many of the other psychedelic pioneers believed that they were "storming heaven," "pushing the envelope" of human potential, and Masters and Houston's synaesthetic visions of the next step in human evolution echoed Rimbaud's Luciferic urge and Scriabin's Pro-metheanism. Like Rimbaud and Scriabin, these authors believed that hearing color or seeing sound were signposts on the path toward becoming what Houston called the Possible Human.

The latest representative of Romanticism to champion synaesthesia, self-described ethnobotanist and psychedelic theoretician Terence McKenna, acquired both his interest in synaesthesia and his expectation of the end of history as we know it by way of the hallucinogenic compound DMT—dimethyltryptamine. Dimethyltryptamine is chemically related to the LSD/psilocybin class of hallucinogenic drugs. It is a serotonin agonist; that is, it mimics the neurotransmitter serotonin but interferes with its normal action. This class of drugs enhances the brain's sensitivity to many kinds of incoming information. McKenna had first encountered its synaesthetic effects in Berkeley during the Summer of Love, and it gave him the feeling of "bursting into a space inhabited by merry elfin, self-transforming machine creatures . . . [who] seemed to be babbling in a visible and five-dimensional form of Ecstatic Nostratic" (McKenna, 1993, p. 7). McKenna and his brother Dennis, charmed by their encounter with the synaesthetic speech and other wonders of the hallucinogenic gnomes, had set out in 1971 for the Amazon to locate a strong aboriginal hallucinogen containing DMT, perhaps *ayahuasca* (known also as *yagé*) or *oo-koo-hé,* a psychedelic brew made by the Witoto tribe of the upper Amazon. But in their quest for the ultimate source of naturally occurring DMT, McKenna and his brother stumbled on a psilocybin-containing coprophilic mushroom—*Stropharia cubensis*—which was so powerful in its mind-altering effects that the brothers focused their investigations on the mushroom instead.

The McKenna brothers felt that the dung-loving mushroom took them deep into an "invisible landscape," where, in addition to encountering elves whose speech was visible, they found that they frequently communicated telepathically between themselves. Terence McKenna's "phenomenological" assessment, characteristically inflated with Irish whimsy, was that the mushroom was "a transdimensional doorway" that could lead to "a transformation of life on the planet" (McKenna and McKenna, 1975, p. 42). Their initial response to this intuition was to try to induce the transformation through what they christened the experiment at La Chorrera. The brothers McKenna had been insatiable readers of science fiction as boys, and so the sort of science fiction they intended to enact during the "experiment" came easily to them: through a process that Dennis McKenna called hypercarbolation, they wished to "exteriorize the soul" by taking a massive dose of *Stropharia* mushrooms and then letting out a howl that would synaesthetically translate sound into a visual image (and then into actual matter) and as a consequence "blow the doors of paradise right off their hinges" (p. 88).

Dennis assured his brother that their effort had succeeded: the wave of hypercarbolation they had set in motion was "sweeping through the human race, eliminating the distinction between the individual and the community as everyone discovered themselves spontaneously pushing off into a telepathic ocean." Terence was "flooded with ecstasy" at the realization that they "were now operating in the first few moments of the millennium" (1993, p. 111). Believing the "experiment" to be the penultimate event, the one before the passing of the old world and the coming of the new, the McKennas were like the faithful Millerites who came down from their hilltops when they were not rapt up into heaven—continuing to forecast apocalypse in the absence of any confirming evidence. Dennis went into a fourteen-day hallucinogenic trance; Terence, meanwhile, came back from hyperspace and fell into a state of portent overdrive: "Clues seemed everywhere; everything was webbed together in a magical fabric of meaning and affirmation and mystery" (p. 129). The most compelling pattern McKenna felt he had discovered in the wake of the "experiment" was the cyclical nature of time, and according to his "timewave" theory, the end of time was due to arrive on December 22, 2012, a date also chosen by Arguelles from his reading of the Mayan calendar. Writing of his discovery twenty-two years afterwards, McKenna admitted that his theory bordered on being a form of private entertainment, but he held to the idea that 2012 would truly mark the end of time. For nearly a decade now, McKenna has earned his living as a psychedelic Millerite, spreading the gospel of DMT and the timewave to an eager public. In proselytizing for the DMT experience, he has also been an enthusiast of synaesthesia, believing that "the relationship of the psyche to the surface of the body, the skin, is synesthetic and emotionally complex under the influence of psilocybin" (p. 216).

As the subtitle of McKenna's *Archaic Revival* ("Speculations on Psychedelic Mushrooms, the Amazon, Virtual Reality, UFOs, Evolution, Shamanism, the Rebirth of the Goddess, and the End of History") suggests, there is more to his vision than just mushrooms, the timewave, and synaesthesia. All manner of "new science" concepts with high metaphorical potential—Gaia, chaos, fractals, morphogenetic fields—and denizens of the beyond, particularly extraterrestrial aliens and transcendental visitors whose visits are facilitated by the use of psilocybin, are incorporated into his psychopolemics. Motivating McKenna's every metaphorical maneuver is the relentless drive for transcendence over rationalism, materialism, the body, the Earth.

In his elevation of the imagination over reason, McKenna joined a venerable group of Romantics who had sought meaning in the psychedelic experience. Authors such as E. T. A. Hoffman, Théophile Gautier, Thomas De Quincey, Charles Baudelaire, Arthur Rimbaud, Havelock Ellis, William James, Heinrich

Klüver, and Aldous Huxley recorded their experience with synaesthesia as an effect of marijuana, peyote, LSD, mescaline, and other hallucinogens, and all of them had the same feeling of liberation from the world of prosaic perception. Why? Was it merely on account of the dazzling beauty of the visual phantasmagoria conjured up before their eyes? For many of these seekers after visions, something more is obviously at work than the mere magical fascination of the gaze. Altered states of consciousness invariably carry with them a dramatic sense of their own importance, as if what is being experienced were the truth behind all illusions, a state of grace hard to verbalize but nonetheless more real than reality. Upon returning to a normal state of consciousness, few people are as keen as Arguelles or the McKenna brothers to make the synaesthetic experience a permanent state, especially because they can see that their visions are not shared by those who are not in an altered state. The visions that they recover from their altered states are not from other worlds but from the world inside their own minds; these are "true hallucinations," true for the hallucinators but for no one else.

Terence McKenna is fond of saying about DMT that "it's the most idiosyncratic thing there is." Idiosyncrasy is certainly characteristic of solipsistic worlds, from the color visions of the synaesthetic state, whether natural or pharmacologically induced, to McKenna's view of time and space as revealed to him in his psychedelic explorations. Those views have made him a celebrity among late twentieth-century Romantics, who share their predecessors' desires for a coherent, vivid world packed with meaning to replace the empty, mechanistic post-Enlightenment universe that they feel they inhabit. And yet there is nothing idiosyncratic about apocalypse as conceived in Scriabin's *Mysterium,* Arguelles's "posthistoric synaesthesia" or McKenna's "experiment." All envisage the end of time for everyone, not just for themselves. Recognizing that their own minds are on the verge of being "snuffed out," they assume that the impending psychic and physical extinction will be universal.

SYNAESTHESIA AND MEANING (REPRISE)

Early in the twentieth century, theorists had often interpreted synaesthesia as a transcendental form of representation, without taking into account Wheeler and Cutsforth's idea that synaesthetic percepts were a *mechanism for* meaning rather than an independent meaning in themselves. In formulating his notion that psychedelically induced synaesthetic photisms were a transcendental Urlanguage, McKenna, similarly, had conveniently overlooked the contemporary extension of Wheeler and Cutsforth's work. For more than twenty years, Harry Hunt, a cognitive psychologist at Brock University in Ontario has worked at developing a phenomenology of mystical and altered states. The subjects of Hunt's studies, who engaged in activities centering on the receptive observation of their immediate consciousness—insight meditation, generation of metaphors via the *I Ching,* and analysis of dream and hypnagogic imagery—experienced radical alterations in perception, affect, and cognition. The results strikingly resembled the experimental outcomes of classic introspectionism, including the work of Wheeler and Cutsforth (Hunt, 1976, 1984, 1985a, 1985b, 1987, 1989; Hunt et al., 1992; Spadafora and Hunt, 1990). As a consequence of his research, Hunt has become a strenuous defender of introspectionism as a technique for studying consciousness, just as Wheeler did.

Although he agreed with Wheeler and Cutsforth that synaesthesiae are *felt* by subjects as thoughts rather than merely as curious sensory effects, Hunt drew on their studies to argue that "simple" synaesthesiae—such as the visual blobs perceived during color hearing—are too stereotyped to qualify as thought. Colored photisms, Hunt argues, are as amorphous and plurisignificant as the fundamental units of language, morphemes and phonemes. Discrete units lacking any structural complexity or precision, they are as inappropriate a primary medium of thought as vocalization (for example, Vygotsky's "inner speech"). According to Hunt, "simple synaesthesias mark the first step in the sequential articulation of a simultaneously given felt meaning and help to show the point of shift between semantics and syntax. . . . We have in simple synaesthesia symbolic phenomena midway between the simultaneity of thought and actual linguistic syntax" (1985b, pp. 938–939). Hunt also noted that Cutsforth's photisms were not the terminus of his introspections; beneath them, he still sensed a separate subjective core of felt meaning. It was from this hidden, impenetrable core—the same wall that the Würzburg and Cornell introspectors ran up against—that the meaningful photisms arose. Wheeler and Cutsforth gave the term "kinaesthesis"—the inner sense of one's own body within space—to the same "imperceptibles" that halted the Würzburg introspectionists. Considering Cutsforth's synaesthesiae to be analogous to what "inner speech" is for most of us, Hunt was left with the question that had stumped the early introspectionists: What was the "stuff" of consciousness?

Hunt's approach to altered states of consciousness has been that they are "a sort of self-generated tachistoscope for mind," that show something fundamental about human symbolic capacity (1984, p. 469). From the outset, Hunt was struck by the ubiquity of synaesthesiae in altered states. Along with "simple" synaesthesiae that mimicked those experienced by idiopathic synaesthetes, Hunt studied "complex" synaesthesiae, borrowing the term "complex" from Heinrich Klüver, who had described complex synaesthesia in his 1966 monograph on the hallucinations induced by peyote. Klüver explained that geometric form constants—spirals, lattices, arcs, honeycombs, and other shapes commonly seen during hallucinations—were received as communications of a mythical or metaphysical nature and were charged with a distinct sense of portent or "meaning." Hence their ubiquity in both shamanic pictorial representations and 1960s "psychedelic art". Hunt recognized these psychedelically generated form constants as the synaesthetic expression of kinaesthesis; the same effect was noticeable with the typical fourfold division of mandala patterns, the arrangement of the chakras—the invisible force centers of the subtle bodies in Hindu, Buddhist, and Taoist meditative practice—and by extension the layered "body armor" described by Wilhelm Reich: "Both the fourfold division of mandalas and much of the specific 'grain' of these patterns— repeated lattices, arcs, angles, bursts—could be taken as synaesthetic translations back and forth between visual structure and an 'abstract' body scheme based on the imaginal reuse of the 'flow' or 'streaming' sensations of specific muscle groups" (Hunt, 1985, p. 918). Hunt's interpretation of thought, consciousness, mind, and ultimately, meaning "as a complex synaesthesia" (1989, p. 210) rescued introspection as the necessary technique for investigating mind and meaning, for it identified the missing "something" between "imperceptibles" and images.

Hunt was particularly struck by the similarity between the reported results of introspectionism and accounts of experience during altered states: both alluded to feelings of "strangeness and the uncanny, sense of timelessness and loss of spatial localization, derealization, and depersonalization, ineffable portent, synaesthesias . . . and the probably related sense of fusion between the observer's "body percept" and the stimulus object" (Hunt, 1984, p. 498). Hunt recovered from the scientific introspectionist literature impressive evidence of the consonance between introspective states and the state of mystical ecstasy. He drew particularly on John Paul Nafe's 1924 study of "feeling," in which observers attempted to analyze their sensations of pleasure and displeasure in response to diverse sensory stimuli. Nafe hypothesized that all positive and negative affect could be understood as a translation of bright and dull pressure sensations. His introspectionist subjects were aware that this is what they would feel, but on performing the introspections, they discovered a different quality. With introspection into smells and tastes, they reported:

Observer B: (Asafoetida) A general, soft diffuse pressure . . . (Caryophylline) Something like the glow of warmth that I feel in the warm sun. It's deeper than warmth. It is soft like warmth and a good deal like pressure too. (Jasmine) The pleasure is like an expansiveness somehow. It's linked up with a bodily state of a pressure sort. . . . (Caryophylline) I'm not ready to say that the pleasure swells; the experience swells and that swelling is attended by, or is, the pleasure. (Rose Geranium) "Massive" is a good word in the sense of spread out indefinitely. It seems to be bigger than my body, and my body is in it. (Vanillin) The spread is indefinite. There is something expansive without limits. . . . (Chocolate) It was a big swell.

Observer M: (Jasmine) There seemed to be a volume to it, and I don't know where I get the volume, for the only thing I get that I can talk about is the soft continuous pressure. It's vague and unlocalized and has no boundaries. . . . It feels as if there's a lot of stuff behind it, but not a surface. It's a deep thing. (Vanillin) It was a big, vague, misty something. It was uniform all the way through, no clouding about it . . . this deep something. [Nafe, 1924, pp. 518–527]

The "deep something" expressed the paradoxical feeling the observers had that although "pleasure" was at first localizable as a pressure originating in the chest cavity that expanded out and up, at a certain point the body percept vanished:

Observer M: (Bergamot) The pleasure is all around, but I don't know where, and I can't say where it ends. (Chocolate) I don't know where it was spread around; it occupied a lot of space but I don't know what space. (Asafoetida) These things are odd; they seem so definitely there that I feel I should be able to touch them, but the trouble is, you're not connected with them, you're not *there* in the sense that they are. (Glue) I think the thing that bothers me is the way I seem to be dissociated from the experience; that is, it seems just as real as a sensory quality, just as existential and just as independent of me, but as a conscious organism I'm not even there. (Jasmine) It's as senseless to talk about pressures you don't feel anywhere as about a color volume you don't see. If you could have a pressure out in the air, that would be it, not localized and with no reference to me. [Nafe, 1924, pp. 537–538]

Hunt also focused on one of the last major introspectionist studies done at Cornell, in which Raymond Cattell described the response of introspectors to the presentation of novel and unexpected visual, aural, gustatory, tactile, and olfactory stimuli. Cattell organized the various accounts to suggest that there were four stages of progressive subjectification:

Level 1: [ticking watch] It was subjective insofar as the sound was only vaguely localized as around my head and it was a tick rather than a watch. . . . [loud blast on mouth organ] unpleasant tone which could be said to be subjective in the sense of being *in* my head.

Level 2: [plaster model of gargoyle] Queer pleasure at the way the light grew, tinged with emotion of wonder. There was a distinct subjectivity as a result of feeling of admiration which changed the cognitive contemplation into a dreamy aesthetic experience in which reality and localization were lost.

Level 3: [gustatory: salt solution] A consciousness which was highly subjective in a sense, which I can only describe as "dreamlike," "unreal." . . . [cushion pressed on chest, solar plexus, abdomen] I fell once again into a passive state and the object and all reference disappeared so that I was only left with consciousness of pressure and some vague meanings that were read into it, making it a nightmare-like experi-ence. . . . [gustatory: sulphuric acid solution] The whole experience might be de-scribed as appearing like a solid lump of awareness in an otherwise fluid field of consciousness. . . . There was some visual synaesthesia—a black and yellow mass round which circled a number of clearer shapes.

Level 4: [odor: pyradine] The whole outside world seemed to have disappeared and it was a state. I can scarcely say "I" was a state for I seemed to lose my personality. There was only smelling. There was no objective reference and no subjective reference. [Cattell, quoted in Hunt, 1986, pp. 259–260]

It was obvious to Hunt that in their introspectionist protocols, Western experimental psychologists had finally stumbled on the same arena of con-sciousness as that cultivated in certain Eastern methods of meditation. Instead of viewing the fusion of subject and object, confusions in modality, and lack of reference to any concrete environment as a failure of the introspectionist method, Hunt saw them as indicators that provided crucial evidence of how perceptual schemata are transformed into thought. He dismissed the idea that synaesthetic building blocks might undergo continual assembly and recom-bination "underneath" consciousness. He also denied that synaesthesia had represented a stage of development—either of individuals or of the human race as a whole. No creature, he reasoned, whether human infant, archaic man, or lower vertebrate, can afford to be confused about what sensory modality is being stimulated, or even worse, to experience a world lacking any spatial or temporal order—as occurred in "Level 4" introspective states in Cattell's ob-servers. Hunt interpreted these sensations of spacelessness and timelessness as "background processes of perceptual and affective functioning which would not be experienced at all were they not exteriorized by the introspective attitude itself" (1986, p. 260). Recognizing that these states had all the attributes of metaphorically self-representational thought, Hunt concluded that they re-vealed the basic "mechanism" of thought.

In interpreting altered states of consciousness as demonstrations of the deep structure of human consciousness, he rejected Freudian and other reductionist views in which mystical experience was interpreted as regression to a primitive mentality. Neither did Hunt embrace the alternative view that mystical experience offered a glimpse at the future course of intellectual development, an interpretation that began with Maurice Bucke, F. W. H. Myers, and William James and runs through the psychologies of Jung, Maslow, and contemporary transpersonalism. Hunt's work brought him face to face with the numinous, and he found that universally, mystical ecstasy in all its myriad manifestations could also be explained as a complex synaesthesia, by means of his theory of consciousness. Even if introspection was an exercise in stilling the mind so that it could watch itself in action, the ultimate stilling of the mind was reached in the various mystical and meditative traditions when the meditator or mystic attempted to quiet the mind long enough to discover the meaning and order of "everything," not just a simple word or word problem as in classical introspection. The mystical literature—Buddhist, Hindu, Gnostic, Christian, indeed, the accounts of mystical ecstasy in all the great religious traditions—invariably describes the resulting insight, when it is successfully experienced, as a "white light of the void." Hunt reasoned that in the intense incubatory states of deep meditation, the degree of dissassembly and satiation of thought processes is at the maximum, and that the synaesthesia expressive of their eventual recombination must also be the most complete possible. Diffuse white light, as the most primitive quale of the visual system (itself the most structurally precise of the sensory modalities able to distinguish distance) is the most inclusive and abstract symbolic vehicle, and it thus occurs as the "answer" to the ultimate human question. In Hunt's words, "To translate the body sense into the empty light of three-dimensional space, as the ultimate answer to the openness of time ahead, may well be to achieve a sense of reconciled and complete understanding of anything that happens" (Hunt, 1986, p. 265). The other complex synaesthesia accompanying mystical ecstasy occurs when the meditator's body becomes kinaesthetically fused with the white light, resulting in a metaphorical annihilation or "snuffing out." The inevitable result of the structural translation of the body image into luminosity is the feeling of death. The seemingly opposite metaphors of the Western mystical tradition—"enlightenment"— and the Buddhist and Hindu traditions—*nirvana*, Sanskrit for "a blowing out," for instance, of the flame of life—can be seen as equally apt phenomenological descriptions of the complex synaesthesia of the mystical union. In archaic shamanic traditions, the same complex synaesthesiae are described as dismemberment (Hunt, 1989, pp. 487–488). Here was the *mysterium tremendum,* the dread Holy; the metaphoric death preceding rebirth was nothing but a complex synaesthesia:

> The *microgenesis* of luminosity—and its unfolding from stages of open glow to geometric contour to specific form—is the perfect vehicle for "insight" into an all-encompassing, "emanating" source outside space and time, that paradoxically (and this also fits with the introspectionist accounts of glow and lustre) is both light and dark at once, and that simultaneously contains and gives rise to all specific forms. The more microgenetically preliminary the perceptual dimension, the more abstract its potential symbolic reference when reused and synaesthetically embodied as metaphor. The synaesthetic embodiment of "glow" would present and evoke an overt *sense* of everything-at-once and constitute the metaphoric vehicle for the sense of an all-encompassing metaphysical absolute common to various cultural traditions.[2]

Hunt's insights suggest why synaesthesia has been such an irresistible idea for so many people; if they had experienced simple synaesthesiae under hypnosis (Baudelaire), hallucinogens (Rimbaud, Baudelaire, Arguelles, and McKenna), or as their given cognitive style (Nabokov and Shereshevsky), there was a good chance that they had also experienced the sort of complex synaesthesiae that Hunt described. The compelling feeling of portent expressed in Baudelaire's correspondences, Nabokov's potustoronnost, Virginia Woolf's epiphanies, Shereshevsky's sense that "something particularly fine was about to happen," and Kandinsky's, Arguelles's, and McKenna's expectations of the advent of a synaesthetic New Age all had as their psychological substrate the complex synaesthesia in which one's sense of personal subjectivity is lost and yet some form of consciousness is retained. Perhaps the reason that synaesthesia so often became a vehicle for Promethean fantasies was that it carried the feeling of finality, of escape from the body, escape from time, escape from the familiar divisions of the five senses—our link to the physical world. Hunt's theories reveal that what the Symbolists and their followers understood as a "lifting of the veil," or what McKenna took to be "out there" in hyperspace, existed in their minds. But Hunt also believes that the "numinous" underlies all thought. McKenna's declaration that the DMT experience is "the most idiosyncratic thing there is" rings true: *thought* is idiosyncratic. Psychedelic drugs, meditation, and introspection merely make it "visible" or "audible" or "palpable," and generally all of these at once, so that it is often unclear to the perceiver through which modality the uncanny is being experienced.

A NEW ROMANTIC METAPHOR: SYNAESTHESIA
AS THE SUBSTRATE OF THE EMOTIONAL SELF

Hunt's interpretation that the experience of "felt meaning" is an abstract pre-sentational metaphor based on synaesthesia has gained as few adherents among contemporary psychologists as Wheeler and Cutsforth's work did in their day. His 1989 book, *The Multiplicity of Dreams,* introduced his theory to psychologists interested in dream research, but although his papers on the wider dimensions of synaesthesia and consciousness have appeared in the journal *Perceptual and Motor Skills,* they have attracted little notice from the mainstream American psychological community. Hunt's work was completely unknown to neurologist Richard E. Cytowic, who, in his book *Synesthesia: A Union of the Senses* (1989), advanced the first new theory for a mechanism of synaesthesia to appear in more than half a century. Cytowic's book was also the first scientific study of synaesthesia since the early twentieth century to include observations of a relatively large number of actual synaesthetes. He encountered his first two subjects by chance, but eventually, in response to popular media coverage of Cytowic's presentations on synaesthesia at professional meetings, forty other idiopathic synaesthetes made contact with him. From interviews conducted with the forty-two synaesthetes, Cytowic gathered information on demography (age, sex, and education), cognitive characteristics (incidence and family history of left-handedness, memory ability, mathematical aptitude, sense of direction), and descriptions of each subject's type of synaesthesia. A majority of the subjects were colored hearers, but Cytowic also found many individuals with forms for numbers, one person with "visual smell," another with "geometrically shaped pain," and three "polymodal" synaesthetes. His "composite" portrait of the individual synaesthete was "a left-handed female, who feels alienated, has a cosmic *Weltanschauung* and a feeling of portentousness that at any moment something quite special will happen to her. Artistic, creative, and sensitive, she runs the emotional gamut from the highest of the highs to the lowest of the lows. She feels, and is, highly intelligent and intuitive, yet there is an abstruseness that may cause others to perceive her as 'dense'" (Cytowic, 1993, p. 49).

Cytowic here referred to the same distress experienced by Shereshevsky and also alluded to by Cutsforth—the occasional tendency of synaesthetic percepts to overwhelm thought and thus hinder communication. The experience of the cosmic perspective in all likelihood reflects states of depersonalization. Hunt identified the experience of depersonalization as a frequent concomitant of introspection, and Nabokov also described it repeatedly in his writings. Among his forty-two subjects, Cytowic found seven who had routinely had paranormal experiences, from precognition and psychokinesis to "the feeling of a presence," which the synaesthete tentatively supposed to be angels. Although Cytowic at first suggested that such experiences "are best left to speak for themselves," he offered his own explanation, likening these synaesthetes' clairvoyant and pre-cognitive feelings to the *déjà vu* and *déjà vécu* (feeling of already having lived through it).

Cytowic emphasized the emotional component of synaesthesia. His comment on this final diagnostic criterion ("There is an unshakable conviction and sense of validity that what the synesthete perceives is real. There is often a 'Eureka' sensation, such as when we have an insight") is reminiscent of Wheeler and Cutsforth's observations regarding the sense of "felt meaning" during synaesthesia, and also of Hunt's hypothesis that the feeling of novelty underlying thought *is* a complex synaesthesia. Cytowic believed that the strong emotional component of synaesthesia indicated that the limbic system might be the "site" of synaesthesia. The limbic system is thought to mediate emotion and memory and is also the part of the brain that allows it to combine sensory information. Cytowic therefore advanced the theory that synaesthetes are "cog-nitive fossils." Cytowic argued that synaesthesia is "more mammalian" than language, for "synesthetic perception is more fundamental to what it means to be a mammal in this world than is ascribing high-level semantic meaning to things."[3]

The aspect of synaesthesia that Cytowic, a nonsynaesthete, found most compelling was the sense of certainty that synaesthetes had about their per-cepts. Interpreting it as further evidence of limbic system involvement, he ascribed that feeling to limbic "intuition" rather than to the rational "knowing" of the neocortex. He synthesized his observations about the implication of the limbic system in synaesthesia by drawing on Paul MacLean's (1973) theory of the "triune brain," in which he posited that three types of "systems" are found in the brain of mammals—reptilian, paleomammalian, and neomammalian. According to MacLean, the reptilian brain, or "R-complex," is the core of the nervous system, consisting of the upper spinal cord, midbrain, diencephalon, and basal ganglia, and is an evolutionary legacy from Therapsid (mammal-like) reptiles that became extinct in the Triassic period. This "instinctual" brain is the home of the stereotyped behaviors relating to territoriality, foraging, breed-ing, and social dominance. The next system in the brain hierarchy, the paleomammalian brain, represented an advance in the mammal's ability to adapt to the environment as well as in the integration of external and internal stimuli. In MacLean's triune brain scheme, the paleomammalian brain essentially corresponds to the limbic system—of interest to Cytowic because of its role in emotion and sensory integration. Cytowic cited studies, including MacLean's, that implicated disruptions of the limbic system in experiences during altered states of consciousness, particularly experiences associated with intuitions of "fundamental truths, feelings of depersonalization, hallucinations, paranoid feelings, and synesthesia" (Cytowic, 1989, p. 174). All these feelings, Cytowic noted, have been documented as occurring during epileptic seizures. The brain structure that "produces" these experiences is the hippocampus, a principal component of the limbic system; the hippocampus is also the nexus for nerve pathways bearing diverse external and internal stimuli. Taking these two functions into account, Cytowic was convinced that synaesthesia was a function of the hippocampus. In Cytowic's view, synaesthetes, because of the relative predominance in their cognitive processes of an evolutionarily older brain structure, might offer clues about the evolution of the mammalian cortex (pp. 175–176).

The neomammalian brain, the expansion of the frontal cortex that has occurred to some degree in primates but most fully in human beings, acts as a kind of foil, in Cytowic's application of MacLean's theory. It is the site of rationality, with all its distancing and alienating tendencies:

> The limbic system in the advanced mammal, such as the human, retains its status as the terminal stage of information processing, that stage for suppressing automatic preexisting biases in favor of newer alternatives to express themselves and where value, purpose, attention, and memory are calculated. This organ for calculating valence, to use a more neutral term, could have had either of two fates. It could have been replaced and suppressed by neocortex, which is to say that one's calculations of value and bias are now to be suppressed by higher calculations, a "better" organ for determining meaning and purpose. That seems to be the quintessential delusion of the intellectual in our midst. He thinks that the goal of thought is to suppress limbic system functions. [1989, pp. 21–22]

Believing that "people who make their choices 'emotionally' . . . are more human than those who make them rationally," Cytowic saw synaesthesia as "a short-cut way of calculating realities, of attaching significance to things" (1989, p. 22). It is possible that Cytowic's emphasis on the synaesthesia–emotion–limbic system triad originated with Paul MacLean. Cytowic recounted that in 1983, after hearing Cytowic present a paper, MacLean had suggested that the hippocampus was the possible anatomical locus of synaesthesia. MacLean had also given Cytowic a reprint of an article in which he tentatively offered this same explanation (Cytowic, 1989, p. 167). In the 1970s and 1980s, when Mac-Lean's triune brain theory was extremely popular and commonly cited as biological evidence that human emotionality was preferable to rationality, MacLean himself had speculated on the social consequences of the paleomammalian brain's continuing role in human behavior. Cytowic was sympathetic to the calls for tempering reason with emotion, and he saw his own approach to neurology as bridging the gap between two cultures. In *Synesthesia: A Union of the Senses,* he repeatedly dwells on the importance and validity of the subjective. He acknowledges its role in scientific work and extols the subjective capacity to make the world more meaningful through art. One chapter contains a long digression on geometry, color, form, and divine proportion and concludes with a section entitled "Personal Visions Arising from the Synaesthetic Sense." Cytowic, in discussing Olivier Messiaen and some of Cytowic's own synaesthetic subjects, including painter and theatrical designer David Hockney, pointed with admiration to the creative use they had made of their synaesthesia and celebrated their ability to describe "visions that transcend what we ordinarily know" (p. 282). (Cytowic mistakenly also included Rimbaud, Kandinsky, and Scriabin in his discussion of artistic synaesthetes.) In the chapter "What is Real?" Cytowic considered various illusions in an attempt to respond to the frequent objection that synaesthesia is not "real." Despite his objections to "New Age" views of synaesthesia, Cytowic lent his own imprimatur to the transcendental interpretation.[4]

Synaesthesia has by now been largely purged of its earlier associations with religion (by way of Swedenborgian "correspondences") and the occult (through the equation of the synaesthetic photisms with astral representations). Yet during the modern upsurge in interest that has spanned the decades from McLuhan to McKenna, synaesthesia has continued to fulfill a popular longing for metaphors of transcendence. Meanwhile, science still is attempting to determine the location of this elusive phenomenon, in the brain or some other part of the human sensory "wiring."

Romantics have credited synaesthesia, in both its psilocybin-induced and naturally occurring forms, with revealing the falsity of the most tenaciously held values of the dominant culture: that we live in a material universe animated ultimately by physical processes and that the empirical truth can be discerned through intellectual application. And yet it has been science— Wheeler and Cutsforth's, in particular—that has most accurately described the phenomena of synaesthesia and provided sound empirical evidence to bolster Romantics' unflagging intuition that cognition is a warmly affective act, not a cold mechanical reaction.

The original Romantic visions of expanded consciousness, and the subsequent historical frameworks outlining the evolution of consciousness, have uniformly reached toward that which is as yet unseen, or seen by only a few. With each phenomenon that seemingly appears from beyond the veil, the same question arises: What is the location of that particular subjective mental image? This issue has been badly bungled by Romantic interpreters of synaesthesia. For more than a century, synaesthesia, a rare mental phenomenon, but entirely one of this world, has been given otherworldly status. The numinous quality of synaesthetic (and eidetic) mental images has repeatedly encouraged the impression that synaesthesia pointed to some transcendental Other. At worst, this mistaking of the mundane for the absolute has contributed to the failure of the Romantic initiative to transform human consciousness; at best, synaesthesia has served as a viable metaphor that has helped bridge the gap between materialist and nonmaterialist conceptions of consciousness. Synaesthetes, however, encounter no invisible beings—merely a visible (or touchable or tastable) representation of their own mental processes.

Even when viewed as fanciful myth or metaphor rather than a fallacy of misplaced concreteness, the Romantic interpretation of synaesthesia and eideticism as forms of transcendental knowledge has served to derail rather than advance the philosophical ideals of spirit over matter, imagination over reason. The popular Romantic image of synaesthesia has functioned as a sort of ersatz mystery, a stand-in for truly transcendental knowledge. Romantic celebrants of synaesthesia never investigated it by applying an epistemologically sound theory of consciousness, even though such a theory had made its debut in the West nearly simultaneously with the beginning of the scientific and extrascientific interest in synaesthesia. The "Theosophical Enlightenment" that began in the 1870s essentially updated humanity's longest-held theory of nature—that man's physical form is merely the reflection of subtler bodies that derive from and are interpenetrated by the spiritual world. Universally, the human being and the study of human anatomy have been seen as the key to the nature of God and the universe. This is the ancient esoteric understanding that became so diluted in the hands of the Symbolists. When Wassily Kandinsky, Sixten Ringbom, and other students of Theosophical and anthroposophical texts imbibed their exegeses of the subtle bodies, they did so somewhat selectively and incompletely, borrowing only those portions of occult doctrines which would help to support their aesthetic and intellectual aims. Though drawn to the superficial similarities between descriptions of the astral plane and the colored visions of synaesthetes, Kandinsky, Ringbom, and others paid little attention to the elaborate details of occult theories of the body.

Not one of the occult interpreters of synaesthesia and eideticism ever mentioned the element posited by esoteric theories as intermediate between the physical and astral bodies—the etheric body. The etheric body or "life body" is, according to one modern account (Rudolf Steiner's *An Outline of Occult Science* [1910]), "an independent member of the human entity, that prevents the physical substances and forces during life from taking their own path, leading to dissolution of the physical body" (p. 23). Steiner constantly clarified both the terms "etheric"—distinct in his application of the word from physicists' use of "ether"—and "body." He stressed that there was nothing physical or material about this etheric or life body; like a body, though, it had shape and form. (Theosophy, borrowing the Hindu terminology, called the etheric body *linga sharira;* and *prana, chi* [*ki*], *mana,* even Wilhelm Reich's "orgone" are analogous terms for the etheric principle). Steiner conceives of the etheric body as the bearer of both life and memory. Like humans, plants and animals possess an etheric organization in addition to their physical constitution. The additional members, which are not possessed by nonhuman living beings—the astral body, absent in plants, and the ego, absent in animals—interact with the etheric to "produce" consciousness in human beings. (The chakras are the sites of interaction between the astral body and the etheric.)

According to Theosophical conceptions, the shift in consciousness that was purported to have begun in the late nineteenth century, away from materialism toward a perception of the supersensible, was based on a change in the relation of the etheric body to the physical and astral bodies. Humanity's mastery of the physical world—and eventually, by the nineteenth century, Western insistence on the sole reality of the physical world—were regarded as coinciding with the period in which the etheric body was most tightly bound to the physical body, thus preventing any cognizance of the supersensible. Theosophy's new age—Kandinsky's "Great Spiritual"—was marked by the etheric body's gradual loosening from its physical fetters, which would bring about a series of predictable physiological and psychological changes in human beings. Although at first those changes would be apparent in only a few individuals, they were expected to become increasingly common.

For all the Romantics' mistaken assertions about the cause and significance of synaesthesia and eideticism, one of their expectations seems to have been borne out—that synaesthesia and eideticism would become increasingly common as humans moved into the new age. Some recent studies estimate that the incidence of synaesthesia is now one in two thousand among the adult population (Yoon, 1997, p. 25). It seems unlikely that this apparent upsurge is entirely a result of more comprehensive reporting. Contrary to Romantic expectations, however, the increase in synaesthesia and eideticism has hardly coincided with any millennial escape from nature and history. The supposedly evolutionarily advanced are still fully engaged in the physical world, muddling their way toward eternity like their nonsynaesthetic and noneidetic neighbors. The case study literature continues to pose challenges for Romantic interpreters of these phenomena. As I was finishing this book, I happened to pick up a copy of Oliver Sacks's book *An Anthropologist on Mars* (1995), because I was aware of his interest in Temple Grandin and her revelations about autism. The very first chapter, "The Case of the Colorblind Painter," tells the story of a sixty-five-year-old artist who, after suffering a concussion when he was struck by a truck, awoke with cerebral achromatopsia, the sort of neurological mystery for the analysis of which Sacks's writing has become justifiably famous. The artist, "Mr. I," who had worked with Georgia O'Keeffe, painted Hollywood backdrops in the 1940s, and been a member of the New York group of Abstract Expressionists in the 1950s, lost all color vision—a man whose life work was to witness and celebrate *color*. In passing, Sacks noted that before the accident, the man had had color hearing for music; after the accident, it too was gone. Sacks's second account is of another artist, Franco Magnani, who, after suffering from a mysterious illness accompanied by a high fever some thirty years ago, suddenly became possessed by eidetic images of Pontito, the Tuscan hill town of his childhood. Like Vladimir Nabokov, Magnani hears the sounds, smells the smells, feels the textures of his natal landscape, in episodes that are like seizures. Sacks notes the similarity of Magnani's images to the sort elicited by Wilder Penfield when he electrically stimulated the brains of patients with temporal-lobe epilepsy. Magnani's images also resemble Shereshevsky's and autistic savants' "verbatim" memories.

The central character in Sacks's chapter "Prodigies" is Stephen Wiltshire. Wiltshire, another visual artist, is also autistic; at age eight, though completely incapable of abstract reasoning, he could instantaneously grasp and retain, then (as well as much later) effortlessly reproduce, the most complex visual, auditory, motor, and verbal patterns, irrespective of their context and meaning. This spectacular memory was paired with an equally spectacular artistic ability; two best-selling books of Stephen Wiltshire's artwork were published before he was sixteen. In 1993, prodigious musical powers "erupted" in Stephen, on the level of those in the musical autistic savants described earlier. In ruminating on the suddenness with which extraordinary abilities are apt to appear or disappear, Sacks mentions Vladimir Nabokov's autobiographical account of losing his calendar calculating ability after suffering from a high fever with delirium at the age of seven. A few autistic individuals, after taking certain prescription drugs (such as Tegretol), lose their eidetic and synaesthetic capacities altogether. The apparent role of shocks and high fevers in synaesthesia and eideticism calls for new scientific exploration. Sacks makes one other provocative incidental observation. Traveling by airplane with Stephen Wiltshire to New York City, Wiltshire's teacher witnessed an event that Wiltshire had told him about in recounting a dream the previous day; Wiltshire had had an image of being invited up into the cockpit as they flew over the Manhattan skyline, an eidetic image of the future event as it came to pass. The coincidence of precognitive and telepathic events with synaesthesia and eideticism cries out for more serious study.

A recent book by the Dutch psychologist and art therapist Ron Dunselman, *In Place of the Self: How Drugs Work,* suggests the fruitfulness of considering synaesthesia and eideticism within an interpretive framework that acknowledges the subtle bodies. Dunselman only incidentally deals with synaesthesia, within the context of his discussion of the effects of LSD, but his discussion points the way to an approach that is empirical, while still holding to the premise that the human being is first and foremost a *spiritual* being. Dunselman views the effects of a whole range of drugs—tobacco, alcohol, marijuana, hashish, opium, cocaine, morphine, heroin, LSD, XTC—through the lens of the subtle bodies, as understood in Rudolf Steiner's spiritual science. The key to understanding LSD's effects is the concept of the etheric body as the bearer of life; the consequence of the separation of the etheric body from the physical is death. Dunselman suggests that people who ingest LSD—which is derived from the highly toxic substance ergot—actually "die" to some extent, that is, their physical bodies experience a temporary and incomplete separation from their life-bearing etheric bodies. (All of the other drugs that are known to produce synaesthesia and eideticism—hashish, psilocybin mushrooms, fly agaric, peyote, mescaline, and MDMA—are also toxic and presumably have the same effect on the etheric body.) The coincidence of certain aspects of the phenomenology of the near-death experience with that of LSD intoxication—particularly the perception of the subjects as "leaving" their body—may possibly support such an interpretation (1995, p. 53). The descriptive literature about autobiographical reports of LSD trips is replete with language that indicates that subjects have had near-death experiences. The literature on both LSD and NDE also contains descriptions of the "life review"—the rapid, sometimes instantaneous, panoramic visual retrospective of the subject's life.

Rudolf Steiner maintained that the etheric body is the repository of all our impressions of the physical world; and that storehouse becomes available at or near death, when, liberated from its role of sustaining the physical body, the etheric body gives itself up to the astral body, which turns the stored memories into vivid pictures. Vladimir Nabokov's fever-induced out-of-body experience and the fever that precipitated Franco Magnani's eidetic abilities would be instances in which the shock of a life-threatening condition led to a loosening of the etheric body. But the typical eidetic receives no such shock; his condition exists from an early age and may persist throughout life. Such individuals may possess etheric bodies that are relatively more independent of the physical body than those of noneidetics. If the concept of subtle bodies is theoretically useful in understanding eidetic imagery, in what way can it help to explain syn-aesthesia? In Dunselman's work on the effects of LSD, he draws on the litera-ture of Steiner's spiritual science for a further differentiation of the etheric body into four distinct principles (1995, pp. 57–61): etheric (or "ethereal") form, which creates the geometric order of matter in crystal formations and which is often visualized during LSD trips as fantastic multicolored geometric hallu-cinations; chemical (or "sound") ether, the order-producing principle in liquid matter, LSD-induced perceptions of which inspired the light shows and lava lamps of the 1960s (and more recently, liquid TV); etheric light (or "conscious-ness")—the universally reported "white light" of LSD literature, and quite possibly that of mystical literature, as well—which is conceived of in anthro-posophical science as forming the link with the astral body; and etheric heat, the medium through which the spiritual world intersects the physical, sensed by some LSD users as a presence of the numinous, of God. Dunselman con-cludes that in LSD intoxication, it is principally the chemical ether and etheric light that become separated from the physical body (p. 61). Despite this differ-entiation, there is no sharp demarcation between the four etheric principles, and frequently the etheric forces released by the effects of LSD connect with the senses at several places at once and produce synaesthetic perceptions.

After quoting from an account of someone experiencing synaesthesia while listening to music under the influence of LSD, Dunselman concludes:

> Several senses are stimulated by the extra forces of ethereal light (consciousness) which are released; the stimulation of one sense immediately evokes 'responses' or

sensations in other senses, because the ethereal body works in several places and is potentially present everywhere. Even slight stimulation of just one of the senses immediately evokes reactions in the ethereal bodies of the other senses because of the presence of extra ethereal forces. The astral body connected to these senses then translates the stimulation into sensory perceptions. [1995, pp. 67–68]

Dunselman also attributes the hyperaesthesia of LSD to the release of etheric forces; the astral body, or consciousness, much more readily receives sensory impressions once the etheric body has been loosened, and sensations are magnified. If a loosening of the etheric body accounts for the autistic individual's synaesthesia and eideticism, perhaps it also is responsible for the painful heightening of sensations so typical of autism.

From G. T. L. Sachs, the albino physician who first heroically reported his synaesthetic perceptions, to the anonymous Parisian who composed a paean to the colors created by passing railway cars, to the individuals described in Oliver Sacks's remarkable case studies, synaesthetes and eidetics have faithfully described the landscapes of their thoughts. For more than a century, a wide range of thinkers of Romantic sensibility have seized on these mental landscapes as harbingers of the redemption of human consciousness from a deadening rationalism and materialism yet have repeatedly failed to offer a persuasive scientific accounting of these psychological mysteries. Frequently their excessive enthusiasm for transcendental human faculties has led to obfuscation and error rather than bringing the vision of synaesthetes and eidetics into the clear light of trained and reasoned observation. Synaesthesia and eideticism may yet become a bridge to a theory of consciousness and its evolution that redeems the human psyche from materialist views, but they will do so only as subjects of an enlightened empiricism, a Romanticism come of age. Esoteric theories of consciousness, the very theories that have for so long been employed by Romantics who have falsely seen the bright colors of synaesthesia and eideticism, may yet help to see them true.

Notes

INTRODUCTION

1. Cytowic, 1989, p. 1. Though the term is frequently spelled "synesthesia," I will use "synaesthesia" throughout this work. This was the original spelling of the word and it continues to be the most common spelling outside the United States. Lawrence E. Marks, a psychologist who has studied synaesthesia for more than twenty years, defines it as "the transposition of sensory images or sensory attributes from one modality to another" (Marks, 1978, p. 8).

2. Letter to editor from Peter C. Lynn, *New York Times* January 6, 1991, p. 4. The other letter was from *New York Times* art critic Jack Anderson, who also related his childhood discovery of his absolute pitch, along with his chromaesthesia, which like that of most synaesthetes, also communicated an emotional quality. Anderson said that he "occasionally fantasize[s] that keys have personalities. Thus for me, D Major is warm and golden."

3. In Simon Baron-Cohen's recent study, for example, nine of his ten synaesthetic subjects were women, and after he was interviewed on a radio program about synaesthesia, of 212 people who called or wrote to identify themselves as synaesthetes, 210 were women. When questioned about other family members who had color hearing, they mentioned only mothers or sisters (Baron-Cohen, Goldstein, and Wyke, 1993, pp. 423–424). The other contemporary researcher who has worked with many synaesthetic subjects, Richard Cytowic, has also noted this gender difference (1989, p. 33).

4. Locke [1690], 1961, vol. 2, p. 30. Two possible explanations contradictory to Locke's reasoning exist: 1) this blind man was synaesthetic, and actually "saw" a red photism at the sound of the trumpet, or 2) he took the testimony of sighted people and created his own subjective, yet intuitively apt, metaphor. On the Molyneux problem, see Morgan, 1977.

5. For information about Castel and his invention, see Mason, 1958; Goethe [1810], 1970, pp. 166, 73.

6. Each year the *MLA Bibliography* cites dozens of scholarly articles that examine so-called synaesthesia in various poets, artists, etc. For a broad survey of the sorts of interpretations of synaesthesia contained in this literature, see Campana, 1981; Ruddick, 1984; Harper, 1989.

7. Examples of synaesthetic photisms are taken from Wheeler, 1930, pp. 358–386 (voice and instrument photisms), 372–373; Wheeler and Cutsforth, 1922b, p. 371 (consonant photism). See Simpson and McKellar, 1955, for a similar typological breakdown.

8. Ahsen, 1977a, p. 6. Another recent definition of eideticism can be found in Marks and McKellar, 1982, p. 1: "any mental imagery projected into the sensory environment which cannot be attributed to a material change in sensory input and which is known to the imager to be subjective. . . . Eidetic imagery is characteristically autonomous, constructive and dynamic, displaying natural progressions and movement." Almost all the experimental and theoretical work on eidetic imagery has focused on visual images, although there has been some experimental work on other senses. The early literature on eideticism sometimes used the term "eidetic image" to refer to other than visual images. See Haber, 1979, p. 620.

9. The literature on "synaesthesia" (i.e., intersensory metaphor) in Romantic poetry is enormous. For a representative example, see O'Malley, 1964.

CHAPTER 1: THE FASCINATION WITH SYNAESTHESIA

1. That Sachs gave no clinical term for the phenomenon and cited no previous works on the subject suggests that his was indeed the first published description. For a review in English of Sachs's dissertation, see Krohn, 1892.

2. Though Müller deals at length with intersensory relations in this work, he makes no mention of Sachs's or any other cases of chromaesthesia.

3. Millet took "synesthésie" from Alfred Vulpian, who in 1874 had given that name to "secondary sensations produced under the influence of a primitive sensation, which is provoked by an exterior or interior sensation." ("Moelle épinière (Physiologie)" in A. Dechambre, ed., 1874, vol. 8, p. 527. Vulpian had also used the term in an earlier work (1866, pp. 274–291) using the term. But in his description of synesthésies, Vulpian included such phenomena as the "photic response" sneeze and the sensation of nausea caused by pressing on the palate.

4. On German Romantics and entoptic phenomena, see Burwick, 1986, pp. 50–79. Burwick's discussion is not entirely clear with regard to the distinction between the various types of entoptic phenomena; he seems to confuse "afterimages" with other subjective visual sensations.

5. Littré, 1865, p. 1241. Most contemporary medical dictionaries retain "synaesthesia" as an

entry, along with "synaesthesialgia," a pain that gives rise to a subjective sensation in a different modality.

6. Marc Legrand's poem is quoted in René Etiemble, 1952, p. 457. The translation is mine; unless otherwise indicated, subsequent translations from the French are also mine.

7. On the "Song of Songs" performance, see Henderson, 1971, and Rudorff, 1972, p. 190; on synthesis in the sense discussed here see Rookmaaker, [1959] 1992, pp. 176–186.

8. Etiemble, 1952: Gourmont is quoted on p. 83; Delahaye and Verlaine are quoted on p. 96; the anonymous quotation appears on p. 459. Etiemble's chapter on "Voyelles" is filled with evidence of just how much of a sensation the poem was, both in artistic and popular culture, in France and elsewhere in Europe. According to Etiemble, "from 1890 to 1905 or 1910, they never stopped speaking about it" (p. 82).

9. Alexandre Axenfeld, *Traité des névroses* (Germer-Ballière: Paris, 1883); Charles Féré, "La famille neuropathique," *Archives neurologiques* 7 (1884): 1–43, 173–191; Ferdinand Brunetière, "Symbolistes et décadents," *Revue des deux mondes,* November 1, 1888, pp. 213–226; Cesare Lombroso, *L'homme de génie,* translated from the Italian *L'uomo delinquente* (Alcan: Paris, 1889).

10. René Etiemble (1968, p. 125), for example, listed six pre-Rimbaud and six post-Rimbaud authors and their vowel colors; none of the predecessors' associations agreed with Rimbaud's, while three of the post-1883 authors had associations identical to Rimbaud's; for Flournoy, see 1893, pp. 240–241; Edouard Claparède (1900) was also concerned with distinguishing true idiopathic synaesthetes—"les vrais voyants"—from "les suggestionnées."

11. Chulkov, 1904, p. 13; the Stevenson story is quoted in Fraser-Harris, 1928, p. 11; Charlotte Felkin, *The Subjection of Isabel Carnaby* (New York: Dodd and Mead, 1906); Richard Pryce, *Christopher* (London: Hutchinson, 1911); Compton Mackenzie, *Youth's Encounter* (New York: Appleton, 1913).

12. Though there are a number of fairly complete bibliographies from which to draw conclusions about the chronological progress of research on synaesthesia, the estimate here is drawn from a chart plotting articles on audition colorée between 1870 and 1926 in Friedrich Mahling, "Das Farbe-Ton-Problem und die selbständige Farbe-Ton-Forschung als Exponenten gegewärtigen Geistesstrebens" (in Lott et al, 1929). According to Mahling's chart, the other two peak years of publication are 1893 (twenty-six papers) and 1925 (thirty-five papers).

13. D'Udine, 1910, p. 39; Clérambault, 1942, p. 703 (quoted in Gordon, 1992, p. 227). Although Gordon's work recovers some poorly known and fascinating aspects of early French psychiatric theory, the discussion of Clérambault's work is hampered by her confusion of "synaesthesia" in Vulpian and Clérambault's sense with the more widely accepted meaning: "The analogy between synesthesia and hysteria is, of course, natural, since both hinge on metaphor. In the former as artistic experience, sound can equal color, odor can equal touch, and so forth; in the latter, the 'wandering womb' makes strangulations of the throat or paralysis of the leg metaphors for the repressed sensation in the sexual organs" (p. 227). In German psychoanalytic circles, synaesthesia was also often seen as pathological: see Hug-Hellmuth, 1912; Pfister, 1912; also Eduard Hitschmann, who is cited in Wellek, 1930.

14. For example, Alfred Ulrich (1903), says that his subject, Ernest, was "born in 1878 to a family of neuropaths but is still a robust and healthy boy" (p. 180). Binet and Beaunis (1892) say that "Mr. X" is "of a nervous temperament" (p. 330). J. Philippe's (1893) "Dr. X" is "a little nervous and subject to periods of depression and sadness" (p. 331).

15. The word "occult" seems to create problems for most everyone who encounters it. In the Middle Ages "occult science" or "occultism" referred primarily to what became known as the physical sciences; at that time, the physical world was as yet unknown, i.e., "occult." The triumph of the physical sciences and philosophic materialism turned what had once been occult into "science," and the word "occultism" into a synonym for contact with the sinister world beyond the reach of objective perception. Mysticism and esotericism are considered subjective in the light of science, and hence "occult." Owen Barfield makes this wonderful comment about "the detested word 'occult'": "an hour or two's receptive reading would be enough to reveal that . . . the word signifies no more than what a more conventionally phrased cosmogony [than contemporary occult sciences such as theosophy and anthroposophy] would determine as 'non-phenomenal,' 'noumenal,' 'transcendental.' Yet, for some reason, it seems almost useless to point this out. It will be the same after you have finished as before you began. Uttered, the term 'occult' will signify 'concealed' (from the senses, because by definition not accessible to the senses, because by definition noumenal): heard, it will still signify 'secret' (because witchery)!" (Barfield, 1966, p. 18).

16. Raynaud, 1888, reprinted in Michaud, 1947, pp. 84–85. Raynaud's concept that material vibrations were the cause of sensory analogies was widely shared and was formalized in the theories of Charles Féré.

17. Segalen, 1981 (originally published in the *Mercure de France* 148 (1902): 57–90), pp. 28, 32, 45. Segalen later recanted his allegiance to synaesthesia in a number of "palinodies."

18. Pommier, 1932 (1967), p. 14. Only rarely do literary commentators on synaesthesia offer explicit explanations of how it is that nonsynaesthetic writers experience the synaesthesiae chronicled in their writings. Pommier here gives voice to the widely held assumption that some poets and other artists can occasionally reach an exalted state of consciousness where synesthesiae occur. June Downey (1912), an early student of literary synaesthesia, makes a similar romantic observation; noting that synaesthesia occasionally occurs in nonsynaesthetes during high fevers, she suggests that poets experience synaesthesia in the "fever of inspiration" (p. 497).

19. Wellek, 1965, p. 444. Recognizing that many students of Symbolism have mistakenly taken synaesthesia to be its central device and that this has caused some to suspect all Symbolist works as "decadent and pathological," Wellek defended Baudelaire against such criticism, denying that synaesthesia was an important technique in his work (p. 445).

20. It is perhaps artificial to separate the "aesthetic" and the "religious," especially in late nineteenth-century Europe, where art was increasingly vested with religious power. In addition, the occult religious view of synaesthesia was well established in French aesthetic theory. For an overview of aesthetic theories in late nineteenth-century France, see Mustoxidi, 1920, with the appended chronological bibliography of French works

on aesthetics up until 1914. Beginning about 1885, the titles suggest a distinct mix of aestheticism, psychology, and occultism.

CHAPTER 2: A TRANSCENDENTAL LANGUAGE OF COLOR

1. Both "Spiritualist" and "Theosophical" are used here as names for widespread nineteenth-century religious and intellectual movements. The lowercase variants of both words refer to more general systems of speculative mysticism.

2. For a brief review of the replacement of older ideas of "mind" and "soul" with the term "consciousness," see Patrick, 1911; Müller, 1887, p. 145.

3. Bucke, 1898 (1901), p. 3; p. 51. Another Whitman devotee, the Englishman Edward Carpenter, preceded Bucke slightly with his own exegesis of the evolution of consciousness, *From Adam's Peak to Elephanta* (1892).

4. Myers, 1903, vol. 1, p. 19. For biographical information on Myers and an assessment of his work, see Cerullo, 1982. Reprints of Myers's American counterpart William James's reviews of *Human Personality* and his tribute to Myers can be found in James, [1901] 1986b.

5. Blavatsky, [1885–1888] 1978–1979, vol. 3, p. 215. Some sense that this "magpie-like accumulation of mysticism, tall stories, and archaeology" (Webb, 1971, p. 46) is really the first modern esoteric examination of the evolution of consciousness is apparent from the index: there are nearly 150 separate entries under "consciousness" and more than 400 under "evolution." For an excellent overview of both Blavatsky and Theosophical ideas, see Carlson, 1993. Carlson accepts the prevalent view that Theosophy "evolved out of" Spiritualism (p. 29); for an alternative interpretation, see Steiner, 1973; Harrison, 1993; Prokofieff, 1993; and Johnson, 1990.

6. Freudenberg, 1908, quoted in Kandinsky, [1912] 1982, vol. 1, p. 44. Sixten Ringbom makes the observation about Kandinsky's underlining the passage in the Freudenberg article—see Tuchman, 1986, p. 132.

7. Kandinsky, [1912] 1947, p. 44. Zakharin-Unkovskaia, a member of the Kaluga branch of the Russian Theosophical Society (closely allied with Rudolf Steiner's Theosophical practice), was a professional violinist who knew many of Europe's leading artists and musicians.

8. Besant and Leadbeater, [1901] 1961, p. 58, quoted in Ringbom, 1966, p. 399. Ringbom pointed out that he was not the first to link Kandinsky's abstract paintings to Theosophical ideas, particularly concerning "thought-forms." In particular he cited T. H. Robsjohn-Gibbings's *Mona Lisa's Mustache: A Dissection of Modern Art* (1947); see pp. 84–86, pp. 148–154.

9. Gombrich, 1991, p. 174. Gombrich had made synaesthesia a central element of his own theories of art as early as the 1950s; see Gombrich, 1963.

10. Long, 1980, pp. 53–55. Though she refers to the "gift of audition colorée" (p. 54), Long does not explicitly argue for or against Kandinsky and Ringbom's occult interpretation of synaesthesia.

11. Hahl-Koch, 1984, pp. 149, 151. Hahl-Koch (who comments approvingly on Ringbom's work—see p. 144) is tentative about whether Kandinsky was "a genuine synesthetic" or

an "emotional" synaesthete; by the latter he means the sort of synaesthesia imagined by Kandinsky in *Concerning the Spiritual in Art* (p. 151).

12. McDonnell, 1990, p. 28; p. 29; pp. 31–32; p. 36; p. 34; The term "Law of Minimization of Mystery" comes from David Chalmers, who spoke at a 1993 conference in Tucson, "Scientific Basis for Consciousness." A more extended discussion of the difficulty with mixing metaphors and theories of new science can be found in Ken Wilber, "Physics, Mysticism, and the New Holographic Paradigm" and "Reflections on the New Age Paradigm—An Interview" in Ken Wilber, *Eye to Eye: The Quest for the New Paradigm* (Shambhala: Boston, 1990).

13. Although Steiner's epistemology was founded on the language and concepts of European philosophy in 1894 (*Philosophy of Spiritual Activity*), the traditionally identified source for his original "occult" exposition of the anthroposophical approach to cognitive development is *How to Know Higher Worlds: A Modern Path of Initiation* (originally published as *Knowledge of the Higher Worlds and Its Attainment;* see Steiner, [1904] 1947.

CHAPTER 3: THE MEANING OF SYNAESTHESIA IS MEANING

1. For a full chronology of the various attempts to create color music, see Peacock, 1988. Peacock's article is especially useful for the "pre-synaesthesia" attempts (that is, those before 1890); for the period of most intense experimentation—1890–1925—see Klein, 1925; Brewster, 1819, p. 135, quoted in Gombrich, 1979, p. 287.

2. Rimington, 1895. This paper was given before a private color music concert that Rimington gave to a group of luminaries—the Duke of Norfolk, the Japanese ambassador to England, Cardinal Vaughan, Alma Tadema, Silvanus Thompson, and other celebrities—at St. James Hall. Luckiesh quoted in Birren, 1941, p. 153; Greenewalt quoted in Gage, 1993, p. 245; Rimington, 1895, p. 5; For a sampling of the critical and popular response to color music from about 1920 to 1930, see Appendix 1 in Klein, 1925.

3. For the full texts of Kandinsky's and Schoenberg's works and commentary, see Watkins, 1988, p. 157–163.

4. See for example Brown, 1953, p. 75. In *The Tuning of the Word: The Musico-Literary Poetics of the Symbolist Movement* (1987), David Michael Hertz says that "synesthesia was the first and most significant lesson the Symbolists learned from Wagner" and that "technically, the [Symbolist] lyric play explores the possibility of synesthesia" (pp. 170, 171). On the origins of Wagner's notions of the Gesamtkunstwerk and the subsequent misunderstandings and misinterpretations to which his idea was subjected, see Vergo, 1993, pp. 11–19; Watkins, 1988, p. 156.

5. Huneker's story was written before Scriabin's *Prometheus*—an uncanny realization of Huneker's fiction—was composed, but Huneker spoofed Scriabin's work (especially the Theosophical theories about the astral realm associated with the work) in a later story, "The Synthesis of the Seven Arts," in Huneker, 1917; see also see "Dusk of the Gods" in the same volume.

6. See, for example, Huneker's "Creative Involution," in Huneker, 1917; "The Medium," in Huneker, 1905; and "Magic," in Huneker, 1922. For biographical sketches of Huneker, see de Casseres, 1925; Huneker, 1905, pp. 29, 96; Huneker, 1922, pp. 22–23.

7. For a full description of Bragdon's experiences with color music, see chapter 14 of his *Secret Springs: An Autobiography* (1938).

8. The other twentieth-century composer who is frequently mentioned as synaesthetic is Olivier Messiaen; for a good analysis of Messiaen's synaesthesia, see Bernard, 1986. Bernard mentions another characteristic typical of tonal chromaesthetes that Messiaen exhibited while Scriabin did not—he saw colors when he *read music as well as when he heard it.*

9. Scriabin also took the text for his *Prometheus* chorus from *The Secret Doctrine.* The chorus text "E-a, o-ho-a, o-ho" was Scriabin's rendering of "OEAOHOO," Blavatsky's term for "Father-Mother of the Gods," or "the Six in One." Scriabin was acquainted with French Symbolist ideas about synaesthesia and the synthesis of the arts, and most writers have assumed that the Wagnerian Gesamtkunstwerk, as well as the various less ambitious attempts at synchronizing colored light and music, such as Rimington's, served as a model for *Prometheus.* It is possible that there was a more immediate source: in June 1906, at the congress of the Theosophical Society in Paris, a production of Theosophist and occult bookseller Edmond Bailly's *Chant des Voyelles* was given. Bailly's composition was essentially a re-creation of an Egyptian magical rite, complete with incense keyed to specific incantations. See Godwin, 1991, pp. 51–52.

10. Faubion Bowers quoted in Critchley, 1977, pp. 223–224. "Sporadic synaesthesia" is Critchley's term—that is, he accepts Bowers's experience as being some form of syn-aesthesia, but as with Kandinsky, nothing about his description would suggest syn-aesthesia as an explanation for the colored visions. That Critchley, a neurologist, consid-ered synaesthesia alongside "ecstatic" responses to music suggests that he, too, interpreted synaesthesia as a sublime experience.

11. Aware of the occasional deviations that Scriabin made in *Prometheus* from the The-osophical scale of tone-colors, Scott questioned whether "he was a reliable psychic or merely an imaginative artist" (1917, p. 116).

12. Clarence Lucas's *Musical Courier* review quoted in Hull, 1927, p. 225. As might be expected, Wassily Kandinsky approved of Scriabin's work: "Scriabin's musical color sensations could represent a theory of which the composers could gradually become aware. . . . Those who listened to 'Prometheus' with the corresponding light effect admitted that the musical impression was in fact absolutely equaled by the corresponding lighting. The power was doubled and increased to the last degree" (Kandinsky and Marc, 1974, p. 131). See also *Nation,* 100 (1915), p. 339.

13. Köhler, 1915, pp. 181–182, quoted in Jakobson, 1980, p. 288. Other languages show that Köhler's intuited sense of cross-modal analogies in speech has been widely shared: Greek *barytonos* comes from *barys* ("heavy") and *oxytonos*—"having the acute accent"—from *axys* ("sharp"). The Latin *gravis* and *acutus,* the direct source of modern linguistic designations of "grave" and "acute" for speech sounds, are ultimately rooted in these haptic metaphors. Aristotle commented on this in *De Anima:* "*Acute* and *grave* are here metaphors transferred from their proper sphere, namely, that of touch. . . . There seems to be some sort of a parallelism between what is acute or grave to hearing and what is *sharp* or *blunt* to *touch.*" Aristotle quoted in Stanford, 1936, p. 49; Köhler, 1947.

14. Hartshorne, 1934, p. 9; p. 11; Merleau-Ponty, 1962, p. 229. On synaesthesia in the philosophy of Hartshorne and Merleau-Ponty, see Odin, 1986. The phenomenological

tradition has retained Merleau-Ponty's sense of synaesthesia (see for example McCurdy, 1978); its influence on aesthetic theory can be seen in Berleant, 1991, 1992.

15. The examples dealing with synaesthetic photisms are taken from Wheeler, 1930, pp. 372–373 (voice and instrument photisms), and Wheeler and Cutsforth, 1922, p. 380 (consonant photism); Wheeler, 1930, p. 359. The neurologist MacDonald Critchley gives an interesting example that appears to back up Wheeler and Cutsforth's observations: After a stroke a synaesthetic man became afflicted with anomia—the inability to name objects. Presented with familiar objects, he would utter various sounds that were phonemically similar to the missing word, but he would be alerted to their incorrectness by the fact that the photisms accompanying his names were not quite right. When he finally hit upon the correct name, he knew it from the appearance of the correctly colored and shaped photism. Also, Critchley tells of two red-green color-blind synaesthetes for whom musical notes with the pitch of G were red. Neither of them could identify this note when it was sounded alone, since they could not see the red photism—it appeared as green (Critchley, 1977, p. 223).

16. One of the first students of synaesthesia as a form of mental imagery, Francis Galton, could be considered a synaesthete by Wheeler and Cutsforth's lights. Galton described his ability to substitute odors for mathematical symbols in simple operations of adding and subtracting. See Galton, 1894; Wheeler, 1920a, p. 360.

17. Marks, 1978, p. 94; Cytowic, 1989, p. 69. In addition to citing the same two publications in his bibliography as Ortmann does in his 1933 review, Cytowic borrows Ortmann's terminology for the various theories of synaesthesia and repeats Ortmann's error of grouping Wheeler and Cutsforth's work with "association theories" of synaesthesia. Wheeler and Cutsforth's research also went unnoticed among literary critics interested in synaesthesia; a 1946 review of synaesthesia in literature cited Wheeler's "Synaesthesia of a Blind Subject" only to inventory the size of his bibliography. See Engstrom, 1946, p. 5, n. 25.

18. See especially Hunt, 1986, pp. 266–268. Hunt points out that the assessment that functionalist psychology leveled at introspection as a criticism—that it was not possible to distinguish the actual underlying meaning from the resulting introspected imagery—was in truth a matter of great pride to the introspectionists, for it meant that they were accomplishing their aim of avoiding the stimulus error. Introspection is a process of deferring the moment when meaning becomes apparent; once "meaning" appears to consciousness, the introspective process has ended.

19. In fact, the few psychologists who took note of Wheeler and Cutsforth's work were interested almost exclusively in its significance for explaining consciousness, not synaesthesia. F. R. Bichowsky of the National Research Council, in adopting Wheeler's theory to explain the neurology of consciousness, noted almost incidentally its importance "from the point of view of the student of synaesthesia, because it breaks down the supposedly sharp line between the synaesthetic and the asynaesthetic process, and because it gives strong confirmatory evidence for the view of Wheeler and Cutsforth that synaesthesia is simply a form of perception, differing from ordinary perception only in that it is of a fixed modality regardless of the modality of the pre-sensation" (Bichowsky, 1925, p. 591).

20. Wheeler and Cutsforth, 1925, p. 151. Subsequent citations from this source in Chapter 3 are noted only by a page number in text.

21. Klein, 1925, p. xvii. Though Klein was interested in abstract color representation, he had harsh words for Wassily Kandinsky's efforts to "paint" music: "He is unquestionably only a decorator, his methods being too haphazard to yield anything but superficial prettiness. He is influenced by a symbolic transcendentalism of a pseudo-theosophical variety" (pp. 35–36). Klein also regretted Scriabin's adoption of Theosophical doctrines in his *Prometheus* and ridiculed Cyril Scott's "pseudo-philosophical" explanations of Scriabin's composition that referred to its effect on the astral and etheric bodies. Woolf, 1922, p. 104.

CHAPTER 4: SENSORY UNITY BEFORE THE FALL

1. For an example of the sorts of investigations by administration of questionnaires to college freshmen, see Calkins, 1895. Harry Helson, a professor of psychology at Bryn Mawr, describes his five-year-old's synaesthesia and eideticism in Helson, 1933, and Anna Kellman Whitchurch describes the synaesthesia of Edgar Curtis, son of Cornell plant physiologist Otis Freeman Curtis, in Whitchurch, 1922.

2. On the history of recapitulation theories, see Gould, 1977.

3. Werner, 1940, pp. 86, 88, 71. Page numbers are given in text for subsequent citations of this work. Harry Hunt notes that "developmental models are ubiquitous" in the literature on non-normal states of consciousness, from the obsession of late nineteenth century psychology with primitivization theory and regression to recent transpersonal theories of higher orders of consciousness (Hunt, 1984, p. 492).

4. See pp. 69–86 of *Comparative Psychology of Mental Development,* for a discussion of Werner's idea of physiognomic perception. Also see Marks, 1978, pp. 182–185. For a more recent view of Werner's idea of "syncretic" perception, see Glicksohn, et al., 1992. In *Boundaries in the Mind: A New Psychology of Personality,* (1991), Ernest Hartmann develops a theory of personality that relies heavily on these ideas about syncretic tendencies. Hartmann's first measurement factor for assessing whether persons have "thick or thin boundaries" is "primary process" thinking, essentially Werner's syncretic processes. The person with "thin boundaries" is one who has many experiences of the self merging with the environment, fluctuating identity, and whose imagery is so vivid that it is hard to distinguish from reality. These persons also routinely experience synaesthesia. (224)

5. Siebold, 1919–1920. Oscar Firkin, in *Power and Elusiveness in Shelley* (1937), agreed with Siebold that Shelley's synaesthetic passages were so intense as to demand metaphysical explanation. Siebold's interpretation continues to enjoy currency in studies of eighteenth-century literature: according to Glenn O'Malley, the eighteenth century virtually "rang from beginning to end with synesthetic speculation" (O'Malley, 1964, p. 18).

6. Arguelles, 1988, p. ix. Page numbers only are given in text for subsequent citations of this work.

7. For a brilliant discussion of the identification of the soul with the sea in the history of Western thought, see Gebser, 1985, pp. 215–219.

8. Prior to Erich Jaensch's research, few psychologists who studied synaesthesia or eideticism tested their subjects for both forms of mental imagery. Close study of the pre-1920

descriptive reports of synaesthetes, however, reveals that many of these subjects were also eidetic. See, for example, Binet and Beaunis, 1892; Phillippe, 1893.

9. Almost all the experimental and theoretical work has focused on visual images, although Haber (1979) acknowledges some experimental work on other senses. In the early literature on eideticism "eidetic image" was sometimes used to refer to other than visual images. Another recent definition of eideticism can be found in Marks and McKellar, 1982, p. 2: "Any mental imagery projected into the sensory environment which cannot be attributed to a material change in sensory input and which is known to the imager to be subjective. . . . Eidetic imagery is characteristically autonomous, constructive and dynamic, displaying natural progressions and movement."

10. Jaensch derived the term from the Greek *eidos* (form). For a full listing of Jaensch's publications up to 1928, see Klüver, 1928. In a later article (1932), Klüver critiques the emphasis in eidetic research (originating with Jaensch) on the relation of eidetic imagery to personality.

11. The quotation is from Jaensch, 1930a, p. 93. Page numbers only are given in text for subsequent citations of this work. See Klüver, 1928, pp. 84–90, for a synopsis of Walther Jaensch's work on "psychophysical types" and their relation to eideticism; Purdy's 1936 paper was reprinted in William R. Corliss, *The Unfathomed Mind: A Handbook of Unusual Mental Phenomena* (1982); Corliss's work, the sixth in a series of handbooks on enigmas, anomalies, and mysteries, discusses a range of phenomena: "dissociative behavior"—automatic writing or speaking, multiple personalities, possession, mass hysteria, and hypnotic behavior; "acquisition of hidden knowledge"—divination and clairvoyance, dermo-optical perception, precognition, and telepathy; and (under "oddities of perception") "psychochromaesthesia," followed by entries on eidetic imagery.

12. It is curious that Jaensch omits German psychologist E. B. Titchener from his chauvinistic listing of eidetics. Titchener, who was a pioneer of the introspectionist method in psychology, was an eidetic who also experienced frequent synaesthesiae. Though Titchener disavows being synaesthetic, in his *Lectures on the Experimental Psychology of Thought Processes* (1909, p. 19), the illustration he gives of his own mental processes suggests otherwise.

13. Jaynes, 1979, p. 607. See also Jaynes, 1987.

14. Jeffrey Herf discusses Klages's contribution to "reactionary modernism" in *Reactionary Modernism: Technology, Culture, and Politics in Weimar and the Third Reich* (1984), an examination of the relation of antimodernist, romantic, and irrationalistic ideas to German nationalism.

Although research on synaesthesia also declined sharply during the reign of behaviorism, interest in the topic continued, particularly among three German psychologists who left Germany—Erich von Hornbostel, Heinz Werner, and Wolfgang Köhler. Hornbostel and Werner were dismissed from their academic posts in 1933 after Hitler's proclamation of the Laws for the Restoration of the Professional Civil Service, which barred all "non-Aryans" from employment by the government. Köhler, who was the only German psychologist to protest the law publicly, left Germany in 1935. See Alfred Geuter, *The Professionalization of Psychology in Nazi Germany* (1992), pp. 66, 178, 55.

15. See for example Arguelles, 1972, p. 28; Lawlor, 1989, p. 383. Lawlor also voices his view of

eideticism as a form of higher consciousness in *Sacred Geometry* (1982). The transcendental interpretation of eideticism is not limited to New Age writers; Joseph Burke (1964) explains William Blake's "spiritual eye" in terms of Jaensch's concept of eidetic images.

16. Before 1943, there was no diagnostic category called "autism," but many of the early twentieth-century reports of eideticism in so-called pathological individuals—schizophrenics, psychotics, and the "feeble-minded"—are clearly cases of autism. See for example Flournoy, 1926; Schilder, 1926; Jaensch and Mehmel, 1928; Jelliffe, 1928; Miskolczy and Schultz, 1929; Wertham, 1930; Miller, 1931a, 1931b; Kao and Lyman, 1944; Neymeyer, 1956. For more recent scientific literature that notes the coincidence of eideticism with autism, see for example Giray, et al., 1976; Giray and Barclay, 1977; Richardson and Cant, 1970; Siipola and Hayden, 1965; Symmes, 1971.

17. Viscott, 1970. For other accounts of musical autistic savants, see Sloboda, Hermelin, and O'Connor, 1985; Miller, 1987; Lucci, Holevas, and Kaplan, 1988; Charness Clifton, and MacDonald, 1988.

18. Howe, 1989, p. 9. Howe's book provides an excellent overview of extraordinary abilities among autistic persons. For a detailed look at the imagery of a nonautistic lightning calculator, see Bousfield and Barry, 1933.

CHAPTER 5: VLADIMIR NABOKOV'S EIDETIC TECHNIQUE

1. Nabokov, 1966b, p. 35. Subsequent cites to Nabokov, except as otherwise noted, are taken from this work, with page numbers only given in text.

2. D. Barton Johnson, in the second of two chapters discussing Nabokov as a "man of letters," interprets Nabokov's alphabetic (and numeric) "physiognomies" as "iconicity," and he sees the use of iconic description, though occasionally only a playful embellishment, as symbolic of Nabokov's belief that some hidden reality lies beyond the phenomenal world. Though they may end up in his fiction as signs pointing to more than their alphabetic meaning, Nabokov's literary evocations of letters and numbers are motivated by his physiognomic perception of them (Johnson, 1985, pp. 28–42).

3. The fact that Nabokov's mother was a synaesthete, and hence responded understandingly to his childhood insistence that letters had particular colors, may partially explain the seeming "hereditary" dimension of synaesthesia. As a child's cognitive development progresses out of the physiognomic perceptual style toward the abstract, logical reasoning of the adult, vestiges of the former style are increasingly dismissed or even ridiculed by peers and parents who have no recollection of having once perceived the world physiogomically. This is what synaesthetes almost universally refer to when asked about when they believe their synaesthesia to have begun; they "hid" their synaesthesia when they discovered that no one else seemed to see the world in the same manner as they did.

4. On this fully sensory quality of eidetic images, see Ahsen, 1977.

5. Nabokov did note, however, in his lectures on *A la recherche du temps perdu,* that the narrator Marcel "saw sounds in color," pointing out the passage where Marcel confesses that the word "Guermantes" always was "suffused by . . . [an] orange tint" (Nabokov, 1981, p. 235).

6. Mathematics, chess, and music, all highly abstract mental activities, are the classic

domain of prodigies. Many hypercalculators are known to have been eidetics. The history of chess is replete with extraordinary visualizers, most of whom presumably relied on eidetic ability. The Russian master Koltanowski began exhibitions by filling the squares of the chessboard with names, telephone numbers, bank note serial numbers, and other information contributed by the audience. Then he took a blindfolded tour of the board, reciting the data on each square. He could even repeat the feat a year after he had last seen the board. Though the mnemonic virtuosity afforded by eidetic ability is extremely helpful to master chess players, it is not essential. Alfred Binet found in his study that expert chess players only occasionally relied on photographic visual imagery; more often their strategizing took verbal or other forms. It is nevertheless possible that these other means of considering possible moves also represent types of eideticism. For a discussion of visualization and memory in chess, see Holding, 1985.

7. In *Despair* the character Hermann shares Fyodor's anxiety that he is not truly the author of his own works. Hermann confesses, "It is not I who am writing, but my memory, which has its own whims and rules" (Nabokov, 1966a, p. 62). When Hermann, reviewing his manuscript, wonders whether he "was reading written lines or seeing visions," he makes another admission on Nabokov's behalf about the dependence of his verbal art on his magic lantern device (p. 212).

8. Whereas Alexandrov seems to suggest that Nabokov's dislike of Plato is based on elitist ideas about political economy, a close reading of Nabokov indicates that he eschews any form of philosophy positing a transcendent realm independent of human consciousness.

9. Alexandrov gives a list of other authors who have emphasized Nabokov's "otherworld" theme (1991, pp. 235–236, n. 7): Foster, 1993, p. 193; Borden, 1979; Rowe, 1981; Boyd, 1985, p. 214; Boyd, 1990b, p. vii; Boyd, 1990a, p. vii; Johnson, 1985, p. 185. For a reading of Nabokov's work (as translated into French) that follows the same lines as Alexandrov's interpretation, see Kouchkine, 1990. Not surprisingly, Terence McKenna is an avid reader of Nabokov and in *True Hallucinations* even ranks Nabokov with other "giants of the human past—Carl Jung, Newton . . . Bruno, Pythagoras, and Heraclitus" (McKenna, 1993, p. 95; also see p. 35).

10. This inability to cope with abstractions had previously only occasionally been noted by researchers on synaesthesia: perhaps the earliest was Sokolov, who also noted his synaesthetic subjects' "lively imagination, deep sensitivity, and predominantly visual imagery" (Sokolov, 1901, p. 51).

CHAPTER 6: CONCLUSION

1. Solomon, 1964, p. 142. The early twentieth-century scientific literature on synaesthesia had frequently noted the occurrence of synaesthesia during mescaline intoxication, and documentation of it continued during the 1960s. In *The Primary World of the Senses: A Vindication of Sensory Experience* (1963), Erwin Straus, in discussing the breakdown in the boundaries of the self induced by mescaline intoxication, observed: "Almost all subjects report a genuine experiencing of cosensing. We find in the protocols testimonies of many kinds of synesthesias that the subjects occasionally are not at all sure which one of their senses it was that gave them certain impressions" (pp. 216–217). Straus quoted a physician

under the influence of mescaline as saying: "You think you're hearing noises and seeing faces and everything is one; I no longer know if I am seeing or hearing" (p. 217).

2. Hunt, 1985a, p. 271. Hunt points out that schizophrenia entails the same experience of this ultimate complex synaesthesia; whereas the somatic crisis of the disappearance of the body is metaphorically incorporated by the shaman or mystic, the schizophrenic cannot stand it because he experiences it as literal rather than metaphorical death. The paranoid quality of McKenna's and Arguelles's belief in the end of time may be due to the hallucinogenically induced nature of their complex synaesthesiae.

3. The use of so provocative a term as "cognitive fossils" prompted Cytowic to attach a disclaimer to his metaphor: "I do not want to be misunderstood as considering synesthesia to be vestigial, more primitive or atavistic, nor comparable to animal psychology, which might [imply] that animals might not separate their senses. Nor do I even want to hint that it is perhaps how early man perceived in his prelinguistic phase" (Cytowic, 1993, p. 21).

4. Cytowic's Romantic side prevailed over his scientific training in his second book about synaesthesia, *The Man Who Tasted Shapes: A Bizarre Medical Mystery Offers Revolutionary Insights into Emotions, Reasoning, and Consciousness* (1993). Attempting to recount a tale of scientific discovery for a popular audience, Cytowic focused on his study of one synaesthetic subject, Michael Watson, who experienced synaesthesia of touch, taste, and smell. In the book, Cytowic was in fact making the same claim for synaesthesia that many Symbolists and twentieth-century Romantics had made, that synaesthesia acted as a bulwark against positivism and rationalism.

Bibliography

Abrams, M. H. 1984. *The correspondent breeze: Essays on English romanticism*. New York: Norton.

Ahsen, Akhter. 1977a. Eidetics: An overview. *Journal of Mental Imagery* 1: 5–38.

———. 1977b. *Psycheye: Self-analytic consciousness: A basic introduction to the natural self-analytic images of consciousness: Eidetics*. New York: Brandon House.

Alard, Marie Joseph Louis Alibert, et. al. 1812–1822. *Dictionnaire des sciences médicales*. Paris: Pancoucke.

Alexandrov, Vladimir. 1991. *Nabokov's otherworld*. Princeton: Princeton University Press.

Alter, Robert. 1991. Nabokov and memory. *Partisan Review* 58: 620–629.

American Psychiatric Association Task Force on Nomenclature and Statistics. 1987. *Diagnostic and statistical manual of mental disorders*. Washington, D.C.: American Psychiatric Association.

Arguelles, José. 1988. *Earth ascending: An illustrated treatise on the law governing whole systems*. Santa Fe: Bear and Company.

———. 1972. *Charles Henry and the formation of a psychophysical aesthetic*. Chicago: University of Chicago Press.

Arnheim, Rudolf. 1969. *Visual thinking*. Berkeley: University of California Press.

Arréat, Lucien. 1893. Review of Max Nordau's *Entartung*. *Revue Philosophique* 35: 436–439.

Axenfeld, Alexandre. 1883. *Traité des névroses*. Paris: Germer-Ballière.

Babbitt, Irving. 1910. *The new Laokoön.* New York: Houghton Mifflin.

Balakian, Anna. 1967. *The Symbolist movement: A critical appraisal.* New York: Random House.

Barfield, Owen. 1966. *Romanticism comes of age.* Middletown, Conn.: Wesleyan University Press.

———. 1965. *Saving the appearances: A study in idolatry.* Middletown, Conn.: Wesleyan University Press.

Barnstone, Aliki. 1968. *The real tin flower: Poems about the world at nine.* New York: Crowell-Collier.

Baron-Cohen, Simon. 1995. *Mindblindness: An essay on autism and a theory of mind.* Cambridge: MIT Press.

Baron-Cohen, John Harrison, Laura H. Goldstein, and Maria Wyke. 1993. Colored speech perception: Is synaesthesia what happens when modularity breaks down? *Perception* 22: 419–426.

Barten, S. S., and M. B. Franklin, eds. 1934. *Developmental processes: Heinz Werner's selected writings.* New York: International Universities Press, 1978.

Baudelaire, Charles. [1860] 1971. *Artificial paradise: On hashish and wine as means of expanding individuality.* New York: Herder and Herder.

———. 1968. *Oeuvres complètes.* Paris: Gallimard.

———. 1961. *Oeuvres en prose.* Paris: Gallimard.

———. 1936. *Flowers of evil,* George Dillon, trans. and ed. New York: Harper and Brothers.

Behr, S., D. Fanning, and D. Jarman, eds. 1992. *Expressionism reassessed.* Manchester, England: Manchester University Press.

Belmont, Ira Jean. 1944. *The modern dilemma in art.* New York: Hartsinger House.

Benoît, Emilien. 1899. *Contributions à l'étude de l'audition colorée.* Paris: Maloine.

Berleant, Arnold. 1992. *The aesthetics of environment.* Philadelphia: Temple University Press.

———. 1991. *Art and engagement.* Philadelphia: Temple University Press.

———. 1962. *Selected writings,* vol. 1. The Hague: Mouton.

Bernard, Jonathan W. 1986. Messiaen's synaesthesia: The correspondence between color and sound structure in his music. *Music Perception* 4: 41–68.

Besant, Annie. [1904] 1972. *A study in consciousness: A contribution to the science of psychology.* Wheaton, Ill.: Theosophical Publishing House.

———. 1897. *The ancient wisdom: An outline of theosophical teachings.* London: Theosophical Publishing Society.

Besant, Annie, and C. W. Leadbeater. 1901. *Thought-forms.* Wheaton, Ill.: Theosophical Publishing House, 1961.

Bichowsky, F. R. 1925. The mechanism of consciousness. *American Journal of Psychology* 36: 585–593.

Binet, Alfred. 1893. L'application de la psychométrie à l'étude de l'audition colorée. *Revue Philosophique* 35: 334–336.

Binet, Alfred, and H. Beaunis. 1892. Sur deux cas d'audition colorée. *Revue Philosophique* 33: 448–460.

Birren, Faber. 1941a. *The history of color in painting.* New York: Reinhold.

————. 1941b. *The story of color: From ancient mysticism to modern science*. Westport, Conn.: The Crimson Press.

Blake, William. 1969. *Complete writings of William Blake*. Oxford: Oxford University Press.

Blavatsky, Helena Petrovna. 1885–1888. *The secret doctrine: The synthesis of science, religion, and philosophy*, 3 vols. Wheaton: Theosophical Publishing House.

Bleuler, Eugen. 1913. Zur Theorie der Sekundärempfindungen. *Zeitschrift für Psychologie* 65: 1–39.

Bleuler, Eugen, and Karl Lehmann. 1881. *Zwangsmässige Lichtempfindungen durch Schall und verwandte Erscheinungen auf dem Gebiete der andern Sinnesempfindungen*. Leipzig: Fues's Verlag.

Bousfield, W. A., and H. Barry, Jr. 1933. The visual imagery of a lightning calculator. *American Journal of Psychology* 45: 353–358.

Boyd, Brian. 1990a. *Vladimir Nabokov: The American years*. Princeton: Princeton University Press.

————. 1990b. *Vladimir Nabokov: The Russian years*. Princeton: Princeton University Press.

Bragdon, Claude. 1938. *The secret springs: An autobiography*. London: Andrew Dakers.

————. 1926. *Architecture and democracy*. New York: Knopf.

Brunetière, Ferdinand. 1888. Symbolistes et decadents. *Revue des Deux Mondes* 11: 88.

Bucke, Richard Maurice. 1901. *Cosmic consciousness: A study in the evolution of the human mind*. Philadelphia: Innes and Sons.

Burke, Joseph. 1964. The eidetic and the borrowed image: An interpretation of Blake's theory and practice of art. In Franz Philipp and June Stewart, eds., *In honour of Daryl Lindsay: Essays and studies*. Oxford: Oxford University Press.

Burwick, Frederick. 1986. *The damnation of Newton: Goethe's color theory and Romantic perception*. Berlin: Walter de Gruyter.

Burwick, Frederick, and Walter Pape, eds. 1990. *Aesthetic illusion: Theoretical and historical approaches*. Berlin: Walter de Gruyter.

Calkins, Mary Whiton. 1895. Synaesthesia, part 2. *American Journal of Psychology* 7: 90–107.

Campana, John. 1981. Vittorini's synaesthetic use of imagery in *Conversazione in Sicilia*. *Canadian Journal of Italian Studies* 5: 72–80.

Capuron, Joseph, and Victor Nysten. 1814. *Nouveau dictionnaire de médecine, de chirurgie, de physique, de chimie et d'histoire naturelle*. Paris: Baillière.

Carlson, Maria. 1993. *"No religion higher than truth": A history of the Theosophical movement in Russia, 1875–1922*. Princeton: Princeton University Press.

Casseres, Benjamin de. 1925. *James Gibbons Huneker*. New York: Joseph Lawren.

Castel, Louis Bertrand. 1740. *L'optique des couleurs, fondée sur les simples observations, et tournée surtout à la pratique de la peinture, de la teinture, et des autres arts coloristes*. Paris: Briasson.

Cerullo, John J. 1982. *The secularization of the soul: Psychical research in modern Britain*. Philadelphia: Institute for the Study of Human Issues.

Chapin, J. H. 1892. Colors of names. *Popular Science Monthly* 40: 414.

Charness, N., J. Clifton, and L. MacDonald. 1988. Case study of a musical 'mono-savant': A cognitive-psychological focus. In L. K. Obler and D. Fein, eds., *The exceptional brain: Neuropsychology of talent and special abilities*. New York: Guilford Press.

Cheney, Sheldon. 1934. *Expressionism in art*. New York: Liveright.

————. 1924. *A primer of modern art*. New York: Boni and Liveright.

Claparède, Edouard. 1900. Sur l'audition colorée. *Revue Philosophique* 49: 515–517.

Clérambault, Gaetan Gatian de. 1942. *L'oeuvre psychiatrique*. Paris: Presses Universitaires de France.

Cohen, Sidney. 1968. *The beyond within: The LSD story*. New York: Atheneum.

Congrès international de psychologie physiologique, 1889. [1889] 1974. Liechtenstein: Kraus Reprint.

Connolly, Julian. 1992. *Nabokov's early fiction: Patterns of self and other*. Cambridge: Cambridge University Press.

Coriat, Isador H. 1913a. A case of synaesthesia. *Journal of Abnormal Psychology* 8: 38–43.

————. 1913b. An unusual type of synesthesia. *Journal of Abnormal Psychology* 8: 109–112.

Cornaz, Edouard. 1848. *Des abnormalités congénitales des yeux et de leurs annexes*. Lausanne: Pierre.

Cottom, Daniel. 1991. *Abyss of reason: Cultural movements, revelations, and betrayals*. Oxford: Oxford University Press.

Crary, Jonathan. 1990. *Techniques of the observer: On vision and modernity in the nineteenth century*. Cambridge: MIT Press.

Critchley, MacDonald. 1977. Ecstatic and synaesthetic experiences during musical perception. In MacDonald Critchley and R. A. Henson, eds., *Music and the brain: Studies in the neurology of music*. London: Heinemann Medical.

Critchley, MacDonald, and R. A. Henson, eds. 1977. *Music and the brain: Studies in the neurology of music*. London: Heinemann Medical.

Cutsforth, T. D. 1925. The role of emotion in a synaesthetic subject. *American Journal of Psychology* 36: 527–543.

Cytowic, Richard. 1993. *The man who tasted shapes: A bizarre medical mystery offers revolutionary insights into emotions, reasoning, and consciousness*. New York: Tarcher/Putnam's Sons.

————. 1989. *Synesthesia: A union of the senses*. New York: Springer-Verlag.

D'Udine, Jean [Albert Cozanet]. 1910. *L'art et le geste*. Paris: Alcan.

Dechambre, A., ed. 1876. *Dictionnaire encyclopédique des sciences médicales*. Paris: Asselin, Labé, Masson and Son.

Delahaye, Ernest. 1905. *Rimbaud: L'artiste et l'être moral*. Paris: Messein, 1923.

Dew-Smith, Alice. 1890. *Soul shapes*. London: Fisher.

Downey, June E. 1925. *Creative imagination: Studies in the psychology of literature*. New York: Harcourt, Brace.

————. 1912. Literary synaesthesia. *Journal of Philosophy, Psychology and Scientific Methods* 9: 490–498.

Dunselman, Ron. 1995. *In place of the self: How drugs work*. Lansdown: Hawthorn Press.

Engstrom, Alfred. 1946. In defence of synaesthesia in literature. *Philological Quarterly* 25: 1–19.

Etiemble, René. 1984. *Rimbaud: Système solaire ou trou noir?* Paris: Presses Universitaires de France.

————. 1968. *Le sonnet des voyelles: De l'audition colorée à la vision érotique*. Paris: Gallimard.

————. 1952. *Le mythe de Rimbaud*, vol. 1, *Structure du mythe*. Paris: Gallimard.

Fechner, Gustav Theodor. [1880] 1966. *Elements of Psychophysics,* D. H. Howes and E. G. Boring, eds. New York: Holt, Rinehart, Winston.

———. 1876. *Vorschule der Aesthetik.* Leipzig: Breitkopf and Hartel.

Felkin, Charlotte (Ellen Thorneycroft Fowler). 1906. *The subjection of Isabel Carnaby.* New York: Dodd and Mead.

Féré, Charles. 1884. La famille neuropathique. *Archives Neurologiques* 7: 1–43, 173–191.

Féré, Charles, and Charles Samson. 1888. *Animal magnetism.* New York: Appleton.

Field, Andrew. 1986. *VN: The life and art of Vladimir Nabokov.* New York: Crown.

Firkin, Oscar. 1937. *Power and elusiveness in Shelley.* London: Oxford University Press.

Flournoy, Théodore. 1926. Eidétisme chez un débile. *Archives de Psychologie* 20: 73–74.

———. 1893. *Des phénomènes de synopsie.* Paris: Alcan.

———. 1892. L'audition colorée. *Archives des Sciences Physiques et Naturelles* 28: 505–508.

Foster, John Burt, Jr. 1993. *Nabokov's art of memory and European modernism.* Princeton: Princeton University Press.

Fraser-Harris, David. 1928. *Colored thinking and other stories in science and literature.* London: Routledge.

Freudenberg, Franz. 1908. Über die Spaltung der Persönlichkeit und verwandte psychische Fragen. *Die Übersinnliche Welt: Monatsschrift für Okkultische Forschung* 16 (1): 18–22; (2): 51–67; (3): 101–112.

Gage, David. 1993. *Colour and culture: Practice and meaning from antiquity to abstraction.* London: Thames and Hudson.

Galton, Francis. 1909. *Memories of my life.* New York: Dutton.

———. 1894. Arithmetic by smell. *Psychological Review* 1: 61–62.

———. 1883. *Inquiries into human faculty and its development.* London: Macmillan.

Gebser, Jean. 1985. *The ever-present origin.* Athens: Ohio University Press.

Gelpi, Barbara C. 1992. *Shelley's goddesses: Maternity, language, subjectivity.* Oxford: Oxford University Press.

Geuter, Ulfried. 1992. *The professionalization of psychology in Nazi Germany.* Cambridge: Cambridge University Press.

Ghil, René. 1886. *Traité du verbe.* Paris: Giraud.

Giray, E. F., W. M. Altkin, and A. G. Barclay. 1976. Frequency of eidetic imagery among hydrocephalic children. *Perceptual and Motor Skills* 43: 187–194.

Giray, E. F., and A. G. Barclay. 1977. Eidetic imagery: Longitudinal results in brain-damaged children. *American Journal of Mental Deficiency* 82: 311–314.

Glicksohn, Joseph, Orna Slainger, and Anat Roychman. 1992. An exploratory study of syncretic experience: Eidetics, synaesthesia, and absorption. *Perception* 21: 637–642.

Godwin, Joscelyn. 1991. *The mystery of the seven vowels: In theory and practice.* New York: Phanes Press.

———. 1987. *Harmonies of heaven and earth.* Rochester: Inner Traditions International.

Goethe, Johann Wolfgang von. 1970. *Zur Farbenlehre.* In *Goethe's Color Theory,* Rupprecht Matthei, trans. and ed. New York: Van Nostrand, Reinhold.

Gombrich, E. H. 1991. *Topics of our time: Twentieth-century issues in learning and in art.* Berkeley: University of California Press.

————. 1979. *A sense of order: A study in the psychology of decorative art.* Ithaca, N.Y.: Cornell University Press.

————. 1963. *Meditations on a hobby horse and other essays on the theory of art.* Greenwich: Phaidon.

————. 1960. *Art and illusion: A study in the psychology of pictorial representation.* New York: Pantheon Books.

Gordon, Rae Beth. 1992. *Ornament, fantasy, and desire in nineteenth-century French literature.* Princeton: Princeton University Press.

Gould, Stephen Jay. 1977. *Ontogeny and phylogeny.* Cambridge: Harvard University Press.

Grandin, Temple. 1995. *Thinking in pictures: And other reports from my life with autism.* New York: Doubleday.

Grandin, Temple, and M. M. Scariano. 1986. *Emergence: Labeled autistic.* Phoenix: Arena Press.

Green, Geoffrey. 1988. *Freud and Nabokov.* Lincoln: University of Nebraska Press.

Grüber, Edouard. 1893. Questionnaire psychologique sur l'audition colorée, figurée, et illuminée. *Revue Philosophique* 35: 499–502.

Haber, R. N. 1979. Twenty years of haunting eidetic imagery: Where's the ghost? *Behavioral and Brain Sciences* 2: 583–629.

Hahl-Koch, Jelena, ed. 1984. *Kandinsky and Schoenberg: Letters, pictures, documents.* London: Faber and Faber.

Harper, Phillip Brian. 1989. Synesthesia, 'crossover,' and blacks in popular culture. *Social Text* 23: 102–107.

Harrington, Alan. 1964. A visit to inner space. In David Solomon, ed., *LSD: The consciousness-expanding drug.* New York: Putnam and Sons.

Hartlaub, G. F. 1917. Die Kunst und die neue Gnosis. *Das Kunstblatt* 6: 166–179.

Hartmann, Ernest. 1991. *Boundaries in the mind: A new psychology of personality.* New York: Basic Books.

Hartshorne, Charles. 1934. *The philosophy and psychology of sensation.* Chicago: University of Chicago Press.

Heinenger, S. K., Jr. 1974. *Touches of sweet harmony: Pythagorean cosmology and Renaissance poetics.* San Marino: Huntington Library.

Helson, Harry. 1933. A child's spontaneous reports of imagery. *American Journal of Psychology* 45: 360–361.

Henderson, John A. 1971. *The first avant-garde, 1887–1894: Sources of the modern French theatre.* London: Harrap.

Henderson, Linda. 1983. *The fourth dimension and non-Euclidean geometry in modern art.* Princeton: Princeton University Press.

Henri, Victor. 1893. Note sur un cas d'audition colorée. *Revue Philosophique* 35: 554–558.

Herf, Jeffrey. 1984. *Reactionary modernism: Technology, culture, and politics in Weimar and the Third Reich.* Cambridge: Cambridge University Press.

Hertz, David Michael. 1987. *The tuning of the word: The musico-literary poetics of the Symbolist movement.* Carbondale: Southern Illinois University Press.

Hill, A. L. 1977. Idiots savants: Rate of incidence. *Perceptual and Motor Skills* 44: 161–162.

————. 1975. An investigation of calendar calculating ability by an idiot savant. *American Journal of Psychiatry* 132: 557–560.

Holding, Dennis H. 1985. *The psychology of chess skill*. Hillsdale, N.Y.: Erlbaum.

Hornbostel, Erich von. 1925. Die Einheit der Sinne. *Melos, Zeitschrift für Musik* 4: 290–297 (reprinted in 1927 as The unity of the senses, *Psyche* 7: 83–89).

Horowitz, M. J. 1975. Hallucinations: An information-processing approach. In R. Siegel and L. West, eds., *Hallucinations: Behavior, experience, theory*. New York: Wiley.

Howe, Michael J. A. 1989. *Fragments of genius: The strange feats of idiots savants*. London: Routledge.

Hug-Hellmuth, H. V. 1912. Über Farbenhören. *Imago* 1: 228.

Hull, A. Eaglefield. 1927. *A great Russian tone-poet: Scriabin*. London: Kegan, Paul.

Huneker, James Gibbons. [1902] 1969. *Melomaniacs*. New York: Greenwood Press.

————. 1922. *Steeplejack*. New York: Scribner's.

————. 1917. *Unicorns*. New York: Scribner's.

————. 1905. *Visionaries*. New York: Scribner's.

Hunt, Harry T. 1995. *On the nature of consciousness: Cognitive, phenomenological, and transpersonal perspectives*. New Haven: Yale University Press.

————. 1989. *The multiplicity of dreams: Memory, Imagination, and Consciousness*. New Haven: Yale University Press.

————. 1987. Metaphor and states of consciousness: A preliminary correlational study of presentational thinking. *Journal of Mental Imagery* 11: 83–100.

————. 1986. A cognitive reinterpretation of classical introspectionism: The relation between introspection and altered states of consciousness and their mutual relevance for a cognitive psychology of metaphor and felt meaning. *Annals of Theoretical Psychology* 4: 245–313.

————. 1985a. Cognition and states of consciousness: The necessity for empirical study of ordinary and nonordinary consciousness for contemporary cognitive psychology. *Perceptual and Motor Skills* 60: 239–282.

————. 1985b. Relations between the phenomena of religious mysticism (altered states of consciousness) and the psychology of thought: A cognitive psychology of states of consciousness and the necessity of subjective states for cognitive theory. *Perceptual and Motor Skills* 61: 911–961.

————. 1984. A cognitive psychology of mystical and altered-state experience. *Perceptual and Motor Skills* 58: 467–513.

————. 1976. A test of the psychedelic model of consciousness. *Archives of General Psychiatry* 33: 867–896.

Hunt, Harry T., Sheryl-Shearing-Johns, Arlene Gervais, and Fred Travis. 1992. Transpersonal experiences in childhood: An exploratory empirical study of selected adult groups. *Perceptual and Motor Skills* 75: 1135–1153.

Jaensch, Erich. 1930a. *Eidetic imagery and typological methods of investigation*. New York: Harcourt, Brace.

————. 1930b. Über den latenten Cartesianismus der modernen Wissenschaft. *Zeitschrift für Psychologie* 16: 28–35.

Jaensch, Erich, and H. Mehmel. 1928. Gedächtnisleistungen eines schwachsinnigen Eidetikers. *Psychiatrisch-Neurologische Wochenschrift* 30: 101–103.

Jakobson, Roman. 1980. *On language.* Cambridge: Harvard University Press.

———. 1978. *Six lectures on sound and meaning.* Cambridge: MIT Press.

Jakobson, Roman, and Krystyna Pomorska. 1983. *Dialogues.* Cambridge: MIT Press.

Jakobson, Roman, and Linda Waugh. 1978. *The sound shape of language.* Bloomington: University of Indiana Press.

James, D. G. 1963. *The Romantic comedy.* Oxford: Oxford University Press.

James, William. 1879. Are we automata? *Mind* 4: 1–22.

———. [1869–1909] 1986a. *Essays in psychical research.* Cambridge: Harvard University Press.

———. [1901] 1986b. Frederick Myers's service to psychology. In *Essays in Psychical Research,* Cambridge: Harvard University Press.

Jaynes, Julian. 1987. Eidetic imagery and Paleolithic art. *Yale University Art Gallery Bulletin* 40: 78–83.

———. 1979. Paleolithic cave painting as eidetic art. *Behavioral and Brain Sciences* 2: 605–607.

Jelliffe, S. E. 1928. On eidetic psychology and psychiatric problems. *Medical Journal and Record* 128: 80–83.

Johnson, D. Barton. 1985. *Worlds in regression: Some novels of Vladimir Nabokov.* Ann Arbor, Mich.: Ardis.

———. 1982. The role of synaesthesia in Jakobson's theory of language. *International Journal of Slavic Linguistics and Poetics* 25 (6): 219–232.

Johnson, Paul. 1990. *In search of the masters behind the occult myth.* Boston: Heddely-Benton.

Jones, H. E. 1926. Phenomenal memorizing as a "special ability." *Journal of Applied Psychology* 10: 367–377.

Judd, C. H. 1910. Evolution and consciousness. *Psychological Review* 17: 77–97.

Kandinsky, Wassily. [1912] 1947. Michael Sadleir, trans., *Concerning the spiritual in art.* New York: George Wittenborn.

Kandinsky, Wassily, and Franz Marc. [1914] 1974. *The Blaue Reiter almanac,* Klaus Lankheit, ed. New York: Viking Press.

Kanner, Leo. 1951. The conception of wholes and parts in early infantile autism. *American Journal of Psychiatry* 108: 23–26.

———. 1943. Autistic disturbances of affective contact. *Nervous Child* 2: 217–250.

Kao, C. C., and R. S. Lyman. 1944. The role of eidetic imagery in a psychosis. *Journal of Nervous and Mental Disease* 100: 355–365.

Karwoski, T. F., and H. S. Odbert. 1938. Color-music. *Psychological Monographs* 50: 117–200.

Kern, Stephen. 1983. *The culture of time and space, 1880–1918.* Cambridge: Harvard University Press.

Klein, A. B. 1925. *Colour music: The art of light.* London: Leadenhall Press.

Klüver, Heinrich. 1966. *Mescal and the mechanisms of hallucination.* Chicago: University of Chicago Press.

———. 1932. Eidetic phenomena. *Psychological Bulletin* 29: 181–203.

———. 1928. Studies on the eidetic type and on eidetic imagery. *Psychological Bulletin* 25: 69–104.

Knapp, Bettina L. 1988. *Music, archetype, and the writer: A Jungian view.* University Park: Pennsylvania State University Press.

———. 1985. *Word/image/psyche.* University: University of Alabama Press.

Koch, Kenneth. 1972. Inspiration and work: How poetry gets to be written. *Comparative Literature Studies* 17: 206–219.

Köhler, Wolfgang. 1947. *Gestalt psychology.* New York: Liveright Publishing.

———. 1915. Akustische Untersuchungen. *Zeitschrift für die Gesamte Psychologie* 72: 1–192.

Kouchkine, Eugène. 1990. Nabokov, ou le don de la transcendance. *Dalhousie French Studies* 19: 32–42.

Krohn, W. O. 1892. Pseudo-chromaesthesia, or the association of colors with words, letters, and sounds. *American Journal of Psychology* 5: 20–41.

Langfeld, Herbert Sidney. 1926. Synaesthesia. *Psychological Bulletin* 23: 599–602.

———. 1914. Note on a Case of Chromaesthesia. *Psychological Bulletin* 11: 113–114.

Lawlor, Robert. 1989. *Voices of the first day: Awakening in the aboriginal dreamtime.* Rochester: Inner Traditions International.

———. 1982. *Sacred geometry.* London: Thames and Hudson.

Le Dantec, Félix. 1894. Rétrécissement du champs auditif dans l'hystérie: Ses relations avec l'audition colorée. *Archives de Médicine Navale* 61: 284–294.

Lee, Martin A., and Bruce Shlain. 1985. *Acid dreams: The CIA, LSD, and the sixties rebellion.* New York: Grove Press.

Lemaître, Auguste. 1901. *Audition colorée et phénomènes connexes chez les écoliers.* Paris: Alcan.

Lewes, George Henry. 1879. *Problems of life and mind.* London: Trübner.

Littré, Emile. 1865. *Dictionnaire de médecine, de chirurgie, de pharmacie, des sciences accessoires et de l'art vétérinaire.* Paris: Baillière.

Locke, John. [1690] 1961. *An essay concerning human understanding.* New York: Dutton.

Lombroso, Cesare. 1889. *L'homme de génie,* trans. from the Italian *L'uomo delinquente.* Paris: Alcan.

Long, Rose-Carol Washton. 1993. *German expressionism: Documents from the end of the Wilhelmine empire to the rise of National Socialism.* New York: G. K. Hall.

———. 1980. *Kandinsky: The development of an abstract style.* Oxford: Clarendon Press.

Lott, Walter, et al., eds. 1929. *Festschrift für Johannes Wolf: Zu seinem sechzigsten Geburtstage.* Berlin: Verlag von Martin Breslauer.

Lucci, D., D. Fein, A. Holevas, and E. Kaplan. 1988. Paul: A musically gifted autistic boy. In L. K. Obler and D. Fein, eds., *The exceptional brain: Neuropsychology of talent and special abilities.* New York: Guilford Press.

Ludlow, FitzHugh. 1857. *The hasheesh eater.* New York: Harper.

Luria, A. R. [1968] 1976. *The mind of a mnemonist: A little book about a vast memory.* New York: Basic Books.

Lyle, Wilson. 1982. Colour and music: An introduction. *The Music Review* 43: 261–264.

McCurdy, John Derrickson. 1978. *Visionary appropriation.* New York: Philosophical Library.

McDonnell, Patricia. 1990. Kandinsky's early theories of synaesthesia. *Art Criticism* 6: 28–42.

McKane, J. P., and A. M. Hughes. 1988. Synaesthesia and major affective disorder. *Acta Psychiatrica Scandinavica* 77: 493–494.

McKenna, Terence. 1993. *True hallucinations: Being an account of the author's extraordinary adventures in the devil's paradise.* San Francisco: Harper.

————. 1991. *The archaic revival: Speculations on psychedelic mushrooms, the Amazon, virtual reality, UFOs, evolution, shamanism, the rebirth of the goddess, and the end of history.* San Francisco: Harper.

McKenna, Terence, and Dennis McKenna. 1975. *The invisible landscape.* New York: Seabury Press.

Mackenzie, Compton. 1913. *Youth's encounter.* New York: Appleton.

MacLean, Paul. 1973. *A triune concept of the brain and behavior.* Toronto: University of Toronto Press.

Mahling, Friedrich. 1929. *Das Farbe-Ton-Problem und die selbständige Farbe-Ton-Forschung als Exponenten gegenwärtiges Geistesstrebens.* In Walter Lott et al., eds., *Festschrift für Johannes Wolf: Zu seinem sechzigsten Geburtstage.* Berlin: Verlag von Martin Breslauer.

Marks, David, and Peter McKellar. 1982. The nature and function of eidetic imagery. *Journal of Mental Imagery* 6: 1–124.

Marks, Lawrence E. 1990. Synaesthesia: Perception and Metaphor. In Frederick Burwick and Walter Pape, eds., *Aesthetic illusion: Theoretical and historical approaches.* Berlin: Walter de Gruyter.

————. 1978. *The unity of the senses: Interrelations and modalities.* New York: Academic Press.

————. 1975. On colored-hearing synesthesia: Cross-modal translations of sensory dimensions. *Psychological Bulletin* 82: 303–331.

————. 1974. On associations of light and sound: The modification of brightness, pitch, and loudness. *American Journal of Psychology* 87: 173–188.

Marvick, Louis W. 1986. Two versions of the Symbolist apocalypse: Mallarmé's *Livre* and Scriabin's *Mysterium. Criticism* 28: 287–306.

Mason, Wilton. 1958. Father Castel and his color clavecin. *Journal of Aesthetics and Art Criticism* 17: 103–116.

Masters, Robert, and Jean Houston. 1978. *Listening to the body: The psycho-physical way to health and awareness.* New York: Delacorte Press.

————. 1972. *Mind games.* New York: Viking.

Matlaw, Ralph E. 1979. Scriabin and Russian Symbolism. *Comparative Literature* 31: 1–23.

Maupassant, Guy de. 1890. *La vie errante.* Paris: Ollendorf.

Mellencamp, Patricia. 1990. *Indiscretions: Avant-garde film, video and feminism.* Bloomington: Indiana University Press.

Mencken, H. L. 1958. *Prejudices.* New York: Vintage Books.

Merleau-Ponty, Maurice. 1962. *Phenomenology of perception.* Atlantic Highlands: Humanities Press.

Michaud, Guy, ed. 1957. *La doctrine symboliste: Documents.* Paris: Librairie Nizet.

Michéa, C. F. 1846. *Du délire des sensations.* Paris: Labé.

Miller, E. 1931a. The eidetic image—An undertone of psychosis: Introduction to a future inquiry. *Proceedings of the Royal Society of Medicine* 24: 223–230.

————. 1931b. Eidetic imagery. *Journal of Neurology and Psychopathology* 12: 1–13.

Miller, L. K. 1987. Determinants of melody span in a developmentally disabled musical savant. *Psychology of Music* 15: 76–89.

Millet, Jules. 1892. *Audition colorée.* Paris: Octave Doin.

Miskolczy, D., and G. Schultz. 1929. Eidetik und Schizophrenie. *Monatsschrift für Psychiatrie und Neurologie* 72: 324.

Morgan, Michael J. 1977. *Molyneux's question: Vision, touch, and the philosophy of perception.* New York: Cambridge University Press.

Morishima, A. 1974. 'Another Van Gogh of Japan': The superior artwork of a retarded boy. *Exceptional Children* 41: 92–96.

Morishima, A., and L. F. Brown. 1976. An idiot savant case report: A retrospective view. *Mental Retardation* 14: 46–47.

Müller, F. Max. 1879. *The sacred books of the East.* London: Oxford University.

Müller, Johannes. 1838, William Baly, trans. *Elements of physiology.* London: Walton. (Translated from *Handbuch der Physiologie des Menschen für Vorlesungen,* 2 vols., Coblenz: Hölscher.)

———. 1826. *Über die phantasischen Gesichtserscheinungen.* Coblenz: Hölscher.

Mustoxidi, T. M. 1920. *Histoire de l'esthétique française,* 1700–1900. New York: Bert Franklin.

Myers, Charles S. 1914. Two cases of synaesthesia. *British Journal of Psychology* 7: 112–117.

———. 1911. A case of synaesthesia. *British Journal of Psychology* 4: 228–238.

Myers, F. W. H. 1903. *Human personality and its survival of bodily death,* 2 vols. London: Longmans, Green.

Nabokov, Dmitri. 1988. Close calls and fulfilled dreams: Selected entries from a private journal. *Antaeus* 61: 299–323.

Nabokov, Vladimir. 1981. *Lectures on literature.* New York: Harcourt Brace Jovanovich.

———. 1974a. *Bend sinister.* New York: Time.

———. 1974b. *Look at the harlequins.* New York: McGraw-Hill.

———. 1973a. *A Russian beauty and other stories.* New York: McGraw-Hill.

———. 1973b. *Strong opinions.* New York: McGraw-Hill.

———. 1970a. *The defense.* New York: Capricorn.

———. 1970b. *Poems and problems.* New York: McGraw-Hill.

———. 1969. *Ada or ardor: A family chronicle.* New York: McGraw-Hill.

———. 1966a. *Despair.* New York: Putnam.

———. 1966b. *Speak memory: An autobiography revisited.* New York: Putnam.

———. 1965. *The eye.* New York: Phaedrus.

———. 1963. *The gift.* New York: Wideview/Perigee.

———. 1962. *Pale fire.* New York: Putnam.

———. 1959. *Invitation to a beheading.* New York: Putnam.

———. 1958. *Lolita.* New York: Putnam.

———. 1957. *Pnin.* Garden City: Doubleday.

Neisser, Ulric. 1976. *Cognition and reality.* San Francisco: Freeman.

Newton, Isaac. 1718. *Opticks.* London: Smith and Walford.

Neymeyer, H. 1956. Über die Pathologie der Eidetismen. *Psychiatrie, Neurologie und Medizinische Psychologie* 8: 234–257.

Nordau, Max. 1895. *Degeneration.* New York: Appleton.

Nüssbaumer, H. 1873. Über subjective Farben-Empfindungen. *Wiener Medizinische Wochenschrift.*

O'Neill, Helena, and J. Edward Rauth. 1934. Eidetic imagery. *Catholic University of America Educational Research Monographs* 8: 3–22.

Onians, R. B. 1954. *The origins of European thought about the body, the mind, the soul, the world, time, and fate.* Cambridge: Cambridge University Press.

Odin, Steve. 1986. Blossom scents take up the ringing: Synaesthesia in Japanese and Western aesthetics. *Soundings* 69: 256–281.

Ortmann, Otto. 1933. Theories of synaesthesia in the light of a case of color-hearing. *Human Biology* 5: 155–211.

Osgood, C. E. 1960. The cross-cultural generality of visual-verbal synesthetic tendencies. *Behavioral Science* 5: 124–128.

———. 1953. *Method and theory in experimental psychology.* New York: Oxford University Press.

O'Malley, Glenn. 1964. *Shelley and synesthesia.* Chicago: Northwestern University Press.

Patrick, G. T. W. 1911. The search for the soul in contemporary thought. *Popular Science Monthly* 78: 460–468.

Peacock, Kenneth. 1988. Instruments to perform color-music: Two centuries of technological experimentation. *Leonardo* 21: 397–406.

Perroud, Claude. 1862. *Mémoires et Comptes Rendus de la Société des Sciences Médicales de Lyon* 2: 37–43.

Pfister, O. 1912. Die Ursache der Farbenbegleitung bei akustischer Wahrnehmungen über das Wesen anderer Synästhesien. *Imago* 1: 265–275.

Philipp, Franz, and June Stewart, eds. 1964. *In honour of Daryl Lindsay: Essays and studies.* London: Oxford University Press.

Philippe, J. 1893. Résumé d'une observation d'audition colorée. *Revue Philosophique* 36: 330–334.

Pocock-Williams, Lynn. 1992. Toward the automatic generation of visual music. *Leonardo* 25: 29–36.

Pommier, Jean. [1932] 1967. *La mystique de Baudelaire.* Geneva: Slatkine Reprints.

Proffer, Carl. 1968. *Keys to Lolita.* Bloomington: Indiana University Press: Bloomington.

Prokofieff, Sergei O. 1993. *The East in light of the West: Two Eastern streams of the twentieth century in light of Christian esotericism,* part 1, *Agni yoga.* London: Temple Lodge.

Pryce, Richard. 1911. *Christopher.* London: Hutchinson.

Purdy, D. M. 1936. Eidetic imagery and plasticity of perception. *Journal of General Psychology* 15: 437–453.

Purkinje, V. J. 1819. *Opera omnia.* Prague: Calve.

Rader, Charles M., and Auke Tellegen. 1987. An investigation of synesthesia. *Journal of Personality and Social Psychology* 52: 981–987.

Raines, Thomas Hart. 1909. Report of a case of psychochromesthesia. *Journal of Abnormal Psychology* 4: 249–252.

Raynaud, Ernest. [1988] 1947. Du symbolisme. In Guy Michaud, ed., *La doctrine symboliste: Documents.* Paris: Librairie Nizet.

Redgrove, Peter. 1989. *The black goddess and the unseen real.* New York: Grove Press.

Reichard, Gladys, Roman Jakobson, and Elizabeth Werth. 1949. Language and synaesthesia. *Word:* 224–233.

Rice, James L. 1985. *Dostoevsky and the healing art: An essay in literary and medical history.* Ann Arbor, Mich.: Ardis.

Richardson, A., and R. Cant. 1970. Eidetic imagery and brain damage. *Australian Journal of Psychology* 22: 47–54.

Riggs, Lorrin, and Theodore Karwoski. 1934. Synaesthesia. *British Journal of Psychology* 25: 29–41.

Rimbaud, Arthur. 1972. *Oeuvres complètes.* Paris: Gallimard.

———. 1967. *Rimbaud: Complete works, selected letters.* Wallace Fowlie, trans. and ed. Chicago: University of Chicago Press.

———. [1891] 1961. *A season in hell.* New York: New Directions.

Rimington, A. W. 1895. *Colour-music, the art of mobile colour.* London: Spottiswoode.

Rimland, Bernard. 1978. Savant capabilities of autistic children and their cognitive implications. In G. Serban, ed., *Cognitive deficits in the development of mental illness.* New York: Brunner/Mazel.

Ringbom, Sixten. 1970. *The sounding cosmos: A study in the spiritualism of Kandinsky and the genesis of abstract painting.* Abo: Abo Academi.

———. 1966. Art in the epoch of the great spiritual: Occult elements in the early theory of abstract painting. *Journal of the Warburg and Courtauld Institutes* 29: 388–418.

Rivers, J. E., and Charles Nicol. 1982. *Nabokov's fifth arc: Nabokov and others on his life and work.* Austin: University of Texas Press.

Robsjohn-Giddings, T. H. 1947. *Mona Lisa's mustache: A dissection of modern art.* New York: Knopf.

Rookmaaker, H. R. 1959a. *Gauguin and nineteenth-century art theory.* Amsterdam: Swets and Zeitlinger.

———. 1959b. *Synthetist Art Theories.* Amsterdam: Swets and Zeitlinger.

Rowe, W. W. 1985. *Nabokov's Spectral Dimension.* Ann Arbor, Mich.: Ardis.

Ruddick, Nicholas. 1984. 'Synaesthesia' in Emily Dickinson's poetry. *Poetics Today* 5: 59–78.

Rudorff, Raymond. 1972. *The Belle Epoque: Paris in the nineties.* New York: Saturday Review Press.

Sachs, G. T. L. 1812. *Historiae naturalis duorum leucaetiopum: auctoris ipsius et sororis eius.* Solisbaci: Sumptibus Bibliopolii Seideliani.

Sacks, Oliver. 1995. *An Anthropologist on Mars: Seven paradoxical tales.* New York: Knopf.

Schilder, Paul. 1926. Psychanalyse und Eidetik. *Zeitschrift für Sexualwissenschaft* 13: 56.

Schlegel, Julius Heinrich Gottlieb. 1824. *Ein Beitrag zur näheren Kenntnis der Albinos.* Meiningen, Germany: Keyssner.

Schloezer, Boris de. 1987. *Scriabin: Artist and mystic.* Berkeley: University of California Press.

Scott, Cyril. [1933] 1950. *Music: Its secret influence throughout the ages.* London: Rider.

———. 1917. *Philosophy of modernism (in its connection with music).* London: Paul, Trench, Trübner.

Segalen, Victor. 1981. *Les synesthésies et l'école symboliste.* Montpellier: Editions Fata Morgana.

Selfe, Lorna. 1977. *Nadia: A case of extraordinary drawing ability in an autistic child.* London: Academic Press.

Senior, John. 1959. *The way down and out: The occult in Symbolist literature.* Ithaca, N.Y.: Cornell University Press.

Serban, G., ed. 1978. *Cognitive deficits in the development of mental illness.* New York: Brunner/Mazel.

Siebold, Erika von. 1919–1920. Synästhesien in der englischen Dichtung des 19. Jahrhunderts. *Englische Studien* 53: 1–157, 196–334.

Simpson, Lorna, and Peter McKellar. 1955. Types of synaesthesia. *Journal of Mental Science* 101: 141–147.

Sinnet, Alfred Percy. [1895] 1919. *Collected fruits of occult teaching.* London: Fisher Unwin.

Sisson, Jonathan Borden. 1979. Cosmic synchronization and other worlds in the work of Vladimir Nabokov. Ph.D. dissertation, University of Minnesota.

Sloboda, J. A., B. Hermelin, and N. O'Connor. 1985. An exceptional musical memory. *Music Perception* 3: 155–170.

Smith, Neal, and Ianthi-Maria Tsimpli. 1995. *The mind of a savant: Language learning and modularity.* Oxford: Blackwell.

Sokolov, P. 1901. L'individuation colorée. *Revue Philosophique* 51: 145.

Solomon, David, ed., *LSD: The consciousness-expanding drug.* New York: Putnam and Sons.

Spadafora, Aurelia, and Harry T. Hunt. 1990. The multiplicity of dreams: Cognitive-affective correlates of lucid, archetypal, and nightmare dreaming. *Perceptual and Motor Skills* 71: 627–644.

Stackelberg, Roderick. 1981. *Idealism debased: From Völkisch ideology to National Socialism.* Kent, Ohio: Kent State University Press.

Steiner, Rudolf. 1994a. *Occult science—An outline.* Hudson, N.Y.: Anthroposophic Press.

———. [1894] 1994b. *Philosophy of spiritual activity.* Hudson, N.Y.: Anthroposophic Press.

———. [1915] 1973. *The occult movement in the nineteenth century and its relation to modern culture.* London: Rudolf Steiner Press.

———. [1904] 1947. *Knowledge of the higher worlds and its attainment.* Hudson, N.Y.: Anthroposophic Press.

———. [1910] 1946. *Theosophy: An introduction to the supersensible knowledge of the world and the destination of man.* Hudson: Anthroposophic Press.

———. [1918] 1945. *Three streams in the evolution of mankind: The connection of the Luciferic-Ahrimanic impulse with the Christ-Jahve impulse.* London: Rudolf Steiner Press.

Stern, Daniel. 1990. *Diary of a baby.* New York: Basic Books.

———. 1985. *The interpersonal world of the infant: A view from psychoanalysis and developmental psychology.* New York: Basic Books.

Stern, M. E., and M. Maire. 1937. Un cas d'aptitude spéciale de dessin chez un imbécile. *Archives de Médicine des Enfants* 40: 458–460.

Stevens, J. S. 1892. Colors of letters. *Popular Science Monthly* 40: 692–697.

Stevens, Jay. 1987. *Storming Heaven: LSD and the American dream.* New York: Atlantic Monthly Press.

Straus, Erwin. 1963. *The primary world of the senses: A vindication of sensory experience.* London: Collier-Macmillan.

Sury, Kurt von. 1950. *Wörterbuch der Psychologie und ihrer Grenzgebiete.* Basel: Schwabe.

Symmes, J. S. 1971. Visual imagery in brain-injured children. *Perceptual and Motor Skills* 33: 507–514.

Tart, Charles. 1969. *Altered states of consciousness.* New York: John Wiley and Son.

Tellegen, Auke, and G. Atkinson. 1974. Openness to absorbing and self-altering experiences ("absorption"), a trait related to hypnotic susceptibility. *Journal of Abnormal Psychology* 83: 268–277.

Titchener, E. B. 1909. *Lectures on the experimental psychology of thought processes*. New York: Macmillan.

Toffler, Alvin. 1970. *Future shock*. New York: Random House.

Tuchman, Maurice, ed. 1986. *The spiritual in art: Abstract painting, 1890–1925*. Abbeville, Calif.: Abbeville Press.

Tucker, Michael. 1992. *Dreaming with open eyes: The shamanic spirit in twentieth-century art and culture*. San Francisco: Harper.

Tuke, D. Hack. [1892] 1976. *Dictionary of psychological medicine*. New York: Arno Press.

Turner, Victor. 1971. *Dramas, fields, and metaphors*. Ithaca, N.Y.: Cornell University Press.

Ullmann, Stephan. 1951. *The principles of semantics*. Glasgow, Scotland: Jackson.

Ulrich, Alfred. 1903. Phénomènes de synesthésie chez un épileptique. *Revue Philosophique* 56: 180–187.

Urbantschitsch, T. 1907. *Über subjektive optische Anschauungsbilder*. Leipzig: Deuticke.

Viscott, David. 1970. A musical idiot savant. *Psychiatry* 33: 494–515.

Vitz, Paul, and Arnold Glimcher. 1984. *Modern art and modern science: The parallel analysis of vision*. New York: Praeger.

Watkins, Glenn. 1988. *Soundings: Music in the twentieth century*. New York: Schirmer Books.

Webb, James. 1971. *The flight from reason*. La Salle, Ill.: Open Court.

Weber, Max. [1904] 1958. *The Protestant ethic and the spirit of capitalism*. New York: Scribner's.

Wellek, Albert. 1970. *Witz-Lyrik-Sprache, Beiträge zur Literatur- und Sprachtheorie mit einem Anhang über den Fortshritt der Wissenschaft*. Bern: Francke.

———. 1950. Goethe und die Psychologie. *Schweizerische Zeitschrift für Psychologie und ihre Anwendungen* 9: 1–24.

———. 1936. Das Doppelempfinden im 18. Jahrhunderts. *Deutsche Vierteljahresschrift für Literatur-Wissenschaft und Geistesgeschichte* 14: 75–102.

———. 1935. Farbenharmonie und Farbenklavier: Ihre Enstehungsgeschichte im 18. Jahrhunderts. *Archiv für die Gesamte Psychologie* 94: 347–375.

———. 1931a. Das Doppelempfinden im abendländischen Altertum und Mittelalter. *Archiv für die Gesamte Psychologie* 80: 120–166.

———. 1931b. Renaissance- und Barock-Synästhesie: Die Geschichte des Doppelempfindens im 16. und 17. Jahrhundert. *Deutsche Vierteljahresschrift für Literatur-Wissenschaft und Geistesgeschichte* 9: 534–584.

———. 1931c. Der Sprachgeist als Doppelempfinder. *Zeitschrift für Ästhetik und Allgemeine Kunstwissenschaft* 25: 226–262.

———. 1931d. Zur Geschichte und Kritik der Synästhesie-Forschung. *Archiv für die Gesamte Psychologie* 79: 325–384.

———. 1930. Beiträge zum Synästhesie-Problem. *Archiv für die Gesamte Psychologie* 76: 193–201.

Wellek, René. 1965. *A history of modern criticism, 1750–1950*. New Haven: Yale University Press.

Wells, F. L. 1918. Symbolism and synaesthesia. *American Journal of Insanity* 75: 481–488.

Werner, Heinz. [1934] 1978. Unity of the Senses. In S. S. Barten and M. B. Franklin, eds., *Developmental processes: Heinz Werner's selected writings.* New York: International Universities Press.

———. 1948. *Comparative psychology of mental development.* New York: International Universities Press.

Wertham, F. 1930. Eidetic phenomena and psychopathology. *Archives of Neurology and Psychiatry* 24: 809–821.

Wheeler, R. H. 1932. *The laws of human nature: A general view of Gestalt psychology.* New York: Appleton.

———. 1928. Persistent problems in systematic psychology, part 4: Structural versus functional analysis. *Journal of General Psychology* 1: 90–107.

———. 1925. Persistent problems in systematic psychology, part 1: A philosophical heritage; part 2: The psychological datum; part 3: The stimulus error and complete introspection. *Psychological Review* 32: 179–191; 251–265; 443–456.

———. 1924. Synaesthesia in the process of reasoning. *American Journal of Psychology* 35: 88–97.

———. 1923. Some problems of meaning. *American Journal of Psychology* 34: 185–202.

———. 1922. The development of meaning. *American Journal of Psychology* 33: 223–233.

———. 1920a. The synaesthesia of a blind subject. *University of Oregon Publications* 1 (entire issue).

———. 1920b. Theories of the will and kinaesthetic sensations. *Psychological Review* 27: 351–360.

———. 1920c. Visual phenomena in the dreams of a blind subject. *Psychological Review* 27: 315–322.

Wheeler, R. H., and T. D. Cutsforth. 1928. Synaesthesia in judging and choosing. *Journal of General Psychology* 1: 497–519.

———. 1925. Synaesthesia and the development of the concept. *Journal of Experimental Psychology* 8: 149–159.

———. 1922a. Synaesthesia: A form of perception. *Psychological Review* 29: 212–220.

———. 1922b. Synaesthesia and meaning. *American Journal of Psychology* 33: 361–384.

———. 1921a. The number forms of a blind subject. *American Journal of Psychology* 32: 21–25.

———. 1921b. The role of synaesthesia in learning. *Journal of Experimental Psychology* 4: 448–468.

Wheeler, R. H., ed. 1930. *Readings in psychology.* New York: Crowell.

Whitchurch, Anna Kellman. 1922. Synaesthesia in a child of three and a half years. *American Journal of Psychology* 33: 302–303.

Wilber, Ken. 1990. *Eye to eye: The quest for the new paradigm.* Boston: Shambhala.

Yoon, Carol. 1997. Synesthesia: The taste of music, the sound of color. *Journal of NIH Research* 9: 25–27.

Zigler, Michael J. 1930. Tone shapes: A novel type of synaesthesia. *Journal of General Psychology* 3: 277–287.

Index

Abrams, M. H., 14, 15

Absolute pitch, 7, 72, 187*n*2

Absorption, 12–13

Abstract art. *See* specific artists

Alexandrov, Vladimir, 141–142, 146, 198*nn*8–9

Allport, G. W., 108

Altered states of consciousness, 15, 41, 171–176, 179. *See also* Psychedelic experiences

Altschuler, Modest, 75

Anderson, Jack, 187*n*2

Archaic cultures, 79, 95–99, 104, 107, 110–112, 168

Arguelles, José, 100–103, 104, 112, 170, 176, 199*n*2

Aristotle, 24, 29, 48, 110, 193*n*13

Arithmetical calculation, 116–117, 139, 197–198*n*6

Arréat, Lucien, 33

Artistic abilities, 116, 183–184. *See also* specific artists

Asperger, Hans, 114

Astral plane/astral body, 51–54, 63–64, 69, 180, 182, 185, 186

Audition colorée. See Color hearing

Auras of humans, 62, 70, 74

Autism, 95, 113–119, 140, 163, 183–184, 186, 197*n*16

Axenfeld, Alexandre, 28

Babbitt, Irving, 35–36

Bailly, Edmond, 193*n*9

Barfield, Owen, 190*n*15

Barnstone, Aliki, 112–113

Baron-Cohen, Simon, 187*n*3

Baudelaire, Charles, 18, 37–42, 59, 61, 68, 73, 98, 100, 102, 104, 105, 169, 176, 190*n*19

Beaunis, H., 35, 190*n*14

Belmont, Ira Jean, 92

Benedikt, Moritz, 5, 20–21

Benoît, Emilien, 43–44

Bergson, Henri, 109, 136